Course Notes

CRIMINAL
LAW

Lisa Cherkassky

HODDER
EDUCATION
AN HACHETTE UK COMPANY

Orders: please contact Bookpoint Ltd, 130 Milton Park, Abingdon, Oxon OX14 4SB.
Telephone: (44) 01235 827720. Fax: (44) 01235 400454. Lines are open from 9.00–5.00,
Monday to Saturday, with a 24 hour message answering service. You can also order through
our website www.hoddereducation.co.uk

If you have any comments to make about this, or any of our other titles, please send them to
educationenquiries@hodder.co.uk

British Library Cataloguing in Publication Data
A catalogue record for this title is available from the British Library

ISBN: 978 1 444 14654 7

First Edition Published 2012

Impression number   10 9 8 7 6 5 4 3 2 1

Year   2015 2014 2013 2012

Hachette UK's policy is to use papers that are natural, renewable and recyclable products and
made from wood grown in sustainable forests. The logging and manufacturing processes are
expected to conform to the environmental regulations of the country of origin.

Typeset by Datapage India Pvt Ltd
Printed and bound in Spain for Hodder Education, an Hachette UK Company, 338 Euston
Road, London NW1 3BH

Contents

Additional chapters 15 and 16 on Inchoate offences and Public order offences can be found on the companion website. Log in at http://www.hodderplus.co.uk/law

Guide to the book

Check new words and essential legal terms and what they mean

Definition

Capacity: understanding, awareness, capability, clear mind, reasoning, ability.

Test your legal knowledge! Practice makes perfect – answer questions on what you've just read

Workpoint

Why is capacity important in criminal law ?

Questions to help you delve deeper into the law and to guide your further reading

Research Point

In 2003 the Parliamentary Joint Committee on Human Rights criticised the age of criminal liability in their Tenth Report of Session 2002-03, HL1/High Court. Look up paragraphs 35 to 38 and make notes on the main arguments below.

Provides examples and extracts from the key cases and judgements you need to know

Case:	
***Antoine* (2000)**	The words "did the act or made the omission" in the 1964 Act refer to the actus reus only. The mental element need not be explored.

Diagrams illustrate key points for visual learners

People who lack
capacity in criminal law

Children under
the age of ten

Corporations

Those with a
mental illness

Tick off what you have learnt and check you're on track

Checkpoint - corporate manslaughter

I can explain the effect of *C v DPP* (1995) on the doctrine of doli incapax	
I can suggest ways in which a Crown Court trial could be made more accessible to a child.	

Provide you with potential real-life exam questions.
Answers are available on the accompanying website.

Potential exam questions

1) Assess the ways in which incapacitated defendants are dealt with in the criminal court system

2) Examine the role of vicarious liability in criminal law

3) Corporations can be indicted for criminal offences the same as individuals can.

Guide to the website

There is useful additional material online to support your learning of criminal law. Login at www.hodderplus.co.uk/law

Interactive questions to help you revise aspects of the law

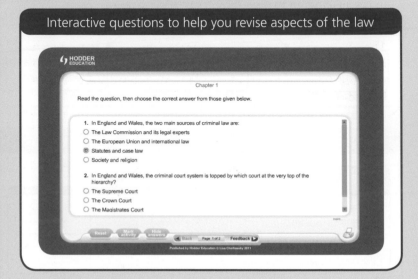

Model Answers

Chapter 1

1. When the criminal law prosecutes and sentences criminals, its purpose is to:

   - incapacitate the criminal
   - punish the criminal
   - deter the criminal and the public
   - reform the criminal
   - educate the criminal and the public
   - affirm moral standards and restore justice in society.

Useful links to websites to help you research further your studies in law

www.parliament.uk
The official Parliament website; use it to track all criminal bills currently before Parliament, explore the role of the House of Lords in law-making, and search for delegated legislation.

www.legislation.gov.uk
The official website for the Stationary Office; use it to search for newly enacted and revised legislation, draft legislation and statutory instruments for the United Kingdom, Scotland, Northern Ireland and Wales.

Acknowledgments

The author would like to thank Jacqueline Martin for her writing guidance throughout this project, Lucy Winder and Sundus Pasha at Hodder for bringing the project together in the final stages, and Jasmin Naim at Hodder for introducing the author to the project.

The author would especially like to thank Professor Alan Reed, who taught her LLB Criminal Law, LLM Criminal Law, and how to exceed even her own expectations.

Preface

This Course Notes series is intended to provide students with useful notes, which are presented in a way that helps with visual learning

The series is also interactive with:

- Workpoints for students to work through

- Research Points where students are invited to further their knowledge and understanding by referring to important source materials

- Checkpoints to see whether the reader has understood/learned the key points on each topic

- Examination style questions at the end of each chapter.

There is also support available on the companion website where students can check their own answers to the examination style questions against the suggested answers on the site, as well as interactive questions and useful links for research.

Jacqueline Martin

Course Notes Criminal Law

This distinctive guide to criminal law covers all the important elements of crime in an innovative and accessible way. All the popular topics are here, including *actus reus* and *mens rea*, theft, criminal damage, causation and homicide (and its numerous special defences). There are even two supplementary chapters on the website for the study of inchoate offences and public order. The book also includes two unique chapters: one on sexual offences, which is widely taught but rarely seen in smaller textbooks, and one on general defences which includes: duress, intoxication, mistake, self-defence, automatism, insanity and consent.

The use of research points and workpoints enables the reader to dissect and engage with the criminal law through leading cases, journal articles and fun case studies, and the inclusion of definition boxes and case boxes illustrates in a simple way what a particular word means and how the criminal law works.

Finally, a number of features make the criminal law even easier to understand. The inclusion of original flow charts, diagrams, charts and boxes all help to illustrate how the law has changed over the years, how it works today, and how cases and statutes can be distinguished from one another. There is a checkpoint at the end of every section to summarise the main points of law and to test the reader, and there are exam questions at the end of each chapter, with suggested answers to these posted on the website to help with the revision process.

Lisa Cherkassky

Table of cases

Table of statutes

Chapter 1
Introduction to criminal law

The criminal law has many different purposes and comes from a wide range of sources. Criminal offences are made up of different elements and are classified into certain groups, and the criminal justice system follows a set hierarchy.

1.1 The purpose of criminal law

- The criminal law has several purposes:

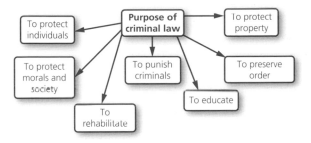

- Some of the purposes listed above have particular aims. For example, when the criminal law punishes criminals, it aims to:
  1. incapacitate the criminal;
  2. punish the criminal;
  3. deter the criminal;
  4. reform the criminal;
  5. educate the public;
  6. affirm moral standards;
  7. restore justice in society.

Workpoint

In 1967 the drink-driving laws in the UK were tightened up, and drivers can now be prosecuted for being over a specified legal limit of alcohol. Before 1967, specific limits were not measured or required; the driver simply had to be 'unfit' to drive. What do you think are the aims of this stricter law?

1.1.1 Enforcing morals

- One of the purposes of the criminal law is to protect morals and society.
- Morals are important in law because they control personal behaviour, and some moral standards are shared by society as a whole (e.g. 'murder is wrong').
- However, morals are also personal to the individual. Every person in society has a different set of morals that are shaped by many different influences.

Workpoint

List five influences on your morals and beliefs.

- The *Wolfenden Committee (1957)* on homosexual offences and prostitution felt that the private lives of individuals should only be regulated by the criminal courts to:
  1. *Preserve* public order and decency;
  2. *Protect* the citizen from offensive and injurious things;
  3. *Provide* safeguards against exploitation and corruption.

Case:	
***R v Brown* (1993)**	Lord Templeman: 'Society is entitled and bound to protect itself against a cult of violence. Pleasure derived from the infliction of pain is an evil thing. Cruelty is uncivilised.'
	Lord Slynn: 'In the end it is a matter of policy in an area where social and moral factors are extremely important and where attitudes could change.'
***R v Wilson* (1996)**	Russell LJ: 'Consensual activity between husband and wife, in the privacy of the matrimonial home, is not, in our judgment, a proper matter for criminal investigation, let alone criminal prosecution.'

The main differences between *Brown* and *Wilson*	
1. *Brown* involved homosexual males	1. *Wilson* involved a married couple
2. *Brown* involved the infliction of injury for sexual gratification	2. *Wilson* involved the infliction of injury for personal adornment
3. *Brown* outraged public decency	3. *Wilson* was a private matter

1.1.2 The changing criminal law

- Below are some examples of how the criminal law can change to reflect or accommodate the changing morals and beliefs of society.

  1. Statutory defences were provided for doctors carrying out abortions in the Abortion Act 1967.
  2. The Criminal Justice and Public Order Act 1994 decriminalised consensual homosexual acts between adults in private for those aged 18 and over (16 in 2000).
  3. As far back as 1736 a wife was assumed to consent to all sexual activity with her husband, but in *R v R* [1994] 4 All ER 260 it was held that men and women were equal partners in marriage and a husband could be prosecuted for raping his wife.
  4. Doctors can withdraw artificial nutrition from a patient in a persistent vegetative state (i.e. not brain dead) as a result of *Airedale NHS Trust v Bland* [1993] 1 All ER 821.

Checkpoint - the purpose of criminal law	
Task:	**Done!**
I can list five purposes of the criminal law	
I can explain the criminal and moral differences between *Brown* (1993) and *Wilson* (1996)	

1.2 Sources of criminal law

- The criminal law comes from two main sources, is overviewed by a third source, and its reform is influenced by a fourth:

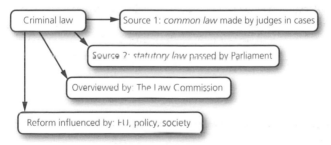

1.2.1 Common law

- Common law (or 'case law') is made by judges in appeal cases.
- Their decision sets a new precedent which all lower courts must follow, thus creating a new law (or updating/reforming the previous law).

- Many criminal offences originate from common law and have been developed over many years (e.g. the offence of murder).
- In *Gibson and another* (1991) the common law offence of outraging public decency was held to exist even though convictions were extremely rare.

Common law offences in crime:	Common law defences in crime:
Murder	Duress
Manslaughter	Automatism
Assault	Insanity
Battery	Intoxication

- Sometimes common law offences will later be enshrined (i.e. incorporated) into statutes.

Common law defence of *provocation* → Formally codified in the Homicide Act 1957 and then updated by the Coroners and Justice Act 2009

- Even when common law offences are enshrined into statutes, judges are still free to interpret the new statutory version according to a number of rules.
- Statutory offences are therefore subject to judicial reform in the same way as common law offences are.

Workpoint

Should judges be allowed to develop the criminal law, or should this be left up to Parliament?

1.2.2 Statutory law

- Much of the criminal law comes from Acts of Parliament.
- Judges interpret and apply these statutes in the courts.

Statute:	Criminal offence:
Offences Against the Person Act 1861	Assault occasioning actual bodily harm, wounding, grievous bodily harm with intent, abortion
Theft Act 1968	Theft, robbery, burglary

Criminal Damage Act 1971	Most forms of criminal damage
Sexual Offences Act 2003	Most sexual offences including rape and sexual assault

1.2.3 Overview of the criminal law

- The Law Commission attempted to codify the whole of the criminal law in 1989 in A *Criminal Code for England and Wales* (1989) (Law Com No 177).
- Parliament did not enact it.
- The Law Commission now takes a 'building block' approach, reviewing small areas of the criminal law at a time.
- When Law Commission reports are enacted into law, they may undergo significant amendment.

Workpoint

Do you think it is a good idea to put the Law Commission in charge of these important tasks, or should Parliament take responsibility for reforming the criminal law?

Law Commission reports:	Resulting changes in crime:
Legislating the Criminal Code: Offences Against the Person and General Principles (1993) Law Com No 218	(review only)
Legislating the Criminal Code: Intoxication and Criminal Liability (1995) Law Com No 229	(review only)
Legislating the Criminal Code: Involuntary Manslaughter (1996) Law Com No 237	Corporate Manslaughter and Corporate Homicide Act 2007
Fraud (2002) Law Com No 276	Fraud Act 2006
Inchoate Liability for Assisting and Encouraging Crime (2006) Law Com No 300	Serious Crime Act 2007
Murder, Manslaughter and Infanticide (2006) Law Com No 304	(review only)
Participating in Crime (2007) Law Com No 305	(review only)

1.2.4 Influences on criminal law reform

- Parliament, judges and the Law Commission will develop the law (or suggest it) if they feel the pressure to do so.

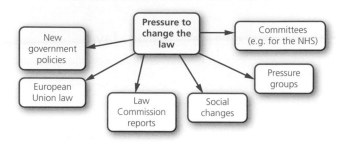

Checkpoint - sources of criminal law	
Task:	**Done!**
I can describe the two main sources of criminal law	
I can explain who overviews the criminal law	
I can describe the influences on criminal law reform	
I can list some common law criminal offences	
I can list some statutory criminal offences	
I understand what the Law Commission does	

1.3 Classification of offences

- Criminal offences can be 'classified' (i.e. 'grouped') together in various ways.
- This helps a student to remember how serious each criminal offence is, where the offence will be tried, and the kind of sanction (punishment) available to the offender.
- Criminal offences can be classified in several ways:

  1. By source (i.e. how the offence was made);
  2. By police powers (i.e. how long police can detain a suspect);
  3. By type of harm caused (i.e. a minor or a serious offence);
  4. By place of trial (i.e. the court the offender will be tried in).

1.3.1 Classification of criminal offences by source

- Criminal offences come from two main sources:

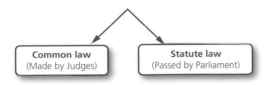

Common law	Statute law
(Made by Judges)	(Passed by Parliament)

1.3.2 Classification of criminal offences by police powers

- The police can detain a suspect for questioning.
- If after questioning they do not charge the suspect with an offence, they must let him go.
- How long the police can detain him depends on the offence he has been arrested for.

	Summary offences	Indictable offences	Terrorism offences
Description:	A basic criminal offence (e.g. assault)	A serious criminal offence (e.g. murder)	Any terrorism offence
Court heard in:	Magistrate's Court	Crown Court	Crown Court
Questioning time:	24 hours	Up to 96 hours with permission from a magistrate	Up to 14 days with permission from a High Court judge
Police power:	The Police and Criminal Evidence Act 1984, s.24	The Police and Criminal Evidence Act 1984, s.42	The Terrorism Act 2000, schedule 8

1.3.3 Classification of criminal offences by harm caused

- For revision purposes, students sometimes like to classify criminal offences according to the resultant harm caused.

- There are three main categories:

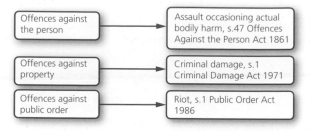

Offences against the person	→ Assault occasioning actual bodily harm, s.47 Offences Against the Person Act 1861
Offences against property	→ Criminal damage, s.1 Criminal Damage Act 1971
Offences against public order	→ Riot, s.1 Public Order Act 1986

1.3.4 Classification of criminal offence by place of trial

- Criminal offences are tried in different criminal courts.
- The reason for this is simple: particularly violent offenders may require a more secure environment in which to be tried.

Court:	Criminal offences:
Magistrate's Court (only):	Assault, minor driving offences
Crown Court (only):	Murder, manslaughter, rape, malicious wounding with intent
Both courts:	Theft, burglary, assault occasioning actual bodily harm

Checkpoint - classification of offences

Task:	Done!
I can list the four ways in which criminal offences can be classified	

1.4 The criminal court system

- Criminal offences are tried in either a Magistrate's Court or a Crown Court.
- Convicted offenders can appeal to higher courts if they feel that they have been treated unjustly, and so the criminal court system follows a hierarchy (i.e. 'order').

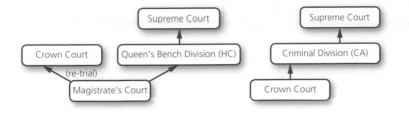

- The accused defendant will have a different trial experience depending on which court his case is tried in.
- He will face different people on the panel and will be given different sentences.

	Magistrate's Court	Crown Court
Panel:	Three magistrates or a District Judge	A judge and a jury of twelve
Qualifications:	Magistrates are not legally qualified but are respected members of the local community. District Judges are solicitors or barristers with at least five years' experience	The judge is legally qualified with many years' experience as a barrister or solicitor. The jury are men and women from the electoral register selected at random
Role:	Hear the case, decide verdict, pass sentence	The judge decides the relevant law and he directs it to the jury. The jury decide whether the law has been broken (i.e. 'guilty' or 'not guilty'). The judge then hands down sentence
Powers:	Six months' imprisonment for one offence, twelve months' imprisonment for two or more offences, fine up to £5,000	Unlimited

	Magistrate's Court	Crown Court
Formalities:	Magistrates must have good character, social awareness, maturity, sound judgement and commitment to be accepted	If the jury decide 'not guilty' the defendant is acquitted. If the defendant pleads guilty, the judge sentences him alone
Trivia:	The Magistrate's Court deals with over 95% of all criminal cases	If the judge decides that the prosecution has not proved the case, he can order that the defendant be acquitted

1.4.1 Appeals from the Magistrate's Court

• There are two routes of appeal from the Magistrate's Court.
• The route taken depends on the reason for the appeal and the party launching the appeal.

	Route 1:	Route 2:
Who is making the appeal?	The convicted defendant	The prosecution or defence
What is the issue?	Appeal against sentence, against conviction, or both	A point of law (e.g. it may have been interpreted incorrectly by the magistrate, or it may contain a loophole)
Where is the appeal heard?	Crown Court	Queen's Bench Division in the High Court
What will the outcome be?	The case is heard by a judge and two magistrates who decide if the defendant is guilty or not guilty and punish him accordingly	Quash the decision, uphold the decision, or send back to Magistrate's Court for a re-trial

1.4.2 Appeals from the Crown Court

• These appeals are slightly more complicated.
• Cases heard in the Crown Court are usually more serious in nature.
• Routes two and three (in the figure below) have no real significance for the defendant – they are simply appeals on points of law only.

	Route 1:	Route 2:	Route 3:
Who is making the appeal?	The convicted defendant	The prosecution	The prosecution or defence
What is the issue?	Appeal against sentence, against conviction, or both	The defendant has been acquitted but an important point of law still needs clarification	A point of law of general public importance needs clarification
Where is the appeal heard?	Court of Appeal (Criminal Division)	Court of Appeal (Criminal Division)	From the Court of Appeal (Criminal Division) up to the Supreme Court
Formalities	The defendant must obtain permission from the Court of Appeal or a certificate from the original trial judge	The Attorney General will refer the case to the Court of Appeal, cited as: *Attorney General's Reference (No.1 of 2012)* (2014)	Permission must be granted by either the Court of Appeal or the Supreme Court
What will the outcome be?	Allow the appeal and quash the conviction, substitute the conviction for a lesser offence, decrease sentence, dismiss the appeal	The ruling of the Court of Appeal will create a new precedent	The ruling of the Supreme Court will create a new precedent

- In appeal judgments, the reference to 'court of first instance' or 'judge at first instance' refers to the original trial that took place in either the Magistrate's Court or the Crown Court.
- The term 'leave to appeal' means 'permission' to appeal.
- The Court of Appeal (Criminal Division) can also order a re-trial for a Crown Court case if new and compelling evidence is discovered.

Workpoint

Answer the questions below (hint: locate the relevant trial court first, and then pick a route of appeal).

(1) Darren has been convicted of assault in the Magistrate's Court. He feels that his sentence is too harsh. What is his route of appeal?

(2) Robin has been convicted of rape but his defence team argue that the law of rape is unclear and that if the trial judge had explained it properly to the jury, Robin would not have been convicted (i.e. there is a point of law which needs clarification). What is their route of appeal?

(3) Joanna is acquitted of manslaughter after she killed her husband after years of domestic abuse. The prosecution believe that the law of manslaughter contains a loophole that allows battered women to walk free and would like this issue clarified. What is their route of appeal?

Checkpoint - the criminal court system

Task:	Done!
I can draw a map of the criminal court system	
I can describe the main differences between a Magistrate's Court and a Crown Court	
I can explain the two routes of appeal from the Magistrate's Court	
I can explain the three routes of appeal from the Crown Court	

1.5 Sentencing

The Criminal Justice Act 2003 lists the numerous purposes of sentencing in criminal law:

Checkpoint - sentencing

Task:	Done!
I can list six purposes of sentencing	

1.6 Elements of a crime

- In criminal law, most criminal offences can be split into two parts: a physical act and a mental element.

Actus non facit reum nisi mens sit rea → The act itself does not constitute guilt unless done with a guilty mind

Definition

Actus reus: physical act of the crime.
Mens rea: mental element of the crime.

- The prosecution must prove that *both* the physical act and the mental element were present when the defendant committed the crime.
- If only one is present, or neither are present, the defendant must be acquitted.

Element of crime:	Latin phrase used:	Example:
The physical act	*actus reus*	• Stabbing (murder) • Shooting (murder) • Taking (theft) • Punching (battery) • Fire (criminal damage) • Threatening (assault) • Intercourse (rape)
The mental element	*mens rea*	• Intention • Reckless • Negligence

- It is not likely that a criminal offence will list the form of *actus reus* required (i.e. 'strangle', 'shoot', 'poison', 'kick' or 'punch').
- The offence will simply be a basic definition with a physical act and a mental element in it.

Section 1 of the Theft Act 1968:

'A person is guilty of theft if he dishonestly appropriates property belonging to another with the intention of permanently depriving the other of it.'

| ***actus reus***: 'appropriates properly belonging to another' | ***mens rea***: 'dishonestly with the intention of permanently depriving the other' |

Workpoint

Shola is 15 and is sitting in her English lesson. She spies her best friend's new designer school bag and decides to hide it in her locker so she can take it home later. At home time, Shola retrieves the bag from her locker and takes it home. Does Shola have both the *actus reus* and *mens rea* of theft? Apply both elements to the facts and give reasons for your answer.

- If a defendant has both the *actus reus* and the *mens rea* of a crime, he can still be acquitted if he can provide a full defence.
- Strict liability offences do not have a mental element, but there are not many of these.

Checkpoint - elements of a crime

Task:	Done!
I can translate *actus reus* and give two examples	
I can translate *mens rea* and give two examples	

1.7 The burden and standard of proof

- Students sometimes confuse 'burden of proof' and 'standard of proof'.
- It may help to use simple translations:

> **Definition**
>
> Burden: load, weight, problem, responsibility, duty, onus, obligation.
> Standard: benchmark, yardstick, level, degree, pattern, measure, norm.

- There are two teams in a criminal trial: the prosecution and the defence.
- Each team has its own job to do, and this is where 'burden of proof' and 'standard of proof' come into play.

- The prosecution have a heavier burden on their shoulders, and a higher standard against which to prove it.

	Prosecution	Defence
Burden of proof:	Burden to prove the defendant committed the crime	Burden to cast doubt on prosecution case
Standard of proof:	Must be proved beyond all reasonable doubt	A reasonable doubt may be raised

- In criminal law, a defendant is always presumed innocent until proven guilty (by the prosecution).
- This was confirmed in the case of *Woolmington* (1935).

Case:	
***Woolmington* (1935)**	Lord Sankey: '...it is the duty of the prosecution to prove the prisoner's guilt. If at the end there is a reasonable doubt as to whether the prisoner killed the deceased, the prosecution has not made out the case and the prisoner is entitled to an acquittal.'

- If the defendant raises the common law defence of insanity or the statutory defence of diminished responsibility, the burden of proof is reversed.
- The burden of proof will be on the *defendant* to prove his defence.
- This is known as the 'reverse onus'.
- The standard of proof on the defendant will be a balance of probabilities – *Carr-Briant* (1943).

Checkpoint - burden and standard of proof

Task:	Done!
I know what the burden of proof is on the prosecution and the defence	
I can explain how the standard of proof differs between sides	

Potential exam questions:

1) What is the purpose of prosecuting and sentencing criminals?
2) Describe the criminal court and appeal system.
3) Explain how the Human Rights Act 1998 impacts on criminal law.

Chapter 2
Actus reus and causation

In criminal law, most crimes are split up into two parts: *actus reus* (physical act) and *mens rea* (mental element). This chapter will look at the *actus reus* component. The *actus reus* must cause the resulting injury (e.g. the victim's death) and so this chapter will also look at causation.

2.1 What is the *actus reus*?

• The defendant must perform the *actus reus* of the criminal offence.
• The *actus reus* may take many forms (e.g. the method of killing).
• Other times, it can be very specific (e.g. theft).

Criminal offence:	Actus reus (i.e. physical act) required:
Murder	Stab, shoot, etc.
Battery	Touch, push, etc.
Actual bodily harm	Punch, bruise, cut, etc.
Theft	Taking property that belongs to another

Case:	
Ahmad (1986)	Facts: a landlord unintentionally disturbed some of his tenants and then failed to rectify the situation. He was convicted under the Protection from Eviction Act 1977 of 'doing acts calculated to interfere with the peace and comfort of a residential occupier'.
	Held: The Court of Appeal quashed the conviction because he had not 'done acts' with the required intent, as was required under the statute.

• There must be a link between the *actus reus* and the outcome (e.g. the stab wound must cause the death if the charge is murder).
• Not every *actus reus* has a consequence.
• Sometimes it is simply enough to perform the *actus reus* of a crime without there being an additional result.

Criminal offence:	*Actus reus* required:	Additional consequence:
Murder	Stab, shoot, etc.	Death
Battery	Touch, push, etc.	–
Rape	Penetrate victim without consent	–
Theft	Take property of victim	Permanently deprive victim

- If there is an additional consequence required, it will be included in the *actus reus* of the criminal offence.

Workpoint

1. The definition of malicious wounding (s.20 of the Offences Against the Person Act 1861) is below. What is the *actus reus* of the offence (i.e. all the physical components of the crime)?

'Whosoever shall unlawfully and maliciously wound or inflict any grievous bodily harm upon any other person, either with or without a weapon or instrument, shall be guilty of an offence and shall be liable to imprisonment for not more than five years.'

2. The definition of criminal damage (s.1 of the Criminal Damage Act 1971) is below. What is the *actus reus* of the offence (i.e. all the physical components of the crime)?

'A person who without lawful excuse destroys or damages any property belonging to another intending to destroy or damage any such property or being reckless as to whether any such property would be destroyed or damaged shall be guilty of an offence.'

2.2 The *actus reus* must be voluntary

- The *actus reus* must be voluntary.
- If the defendant's act is the result of a muscle spasm, for example, the defendant will not be liable.

Case:	
Bratty v Attorney-General of Northern Ireland (1963)	Lord Denning: 'The requirement that [the act of the accused] should be a voluntary act is essential...in every criminal case. No act is punishable if it is done involuntarily.'

- If a person sets off a chain of events, he or she will be responsible for all of the harm caused.

Case:	
***Mitchell* (1983)**	Facts: the defendant pushed someone in a queue who then knocked over the elderly victim, who died.
	Held: The defendant performed the voluntary act. The pushed bystander knocked the elderly victim over unwilfully and accidentally.

Checkpoint - *actus reus*

Task:	Done!
I can define '*actus reus*'	
I can locate the *actus reus* in the definition of a statutory offence	
I can explain the voluntary requirement as established in *Bratty v Attorney-General of Northern Ireland* (1963)	

2.3 Omissions

Definition

Omission: failure to act.

- The phrase 'commission by omission' simply means that a criminal offence can be committed by an omission.
- The *actus reus* of a criminal offence usually requires a physical act, but in some instances the *actus reus* is replaced by an omission.
- Omissions liability is limited in criminal law to instances where a defendant has a duty to act and then fails to do so.

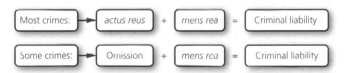

Workpoint

Can you think of an instance where a failure to act may be a criminal offence?

- An omission is culpable (i.e. blameworthy) in criminal law if the defendant had a *duty* to act and then failed to do so.

- A duty to act can arise in a small number of situations:

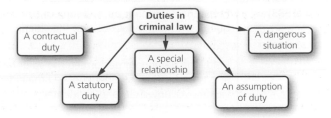

- The jury must decide whether a duty to act existed in the circumstances, and then whether that duty was breached.
- If a jury is not sure that a duty to act existed, then the defendant should be acquitted – *Khan and Khan* (1998).

2.3.1 A contractual duty

- A person working within a contract is under a duty to act.
- This includes all professionals, such as lifeguards, police, teachers and doctors etc.
- An omission in these circumstances will attract criminal charges if it leads to some harm (especially death).

Case:	
Pittwood (1902)	Facts: a signalman was employed to look after a level crossing. He left the gate open and left his post when a train came and a pedestrian was killed. He argued that he only had a duty towards his employer.
	Held: the defendant had a duty towards his employer *and* fellow pedestrians to ensure that they were safe.
Adomako (1995)	Facts: an anaesthetist failed to notice that the patient was deprived of oxygen during surgery. The patient died.
	Held: the defendant was under a contractual duty of care; that duty had been breached; the breach caused the patient's death; and the breach was so gross that it was deemed to be criminal.
Singh (1999)	Facts: carbon monoxide poisoning from a defective fireplace killed a tenant. The landlord's son – who collected rent for him and maintained the flats – was convicted of manslaughter.
	Held: the son was held to have a duty of care over the tenants because he helped to maintain each flat.

Professor Mark was a lecturer in criminal justice. During a lecture one day he left the lecture hall to rush to the bathroom. He said to his students to stay where they were. While he was away, a fire started in the back of the hall and fire alarms went off, but the students didn't know what to do. They remained where they were, waiting for Professor Mark but he never came back. They all suffered serious smoke inhalation. Does Professor Mark have a duty of care and has he breached that duty by omitting to retrieve them? Give reasons for your answer.

2.3.2 A statutory duty

- A statutory duty to act can be imposed upon a person, rendering their omission a criminal offence.
- Some typical examples are listed below:

Statute:	Offence:
Section 6 of the Road Traffic Act 1988	Failing to provide a police officer with a specimen of breath when required to do so
Section 170 of the Road Traffic Act 1988	Failing to stop and provide a name and address to any person requiring it after your vehicle has been in an accident resulting in injury or damage
Section 19 of the Terrorism Act 2000	Failing to give the police information about another person who is committing certain terrorist offences

- Statutory omissions do not always include a particular consequence (e.g. death).
- It is simply enough to fail to perform the statutory duty.
- Where there *has* been a consequence, a person can be charged with the additional criminal offence as well as breaching their statutory duty.

Case:	
Dytham (1979)	Facts: a police officer was on duty near a nightclub. A man was thrown out of the nightclub and was kicked to death in full view of the police officer, who simply watched before driving away. Held: the police officer was convicted of misconduct but was not charged with manslaughter because it was very difficult to prove that his omission *caused* the death.

2.3.3 A special relationship

- Family members have a duty of care towards each other.

- There are no clear rules when it comes to the expiration of this particular duty, or how far it stretches.
- Parents have a duty towards children – *Gibbins and Proctor* (1918).
- Spouses have a duty towards each other – *Smith* (1979).

> ### Research Point
>
> Look up the case *Hood* [2003] EWCA Crim 2772. Do you agree that all spouses should have a duty to act? When do you believe this duty should cease? What about life-partners, cousins and siblings – should they burden a duty to act?

2.3.4 An assumption of duty

- A duty to act will be *imposed* upon someone who voluntarily *assumes* a *duty* over a dependent person.
- When a duty of care is *assumed* by a person and *relied upon* by the victim, harm or death may result if the care is suddenly and unexpectedly withdrawn.
- When a grandparent takes a grandchild into her home permanently, the grandparent voluntarily assumes a duty over that grandchild – *Nicholls* (1874).
- When a person moves in with an older relative who becomes dependent, an omission to feed that relative may result in manslaughter – *Instan* (1893).
- Deliberately omitting to feed a child may constitute the *mens rea* for murder and the omission will constitute the *actus reus* for murder – *Gibbins and Proctor* (1918).

Case:	
***Stone and Dobinson* (1977)**	Facts: the victim moved in to her brother's home. She became very ill and refused to eat. He attempted to find a doctor and seek help, but the sister died.
	Held: the defendants were found to have voluntarily assumed a duty of care which they then breached through their feeble attempts to seek help. They were convicted of manslaughter.

2.3.5 A dangerous situation

- A recent addition to the common law duties to act arose in the case of *Miller* (1983).
- When a person *creates* a dangerous situation, becomes *aware* of it and then *fails* to take steps to control or minimise it, he is held responsible for the resulting harm or damage.
- This is an alternative way of finding liability when no *actus reus* is apparent.

Case:	
***Miller* (1983)**	Facts: the defendant was squatting in a house. He awoke to find his mattress on fire from his cigarette. He simply moved to another room and went back to sleep. The resulting fire caused £800 of damage. The Criminal Damage Act 1971 required an *actus reus*, whereas the defendant had simply failed to act.
	Held: the creation of a dangerous situation imposes a duty upon the defendant to do something to alleviate (i.e. minimise) that danger. His criminal damage conviction was upheld.

- The *Miller* duty was enshrined into the Law Commission's Draft Criminal Code (1989) at clause 23.

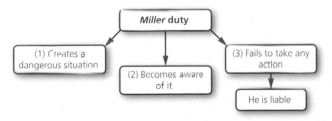

- Pushing a victim into a river knowing that he can't swim creates a duty to act under the *Miller* principle – *Matthews and Alleyne* (2003).
- Lying to a policewoman about carrying sharp objects creates a duty to act under the *Miller* principle – *DPP v Santana-Bermudez* (2003).

- *Santana* may turn on its facts (i.e. be a one-off), but technically, an assault was deemed to have been committed when the defendant failed to act.
- It is controversial to say that an assault can be committed by an omission.

Case:	
Evans (2009)	Facts: the defendant gave the victim (her half-sister) some heroin, which she self-injected. The defendant knew that the victim was unwell and put the victim to bed. The victim had overdosed and she died. The defendant was convicted of manslaughter based on the *Miller* principle.
	Judge LJ: 'When a person has created or contributed to the creation of a state of affairs which he knows, or ought reasonably to know, has become life threatening, a consequent duty on him to act by taking reasonable steps to save the other's life will normally arise.'

Workpoint

Jack drove a minicab to pick up a wedding party. They all got in the car. On the way to the church he stopped at traffic lights and the brakes and handbrake felt soft. Jack drove past his local garage and could have pulled in for repairs, but the wedding party was late so he carried on. He stopped outside the church and put the handbrake on. When he walked away the minicab rolled down the hill, injuring all the people on board. Could Jack be liable under the *Miller* principle? Give reasons for your answer.

2.3.6 When is someone released from their duty?

- An omission may give rise to criminal liability if the defendant has a duty to act.
- The courts have struggled to define exactly when such a duty may expire.
- This is particularly so in instances where the defendant has voluntarily assumed a duty (e.g. *Stone and Dobinson*), or is part of a special relationship.
- In light of *Stone*, even a person of low intelligence may voluntarily assume a duty.
- A duty to care for a patient comes to an end when they competently refuse medical treatment – *Re B* (*Consent to Treatment: Capacity*) (2002).
- *Re B* may be applied when a person has voluntarily assumed a duty of care over a relative if the relative has competently refused care.

- However, if circumstances are grave, a delicate balance must be struck between the relative's wishes and the defendant's duty to provide care – *Smith* (1979).
- In extreme cases, a duty to preserve life will end when the patient has no best interests in being alive.

Case:	
***Airedale NHS Trust v Bland* (1993)**	Facts: Tony Bland was injured in the Hillsborough Stadium disaster. He was in a persistent vegetative state (i.e. a coma) for three years. The hospital authorities applied for judicial permission to withdraw his artificial feeding and hydration, which would, technically, be murder.
	Held: when a patient has no best interests in being kept alive, the doctors no longer have a duty to care, and so artificial feeding and hydration can be withdrawn. The withdrawal is not the *actus reus* of murder; it is an omission, but the omission will not lead to liability because the duty to care has expired.

Research Point

Look up the case *Airedale NHS Trust v Bland* [1993] AC 789. On what grounds did the Lords justify their decision that the doctors no longer had a duty to care?

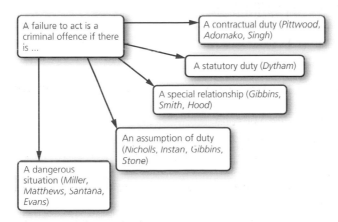

A failure to act is a criminal offence if there is ...

A contractual duty (*Pittwood, Adomako, Singh*)

A statutory duty (*Dytham*)

A special relationship (*Gibbins, Smith, Hood*)

An assumption of duty (*Nicholls, Instan, Gibbins, Stone*)

A dangerous situation (*Miller, Matthews, Santana, Evans*)

2.3.7 Reform in this area

There has been considerable discussion about omissions and criminal liability, so an exam question may well ask you to evaluate this area of law.

Research Point

The leading argument for imposing criminal liability for all omissions is: Andrew Ashworth, 'The Scope of Criminal Liability for Omissions' (1989) 105 LQR 424. Look this article up. What are his main arguments for imposing criminal liability for omissions?

There are some very strong arguments against this idea, some of which are listed below:

- How exactly would a 'social duty to act' be defined by law?
- Would society adhere to the same set of moral rules?
- Should we force strangers to rescue each other when taxes already pay for rescue services?
- Would the emergency services be stretched if a bystander misjudges a situation and makes things worse for himself or others?
- Could the law become too intrusive if strangers attempted to rescue us at every turn?
- What would be the difference between a 'rescuer' and a 'bystander', or would everybody in the vicinity be arrested for failing to act?

Workpoint

Can you think of any more disadvantages to a social duty to act?

Checkpoint - omissions

Task:	Done!
I understand that an *actus reus* can sometimes be replaced by an omission	
I can give a legal example of when a contractual duty gives rise to liability for omissions	
I can give a legal example of when a statutory duty gives rise to liability for omissions	
I can give a legal example of when a special relationship gives rise to liability for omissions	
I can give a legal example of when a voluntary assumption of duty gives rise to liability for omissions	
I can explain when a dangerous situation gives rise to liability for omissions	

Task:	Done!
I understand when someone is released from their common law duty to act	
I can argue against the imposition of a general duty to act	

2.4 Causation

- When a defendant is charged with a result crime (i.e. a crime that has a consequence such as grievous bodily harm), it is not enough to prove that the defendant had the *actus reus* and *mens rea* of that crime.
- He must also have *caused* the outcome.
- This is because sometimes a defendant can have both the *actus reus* and the *mens rea* of an offence, but the victim's resulting injury was actually caused by something or someone else!

> **Definition**
>
> Causation: the defendant must *cause* the outcome.

- This doctrine is known as causation, and it means that the prosecution must prove that the defendant *caused* the outcome.
- This is sometimes difficult to prove, especially if there are several causes to juggle with.
- If it cannot be proved that the defendant caused the outcome, he will be acquitted of the offence.

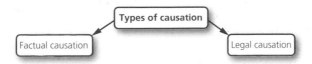

- In criminal law there are two types of causation – factual causation and legal causation.
- Both types of causation must be met.
- The jury will decide whether or not causation has been met.

Case:	
***Pagett* (1983)**	The usual jury direction may read as follows: 'in law the accused's act need not be the sole cause, or even the main cause, of the victim's death, it being enough that his act contributed significantly to that result'.

2.4.1 Factual causation

Definition

Factual causation: it is a physical fact that the defendant caused the outcome.

- Factual causation requires the defendant to have caused the outcome as a fact (i.e. if he was taken out of the equation, it would never have happened).
- This is often called the 'but for' test:

> '...but for the defendant's action, the victim would not have been hurt...'

- If the answer to the 'but for' test is: '...the victim *would still have been* hurt...' then the defendant will not be the factual cause.
- A good way to understand factual causation is to refer to *White* (1910).

Case:	
White (1910)	The defendant put cyanide in his mother's drink in order to kill her. She drank a quarter of the cup and died of a heart attack. It transpired that her heart attack was not caused by the cyanide, but from natural causes. As a result, the defendant could not be convicted of murder because he was not the factual cause of her death. He was, however, convicted of attempted murder instead.

- If factual causation is met, this is not enough to establish that the defendant caused the outcome.
- Legal causation must also be met.

2.4.2 Legal causation

Definition

Legal causation: this is concerned with the *number* of causes, who was the *significant* cause, which cause was *operating* (i.e. 'active') at the time of injury/death, etc.

- Legal causation aims to pinpoint who is really at fault by finding the 'operating' and 'significant' cause.

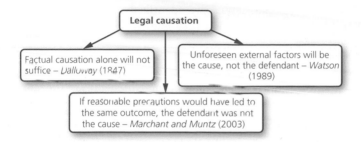

Legal causation

Factual causation alone will not
suffice – *Dalloway* (1847)

Unforeseen external factors will be
the cause, not the defendant – *Watson*
(1989)

If reasonable precautions would have led to
the same outcome, the defendant was not
the cause – *Marchant and Muntz* (2003)

Workpoint

Alice invites Darren over to her house for a party. Darren agrees. Later
that night, Darren crosses the road to reach Alice's house when he is
hit by a car and killed. Is Alice the factual and legal cause of Darren's
death? Give reasons for your answer.

- Legal causation has many different elements to it (four are listed below).
- A jury must ensure that all of these issues are addressed when
  deliberating causation.

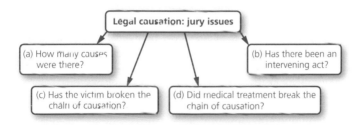

Legal causation: jury issues

(a) How many causes
were there?

(b) Has there been an
intervening act?

(c) Has the victim broken the
chain of causation?

(d) Did medical treatment break the
chain of causation?

2.4.2.1 How many causes were there?

- When a group of individuals set upon a victim with several different
  modes of attack, causation is not straightforward.
- Which *actus reus* was the legal cause of the outcome?
- What if all seven defendants caused the outcome but in varying
  degrees?
- When juries are deliberating these issues, the *de minimis* rule applies.

Definition

De minimis: ignore trivialities.

- In criminal law, very trivial contributions may be ignored (e.g. a
  scratch on the finger compared to a stab wound to the heart).

- However, if several causes are identified and they are all more than 'slight' or 'trifling' then they must all be considered – *Kimsey* (1996).

2.4.2.2 Has there been an intervening act?

- An unforeseeable incident may occur which breaks the chain of causation.
- This new and intervening act will overtake all previous causes as the new cause.

Latin: *'novus actus interveniens'* ⟶ English: 'new act intervening'

- If there is a *novus actus interveniens*, the original defendant is absolved from all liability.
- This is because his original actions can no longer be said to have caused the outcome (he may still be a factual cause, but this will not suffice alone).

Defendant's *actus reus* (e.g. punching) ⟶ Intervening act (e.g. building collapses) ⟶ Chain from defendant is *broken*. New cause

- However, in order for a *novus actus interveniens* to fully absolve a defendant from all liability, it must be unforeseeable. (i.e. the defendant must have no idea that an intervening act is about to occur).
- If the defendant can *foresee* the intervening act, then it is simply part of his plan, and therefore it does *not* intervene as the new cause – *Pagett* (1983).

Research Point

Look up the facts of the case *R v Pagett* [1983] Crim LR 393. The defendant argued that there was an unforeseeable intervening act which caused his girlfriend's death. What was this intervening act and do you agree with him? What did the courts decide? What do you think about the decision?

2.4.2.3 Has the victim broken the chain of causation?

- It is not unheard of for a victim to be the *novus actus interveniens* of his or her own injury or death.
- The courts have seen a number of these kinds of cases in recent years, including:

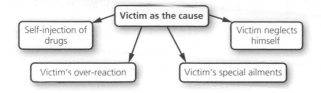

- The same causal rules apply to the acts of victims: if the victim's new intervening act is unforeseeable, it will overtake the original cause and absolve the defendant from all liability.

Self-injection

- There is a causal difference between *receiving* an injection of heroin and *self-injecting* the heroin.
- If the defendant injects the victim, the defendant is the cause of death – *Cato* (1976).
- If the victim injects himself, he is the new cause – *Dalby* (1982), *Dias* (2002) and *Kennedy* (2007).

Case:	
Kennedy (2007)	Lord Bingham: 'The criminal law generally assumes the existence of free will. Thus [D] is not to be treated as causing [V] to act in a certain way if [V] makes a voluntary and informed decision to act in that way rather than another. The finding that [V] freely and voluntarily administered the injection to himself, knowing what it was, is fatal to any contention that [D] caused the heroin to be administered to [V] or taken by him.'

Workpoint

A *novus actus interveniens* can only break the chain of causation and absolve the defendant from all liability if it is **unforeseeable** (*Pagett*). In *Kennedy*, it was held that a victim's self-injection breaks the chain of causation. Has the rule in *Pagett* been followed or ignored here?

Over-reactions

- Victims who escape from dangerous situations (real or imagined) can cause their own injury or death.
- As always, if the victim's response is unforeseeable, it will break the chain of causation and absolve the defendant from all liability.
- These cases are also known as 'fight or flight' cases.

Case:	
Roberts (1972)	Facts: a female passenger jumped from the defendant's car after he tried to remove her coat. He was charged with actual bodily harm.
	Stephenson LJ: 'The test is: was [V's reaction] the natural result of what [D] said and did? If of course [V] does something so "daft" or so unexpected that no reasonable man could be expected to foresee it, then it is only in a very remote and unreal sense a consequence of [D's] assault.'

- The jury must consider whether the victim's reaction was 'within the range of expected responses' – *Williams and Davis* (1992).
- A 'daft' reaction from the victim will break the chain of causation – *Corbett* (1996) and *Marjoram* (1999).
- The test is now one of 'daftness' – a daft and unforeseeable reaction by a victim will break the chain of causation.

Workpoint

Are the following reactions 'expected' or 'daft'? Remember, 'daft' reactions will break the chain of causation and absolve the original defendant.

(a) Craig walks towards Louise with mistletoe and she runs out onto the balcony, falls over it and dies.

(b) Keith touches Mary's leg when he is driving at 68mph. She jumps out of the car onto the M6 and suffers terrible injuries.

(c) Barry stalks Jill along the coast and Jill jumps 20ft over the cliff.

(d) Dawn jumps out from a hedge to scare Matthew and he backs into an oncoming car.

Take your victim as you find him

- The accused may like to argue that the victim broke the chain of causation because they were particularly susceptible to injury (e.g. brittle bones).
- The courts have stated that defendants must 'take their victims as they find them'.
- It is also known as the 'egg-shell skull rule' in reference to the victim's frailty.
- A defendant will be responsible for the death of a victim if they die of fright from a weak heart condition if the death follows a threat of violence – *Hayward* (1908).
- This rule is not limited to physical ailments – it includes religious beliefs too.

Case:	
Martin (1832)	Parke J: 'It is said that [V] was in a bad state of health; but that is perfectly immaterial, as, if [D] was so unfortunate as to accelerate her death, he must answer for it.'
Blaue (1975)	Facts: the defendant stabbed the victim four times, puncturing her lung. A blood transfusion would have saved her life, but she refused because she was a Jehovah's Witness. She died. The defendant argued that her refusal was unreasonable and broke the chain of causation.
	Lawton LJ: 'It has long been the policy of the law that those who use violence on other people must take their victim as they find them. The question for decision is what caused her death. The fact that the victim refused to stop this end coming about did not break the causal connection between the act and the death.'

Workpoint

Should a defendant be convicted of any crime if the victim refuses life-saving treatment? Give reasons for your answer.

Victim neglect

- It has been argued that when a victim neglects or re-opens his or her wounds and exacerbates the injuries, he or she is the new cause of death.
- This has been rejected by the courts, because the defendant caused the injury in the first place.
- When a wound becomes infected and the victim refuses to treat it, the defendant is still liable for the eventual death – *Holland* (1841).
- If a victim re-opens his wounds or fails to stop the blood flow, the defendant is still the operating and substantial cause of death – *Dear* (1996).

Victim action:	Cause of death?	Cases:
Self-injection	Victim	*Dalby* (1982) *Dias* (2002) *Kennedy* (2007)
Victim's over-reaction is daft	Victim	*Roberts* (1972) *Williams and Davis* (1992) *Corbett* (1996) *Marjoram* (1999)

Victim action:	Cause of death?	Cases:
Weak heart condition	Defendant	*Hayward* (1908)
Victim is in bad health generally	Defendant	*Martin* (1832)
Religious refusal of treatment	Defendant	*Blaue* (1975)
Victim refuses treatment	Defendant	*Holland* (1841)
Victim makes injury worse	Defendant	*Dear* (1996)

Checkpoint - causation (1)

Task:	Done!
I can define 'causation'	
I know the difference between factual and legal causation	
I can define 'novus actus interveniens'	
I can explain the rule in *Pagett* (1983) in relation to the foreseeability requirement	
I can list the three instances in which a victim may break the chain of causation	
I understand the causative rules regarding self-injection and can list one relevant case	
I understand the causative rules regarding the over-reaction of a victim and can list two relevant cases	
I can define and explain the 'egg-shell skull rule' and list one relevant case	
I understand the causative rules regarding victim neglect of wounds and can list one relevant case	

2.4.2.4 Did medical treatment break the chain of causation?

- The final issue that a jury must untangle in legal causation is that of medical negligence.
- It has been accepted by the courts that extraordinary medical negligence will constitute a *novus actus interveniens* and break the chain of causation.
- This is extremely rare.

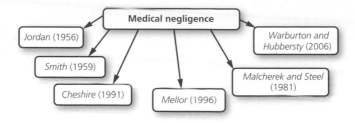

Case:	
Jordan (1956)	Facts: the defendant stabbed the victim and emergency surgery was required. The wounds were healing when the doctors injected the victim with a drug he was allergic to, and waterlogged his lungs causing bronchopneumonia which led to the victim's death. Held: the murder conviction was quashed by the Court of Appeal. Had the jury heard all the evidence, they would not have been able to say that the stab wound was the cause of death.
Smith (1959)	Lord Parker CJ: 'If at the time of death the original wound is still an operating cause and a substantial cause, then the death can properly be said to be the result of the wound. Putting it another way, only if the second cause is so overwhelming as to make the original wound merely part of the history can it be said that the death does not flow from the wound.'
Cheshire (1991)	Beldam LJ: '[D] need not be the sole cause or even the main cause of death, it being sufficient that his acts contributed significantly to that result. Even though negligence in the treatment of [V] was the immediate cause of his death, the jury should not regard it as excluding the responsibility of [D] unless the negligent treatment was so independent of [D's] acts that they regard the contribution made by [D's] acts as insignificant.'

- Beldam LJ in *Cheshire* used the terms 'independent' and 'extraordinary' to describe whether medical negligence had broken the chain of causation.
- Any negligent medical treatment must now be independent of the defendant's original act (i.e. not connected) and extraordinarily bad.
- This makes any negligent medical treatment flowing from the defendant's act even more unlikely to break the chain of causation.

Research Point

Look up the case of *Cheshire* [1991] 3 All ER 670. What happened to the victim before he reached hospital? How did his medical treatment contribute to his death? On what grounds did Beldam LJ justify the need for medical treatment to be 'independent' and 'extraordinary'?

- Sometimes there may be supervening (i.e. 'other') events that may contribute to the victim's death.
- These will not break the chain of causation because the defendant is still the substantial cause of death – *Mellor* (1996).

Supervening acts may include:		
A delay in the arrival of the ambulance	A delay in resuscitation	The victim's reaction to treatment
The victim's bad health	The quality of medical care	The victim's refusal of treatment

- Switching off a life support machine is not an intervening act which breaks the chain of causation – *Malcherek and Steel* (1981).
- Switching off a life support machine is simply allowing the patient to die from the original pre-existing condition – *Airedale NHS Trust v Bland* (1993).
- The correct test as a result of the cases of *Cheshire* and *Mellor* is: 'did the acts for which the defendant is responsible significantly contribute to the victim's death?' – *Warburton and Hubbersty* (2006).

Causation	
Factual causation:	
'but for' test	*White* (1910)
Legal causation:	
Factual and legal causation required	*Dalloway, Watson, Marchant*
More than a minimal cause	*Kimsey*
An intervening act	*Pagett*
Victim breaks the chain	*Cato, Kennedy, Roberts, Williams, Corbett, Marjoram, Martin, Hayward, Blaue, Holland, Dear*
Medical treatment	*Jordan, Smith, Cheshire, Mellor, Warburton, Malcherek*

Checkpoint - causation (2)

Task:	Done!
I can identify the circumstances in which medical negligence breaks the chain of causation and list three relevant cases	
I can distinguish *Jordan* (1956) from *Cheshire* (1991) in terms of legal causation	
I can define the current test as set out in *Warburton and Hubbersty* (2006)	
I can explain why a doctor does not break the chain of causation when he switches off a life support machine	

Potential exam questions:

1) Chris stabs his wife Jo in an argument at home. She is taken to hospital. The doctor who sees her is a young trainee working the nightshift and has been on duty for 36 hours. He gives Jo a powerful painkiller while she awaits surgery. Jo is allergic to the painkiller and her brain begins to swell. She is taken into surgery but her swelling is not noticed. She suffers brain damage as a result of the swelling and dies on the operating table when she loses the capacity to breath for herself. Who has caused Jo's death?

2) Chris returns home later that night after the police interview him feeling very stressed. He is awoken in the early hours by a noise. He goes downstairs to find a gang of burglars. He managed to chase them away two months ago, but this time Chris has a heart attack and dies. The defendants, when charged with burglary and unlawful act manslaughter, argue that they did not cause his death. Are they correct?

Chapter 3

Mens rea

As discussed in the previous chapter, almost all criminal offences require some kind of physical act (*actus reus*). That is not all that is needed to prove that a criminal offence was committed. The accompanying mental element (*mens rea*) must also be present.

3.1 What is a *mens rea*?

Definition

> *Mens rea*: guilty mind

- The mental element of a criminal offence is known as the *mens rea*.
- This is the guilty mind of the criminal.
- As a general rule, every *actus reus* comes with an accompanying *mens rea*.

Workpoint

Write your own definition of each *mens rea*: intention, recklessness, negligence and dishonesty.

- Some crimes will require intenion only ('specific intent crimes').
- Some crimes will accept recklessness as a *mens rea* ('basic intent crimes').
- Negligence is also seen occasionally in criminal law.
- Some crimes will require no *mens rea* whatsoever (strict liability offences).

3.2 Why bother with a *mens rea*?

- *Mens rea* is vital in criminal law – the courts are generally reluctant to punish those who act without awareness.
- A person who performs a criminal act with the accompanying *mens rea* is far more blameworthy than a person who performs a criminal act accidentally or mistakenly.
- If an *actus reus* is accidental (i.e. there was no intention or recklessness as to the physical act), then the person has not committed a crime and will not be punished.
- The only exception to this is strict liability offences where only an *actus reus* is required.

Workpoint

Jack is standing in a post office queue. He trips over his shoelace and falls into Betty, who breaks her hip. Later that afternoon in the same post office, Dean is tired of queuing and pushes Lisa in front, who also falls over and breaks her wrist. Betty and Lisa suffer actual bodily harm under s.47 of the Offences Against the Person Act 1861, which requires intention or recklessness as a *mens rea*.

(a) Does Jack have the *actus reus* and *mens rea* of actual bodily harm? Give reasons for your answer.
(b) Does Dean have the *actus reus* and *mens rea* of actual bodily harm? Give reasons for your answer.

- Criminal offences must clearly state which *mens rea* will suffice for a conviction.

Criminal offence:	*Mens rea* (i.e. mental element) required:
Murder	Intention to kill or cause GBH
Assault	Intention or recklessness
Battery	Intention or recklessness
Actual bodily harm	Intention or recklessness
Criminal damage	Intention or recklessness
Gross negligence manslaughter	Negligence (on a gross level)
Theft	Intention and dishonesty

- Very serious crimes (e.g. murder) require intention only.
- Individuals who recklessly kill another person cannot be charged with murder.

- Recklessness will also not suffice for a theft.
- Assault, battery, actual bodily harm and criminal damage will accept recklessness as a *mens rea* if intention cannot be proved.

3.3 Intention

- A popular *mens rea* in criminal law is intention.
- This alludes to a desire or aim to commit a criminal act, making the defendant particularly blameworthy.

→ Murder
→ Grievous bodily harm (s.18 OAPA 1861)
→ Malicious wounding (s.20 OAPA 1861)   Some criminal
→ Actual bodily harm (s.47 OAPA 1861)   offences requiring
→ Assault and battery   intention
→ Theft
→ Criminal damage
→ Burglary
→ Rape
→ Riot

- It is sometimes difficult for the prosecution to prove that the defendant had an intention to do a particular act or intended a particular consequence.
- There needs to be proof, therefore, that the defendant developed the required intention.

Workpoint

Darren purchases a gun and sets out to find Wendy, his ex-girlfriend who cheated on him. He finds her in the law library. He tells everybody to leave and takes Wendy to the nearby park where he spent four hours the previous night, digging a big ditch. He shoots Wendy directly through the heart and she lands in the ditch. Darren attempts to bury her but a neighbour sees everything and calls the police. Darren is arrested and charged with murder.

You are acting for the prosecution. What *evidence* can you find that Darren had an intention to kill Wendy?

- There are two types of intent in criminal law – direct intent and oblique intent – and either one will suffice.

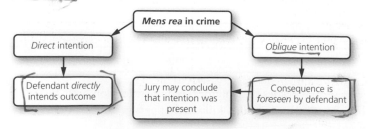

- There has been doubt in the criminal law as to whether oblique intention actually exists, because it is simply an alternative way of finding direct intention.

Checkpoint - intention (1)

Task:	Done!
I can translate the Latin phrase *mens rea*	
I can list the four most common forms of *mens rea* in criminal law	
I can list at least five criminal offences that require intention	
I can distinguish the two different types of intention	

3.3.1 Direct intention

Definition

Direct intention: the defendant directly aims or desires the consequence (e.g. death).

- Direct intention is straightforward: the defendant directly intends (i.e. aims or desires) to perform the *actus reus* of a criminal offence and the prosecution can prove that this was the case.
- A professional hit man who kills for money still has the direct intention to kill – *Calhaem* (1985).
- A sadistic psychopath who enjoys killing people still has the direct intention to kill regardless of the fact that he is motivated by a mental abnormality – *Byrne* (1960).

Workpoint

The definition of theft (s.1 of the Theft Act 1968) is below. What is the *mens rea* of the offence (i.e. all the mental components of the crime)? What must the defendant possess as a state of mind?

'A person is guilty of theft if he dishonestly appropriates property belonging to another with the intention of permanently depriving the other of it.'

Complete the sentence: The *mens rea* of theft is:

3.3.2 Oblique intention

> **Definition**
>
> Oblique intention: the defendant foresees the consequence (e.g. death) as virtually certain so therefore the jury may conclude that intention was present.

- Oblique intention was developed through case law as an alternative way of finding direct intention.
- It will still suffice as the required intention once it is found, thus ensuring that the defendant has still met the *mens rea* of his criminal offence.

> **Definition**
>
> Oblique intention test: does the defendant foresee the consequence as virtually certain? If so, the jury are free to find that he intended it.

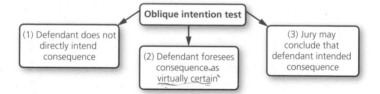

- Oblique intention places an emphasis on foreseeing a consequence rather than directly intending it.
- The defendant's foresight is not treated as intention; it is treated as evidence of intention – *Moloney* (1985).
- The jury will decide whether the defendant's foresight really amounted to intention – *Moloney* (1985).

> **Research Point**
>
> Look up the judgment of Lord Bridge in *R v Moloney* [1985] AC 905. What is Lord Bridge's opinion when it comes to foresight, evidence, intention and directing juries, known as Lord Bridge's 'golden rule'?

- The jury direction on oblique intention was altered in *Nedrick* (1986).
- If a defendant recognised a consequence as virtually certain, the jury could 'infer' (i.e. 'assume') intention.

Case:	
Nedrick (1986)	Lord Lane: 'If the jury are satisfied that at the material time [D] recognised that death or serious harm would be virtually certain to result from his voluntary act, then that is a fact from which they may find it easy to infer that he intended to kill or do serious bodily harm, even though he may not have had any desire to achieve that result'.

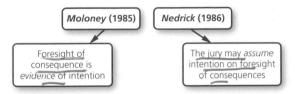

Moloney (1985) → Foresight of consequence is *evidence* of intention

Nedrick (1986) → The jury may *assume* intention on foresight of consequences

---

Workpoint

If you foresee that bad exam results are a virtually certain consequence of you skipping lectures, is a jury right to infer (i.e. assume) that you intend to get bad exam results? Give reasons for your answer.

- The word 'infer' in the *Nedrick* direction was interpreted as saying that a jury could convict a defendant of murder if he *recognised death as virtually certain*.
- This was controversial because the *mens rea* for murder is a direct intention to kill.
- *Woollin* (1998) slightly altered the jury direction again, but is the current leading case.

Case:	
Woollin (1998)	Lord Steyn: 'Where the charge is murder, the jury should be directed that they are not entitled [to find] the necessary intention, unless they feel sure that death or serious bodily harm was a virtual certainty as a result of [D's] actions and that [D] appreciated that such was the case'.

- Lord Steyn in *Woollin* swapped the word 'infer' for the word 'find'.
- It returns the freedom to the jury to find (i.e. freely decide) intention based on the evidence, as opposed to simply assuming it once foresight was found.

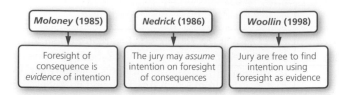

Moloney (1985)	Nedrick (1986)	Woollin (1998)
Foresight of consequence is *evidence* of intention	The jury may *assume* intention on foresight of consequences	Jury are free to find intention using foresight as evidence

Workpoint

David collects his petrol flask, some long matches, and runs over to Jill's house to burn her house down. He can see that a new car is parked in her driveway – it might be her new boyfriend – but David will not allow himself to become distracted. David lights the match and drops it through the letterbox. He stands back and watches the house burn. It turns out that Jill, her new boyfriend and a child were all killed in the fire. David is charged with three counts of murder.

(a) What does he directly intend?
(b) What is the current test for oblique intention and does he obliquely intend anything?
(c) In conclusion, what can he be charged with?

3.3.3 Dealing with oblique intention

- Lord Bridge's 'golden rule' in *Moloney* (1985) states that a judge should avoid any elaboration on intent unless it is strictly necessary.
- This is because the whole concept of oblique intent is very confusing for a jury.
- If a trial judge does feel the need to direct a jury on oblique intention, the defendant will be likely to appeal on the grounds that the jury were unnecessarily confused – *Fallon* (1994).
- It would now be wrong to direct the jury that if a defendant had foreseen death or serious injury as virtually certain, he had intended it – *Scalley* (1995).
- The jury should not be confused with questions of purpose, foresight of consequences or awareness of risk – *Wright* (2000).
- If a jury were to conclude, based on the facts of the case, that the defendant appreciated a virtual certainty of death, they probably would have found intention – *Matthews and Alleyne* (2003).

Case:	Direction on oblique intention:
Moloney (1985)	Avoid elaboration, foresight is only evidence of intention
Nedrick (1986)	Foresight of a virtually certain consequence is intention
Woollin (1998)	The jury may find intention on foresight of a virtually certain consequence
Fallon (1994)	Lord Bridge's 'golden rule' is good law
Scalley (1995)	Foresight of a virtually certain consequence is not the same as intention
Wright (2000)	Oblique intention does not have to be raised when the intention issue is straightforward
Matthews and Alleyne (2003)	Foresight of a virtually certain consequence is still not the same as intention

Research Point

You may be asked to critically analyse the law on intention in your exam, and oblique intention is definitely worthy of criticism. Find one of the listed articles below and read it. What are the main arguments of the author?

- Lord Goff, 'The Mental Element in the Crime of Murder' (1988) 104 *Law Quarterly Review* 30;
- G. Williams, 'The *mens rea* for Murder - Leave it Alone' (1989) 105 *Law Quarterly Review* 387;
- N. Lacey, 'A Clear Concept of Intention' (1993) 56 *Modern Law Review* 621;
- M.C. Kaveny, 'Inferring Intention from Foresight' (2004) 120 *Law Quarterly Review* 81.

3.3.4 Reform of oblique intention

- In 2006, the Law Commission recommended that oblique intent as established by *Woollin* should be codified along with direct intention.
- This recommendation has not been implemented.

Law Commission report: *Murder, Manslaughter and Infanticide* (2006):

'1. A person should be taken to intend a result if he or she acts in order to bring it about.

2. In cases where the judge believes that justice may not be done unless an expanded understanding of intention is given, the jury should be directed as follows: an intention to bring about a result may be found if it is shown that the defendant thought that the result was a virtually certain consequence of his or her action.'

Checkpoint - intention (2)

Task:	Done!
I can write my own definition of direct intention	
I can explain Lord Bridge's 'golden rule' in *Moloney* (1985)	
I can distinguish *Nedrick* (1986) from *Moloney* (1985) and *Woollin* (1998)	
I can recite the current oblique intention direction in *Woollin* (1998)	
I understand why *Matthews and Alleyne* (2003) may turn on its facts	

3.4 Recklessness

- In addition to intent – whether direct or oblique – a defendant can also possess a reckless state of mind when performing an *actus reus*.
- As a result, recklessness is a *mens rea* for several offences.

Workpoint

What is your own definition of 'reckless behaviour'?

- Recklessness is currently defined by the criminal law as the defendant's foresight of an unjustifiable risk.
- In simpler terms, the defendant sees a risk of injury or loss and goes ahead anyway.

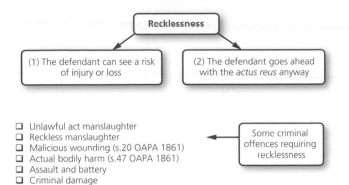

Recklessness

(1) The defendant can see a risk of injury or loss

(2) The defendant goes ahead with the *actus reus* anyway

❑ Unlawful act manslaughter
❑ Reckless manslaughter
❑ Malicious wounding (s.20 OAPA 1861)
❑ Actual bodily harm (s.47 OAPA 1861)
❑ Assault and battery
❑ Criminal damage

Some criminal offences requiring recklessness

Workpoint

The definition of criminal damage (s.1 of the Criminal Damage Act 1971) is below. What is the *mens rea* of the offence (i.e. all the mental components of the crime)? What must the defendant possess as a state of mind?

'A person who without lawful excuse destroys or damages any property belonging to another intending to destroy or damage any such property or being reckless as to whether any such property would be destroyed or damaged shall be guilty of an offence.'

Complete the sentence: The *mens rea* of criminal damage is:

• The test for recklessness has been in a state of flux over the last few decades.
• It is currently a subjective test, although it was objective for a short time.

Definition

Subjective: through the eyes of the defendant (i.e. the 'subject').
Objective: through the eyes of the reasonable man (i.e. who is 'objective').

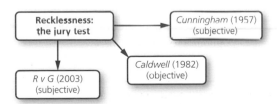

Recklessness: the jury test

Cunningham (1957) (subjective)

Caldwell (1982) (objective)

R v G (2003) (subjective)

• The leading case on recklessness is *Cunningham* (1957).

- Reckless behaviour should be considered from the defendant's point of view, making it *subjective* recklessness.

Cunningham (1957)
(subjective recklessness)

(1) The accused has foreseen that the particular kind of harm might be done...

(2) ...and yet has gone on to take the risk of it

- As a result of *Cunningham*, the old-fashioned *mens rea* of 'malice' was split into two: intention or recklessness.
- The *Cunningham* definition of recklessness has been applied to numerous criminal offences, including all non-fatal offences and criminal damage.
- The defendant must have an appreciation of risk of some damage, even if this is suppressed or driven out – *Stephenson* (1979).

Workpoint

Darren is sleeping over at Stacey's house. They light candles, burn incense and watch TV. Darren and Stacey leave the room to retrieve their dinner from the oven. Darren knows that candle wax is dripping onto the floor and hesitates before he leaves the room. He picks the big candle up and puts it on top of the TV. Ten minutes later, the TV explodes causing a fire and Darren is charged with causing criminal damage. Does his behaviour constitute subjective recklessness? Give reasons for your answer.

- The *Caldwell* case came along in 1982, reverting the subjective recklessness test to an objective one.
- The objective test considered what the ordinary, prudent individual would have foreseen, not the defendant himself.

Case:	
Caldwell (1982)	Lord Diplock: 'A person under the Criminal Damage Act 1971 is reckless if (1) he does an act which in fact creates an obvious risk that property will be destroyed or damaged and (2) when he does the act he either has not given any thought to the possibility of there being any such risk or has recognised that there was some risk involved and has nonetheless gone on to do it.'

- The use of the word 'obvious' was particularly significant in Lord Diplock's judgment in *Caldwell*.

Workpoint

What are the specific words in the quote below that make Lord Diplock's judgment an objective test?

'(1) he does an act which in fact creates an obvious risk that property will be destroyed or damaged and (2) when he does the act he either has not given any thought to the possibility of there being any such risk or has recognised that there was some risk involved and has nonetheless gone on to do it.'

- *Caldwell* recklessness was applied to several other offences including causing death by reckless driving – *Lawrence* (1982).
- It was also applied to reckless manslaughter in *Seymour* (1983) and assault occasioning actual bodily harm (under s.47 OAPA 1861) in *DPP v K (a minor)* (1990).
- McCowan LJ stated in *Spratt* (1991) that *DPP v K* had been wrongly decided, and that the real test was 'taking a risk with foresight of harm'.
- Lord Ackner in *Savage and Parmenter* (1992) confirmed that for malicious wounding (under s.20 OAPA 1861) the defendant 'must foresee that his act would cause harm'.
- *Caldwell* was finally overruled in *R v G* (2003) for being manifestly unfair and subjective recklessness under *Cunningham* was restored.

Research Point

Look up the case *R v G (and another)* [2003] UKHL 50. Lord Bingham listed several reasons why *Caldwell* recklessness should be over-ruled. List these reasons.

Case:	Direction on oblique intention:
Cunningham (1957)	Maliciousness is intention or subjective recklessness
Stephenson (1979)	Defendant must appreciate the risk (subjective)
Caldwell (1982)	*Obvious* risk of which defendant may be ignorant (objective)
Lawrence (1982)	Reckless driving applied objective recklessness

Case:	Direction on oblique intention:
Seymour (1983)	Reckless manslaughter applied objective recklessness
DPP v K (a minor) (1990)	Actual bodily harm applied objective recklessness
Spratt (1991)	Defendant must appreciate the risk (subjective)
Savage and Parmenter (1992)	Malicious wounding applied subjective recklessness
R v G (2003)	*Caldwell* is overruled – return to subjective recklessness

Checkpoint - recklessness

Task:	Done!
I can list two criminal offences that require recklessness	
I can distinguish *Cunningham* (1957) from *Caldwell* (1982)	
I can list three reasons why *Caldwell* was over-ruled	
I can recite the current subjective recklessness test to be put to a jury	

3.5 Negligence

• Negligence can also suffice as a *mens rea* to certain criminal offences, but not many. Negligence is another word for 'mistake' or 'ignorance'.

Definition

Negligence: mistake, ignorance, failing to appreciate consequences that would have been appreciated by a reasonable man.

• We all make trivial mistakes from time to time. It is only rarely that mistakes lead to serious harm or death.
• In civil law (i.e. tort) negligence occurs when a person behaves below a *reasonable standard* of care.
• In criminal law this is not blameworthy enough – only *gross* negligence will suffice for a criminal offence.

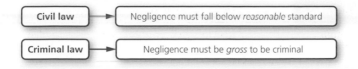

| Civil law | → | Negligence must fall below *reasonable* standard |
| Criminal law | → | Negligence must be *gross* to be criminal |

Case:	
***Andrews v DPP* (1937)**	Lord Atkin. 'Simple lack of care as will constitute civil liability is not enough. For purposes of the criminal law there are degrees of negligence, and a very high degree of negligence is required to be proved before the [crime] is established.'

Workpoint

Why do you think the criminal courts are only interested in prosecuting *gross* negligence?

- The most well-known criminal offence requiring gross negligence is gross negligence manslaughter, explored in detail in Chapter 9.

3.6 Other forms of *mens rea*

- One additional mental element which can be found in the Theft Act 1968 and the Fraud Act 2006 is 'dishonesty'.
- Dishonesty has not been defined by statute or common law, but it is explored in detail in Chapter 12.

Definition

Dishonest: intentionally deceptive, a desire to trick or defraud people.

3.7 Transferred malice

- A defendant can perform the *actus reus* of a criminal offence (e.g. throwing a punch) with the required *mens rea* (e.g. intention or recklessness) but an unforeseen victim feels the full force instead of the anticipated victim.

- Defendants have argued in the past that they do not possess the *mens rea* of the criminal offence if they unintentionally harm a complete stranger.

- The courts have rejected this argument: the malice that the defendant possesses for the first victim is simply 'transferred' over to the unforeseen victim.

Transferred malice: malicious intention towards one victim is transferred to another victim

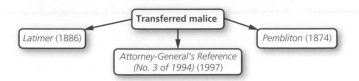

- The doctrine of transferred malice is an old and well-settled one in criminal law.

- If a person is harmed, it does not matter that the defendant intended the injury to be inflicted upon somebody else.

Case:	
Latimer (1886)	The defendant took his belt off and swung it at the victim. The belt missed the victim and hit a complete stranger with full force. The defendant's malice was transferred and he was convicted of malicious wounding under s.20 OAPA 1861.
Attorney-General's Reference (No. 3 of 1994) (1997)	The defendant stabbed his pregnant girlfriend who then gave birth prematurely. The baby died some months later. The defendant was charged with murder. The Court of Appeal transferred his malice from the mother to the foetus, and then to the child (two transfers) and said that a murder conviction was possible. The House of Lords disagreed: transferred malice could not be transferred twice and a foetus was not a person in law.

Research Point

Look up the case *Attorney-General's Reference (No. 3 of 1994)* [1997] 3 WLR 421. How did Lord Mustill define the doctrine of transferred malice and why was the Court of Appeal overruled?

- If a defendant intends one offence (e.g. assault), but accidentally performs a completely different offence (e.g. criminal damage), malice cannot be transferred.

- You cannot mix-and-match the *actus reus* of criminal damage to the *mens rea* of assault – the intended crime and the actual crime must be the same.

Case:	
Pembliton (1874)	The defendant was involved in a big brawl outside a pub. He separated from the group and threw a stone towards the group which smashed a window. His conviction for malicious damage was quashed: he did not have the *mens rea* for malicious damage; he intended to hurt a person.

- Transferred malice was preserved in the Law Commission's *Draft Criminal Law Bill* (1993):

> 'Clause 32(1): In determining whether a person is guilty of an offence, his intention to cause, or his awareness of a risk that he will cause, a result in relation to a person being capable of being the victim of the offence shall be treated as an intention to cause or, as the case may be, an awareness of a risk that he will cause, that result in relation to any other person affected by his conduct.'

Checkpoint - negligence and transferred malice

Task:	Done!
I understand the current standard of negligence required in criminal law	
I can define the doctrine of transferred malice as stated in *Latimer* (1886)	
I can explain why transferred malice was not a route to conviction in *Attorney-General's Reference (No. 3 of 1994)* (1997)	

3.8 Coincidence of *actus reus* and *mens rea*

- The *actus reus* and a *mens rea* of a criminal offence must coincide with each other.

Definition

> Coincidence in crime: the physical act and mental element must happen at the <u>same time, or at least meet at some point.</u>

- If an *actus reus* occurs first and then a *mens rea* is formed later on, a criminal offence has not been committed.
- This is because an *actus reus* (e.g. theft) without its *mens rea* is simply an innocent action.
- A *mens rea* without its accompanying *actus reus* is also not culpable – it is simply a thought or a fantasy.
- What if the *actus reus* takes place over a long period of time and the *mens rea* in comparison is relatively short?
- Alternatively, what if the *actus reus* takes several forms and a *mens rea* is formed during one of these?

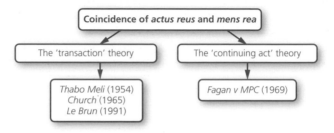

Case:	
Thabo Meli **(1954)**	The defendants took the victim to a hut and beat him. Thinking he was dead, they rolled his body over a cliff. The victim was not dead but died from exposure. The defendants appealed their convictions of murder on the grounds that the *actus reus* (exposure) was separated from their intention to kill. They lost: it was all one long plan and they simply thought the death occurred before it did.

- As a result of *Thabo Meli*, when a combination of events occurs and the *actus reus* is a part of that combination, the *mens rea* may occur at any point during that time.
- This is known as the 'transaction' theory.
- In *Church* (1965), the transaction theory was applied to unlawful act manslaughter where the *mens rea* occurred at the beginning of 'a sequence of acts designed to cause death'.
- *Le Brun* (1991) is a more recent application of the 'transaction' theory.

Case:	
Le Brun (1991)	The defendant punched his wife unconscious while walking home one night. He dragged her dead body home and dropped her. The head injury from the kerb killed her. He appealed against unlawful act manslaughter on the ground that there was a significant time lapse between the original assault (*mens rea*) and the eventual death (*actus reus*).
	Lord Lane CJ: 'Where the unlawful application of force and the eventual act causing death are parts of the same sequence of events, the same transaction, the fact that there is an appreciable interval of time between the two does not serve to exonerate [D] from liability'.

Workpoint

X and Y are drug dealers and drag C to a nearby bridge. C failed to complete a drug deal and owes X and Y a lot of money. He is only a teenager and refuses to break into his neighbour's house. He also cannot swim. X and Y are aware of this, and beat C up until he is almost certainly dead before throwing him over the bridge. C is found dead a week later and his autopsy shows that he drowned. X and Y are charged with murder.

(a) Have X and Y performed the *actus reus* of C's murder? Give reasons for your answer.
(b) Did X and Y possess the *mens rea* of murder on the night in question? Give evidence for your answer.
(c) If the answer is 'yes' to both of the questions above, what might X and Y argue in relation to the coincidence of the *actus reus* and *mens rea*?

- The 'continuing acts' theory is simpler.
- When the *actus reus* is one long continuing act, the *mens rea* can form at any point during that act.

Case:	
Fagan v Metropolitan Police Commissioner (1969)	The defendant accidentally drove his car onto a policeman's foot. The policeman shouted at the defendant to remove it but he refused and switched off his engine. He was convicted of a battery but appealed on the ground that when he committed the *actus reus* of driving onto the policeman's foot, he did not have the required *mens rea* to complete the offence. The Court of Appeal held that a *mens rea* can be placed onto a continuing act at any point to constitute the offence.

Fagan v MPC (1969)

One long *actus reus* of battery: car on policeman's foot

The battery takes place in *Fagan* when the *actus reus* and *mens rea* touch each other.

Shorter *mens rea* when defendant intentionally remains on victim's foot

Coincidence theory:	Case:
'Transaction'	*Thabo Meli and others* (1954)
	Church (1965)
	Le Brun (1991)
'Continuing act'	*Fagan v Metropolitan Police Commissioner* (1969)

Workpoint

Darren and Lorena are unhappily married. Lorena moves out. She takes Darren's wide-screen TV, sports car and laptop. Darren is very angry and forms an intention to kill her when he finds out. Later on that day when Darren has calmed down, he retrieves his sports car but accidentally runs over Lorena in her mother's garage and kills her.

(a) Can Darren be charged with murder (i.e. does he have the *actus reus* and *mens rea*)? Give reasons for your answer.
(b) What if Darren was still intending to kill Lorena (e.g. by poison or strangulation) when he ran her over? Do you think it matters that the mode of death happens to be different to what Darren planned? Give reasons for your answer.

Checkpoint - coincidence of *actus reus* and *mens rea*

Task:	Done!
I can explain why coincidence of *actus reus* and *mens rea* is vital in criminal law	
I can list the two theories of coincidence in criminal law	
I can distinguish *Thabo Meli and others* (1954) from *Fagan v Metropolitan Police Commissioner* (1969) and explain why they represent two different coincidence theories	

Potential exam questions:

1) Derek, a religious extremist, plants a bomb in a shopping centre. He intends for it to go off on a busy Saturday at 12 pm to bring attention to his religious cause. He calls the centre security and informs them to evacuate the building at 11:45 am, knowing that this will be a tight timeframe in which to save everybody. Some families are busy in the crèche and do not hear the warning, and other special-needs shoppers require additional help to evacuate. The bomb goes off and 25 people are killed. Derek is charged with terrorist offences, criminal damage and murder.

   (a) The definition of criminal damage under section 1 of the Criminal Damage Act 1971 is as follows: 'A person who without lawful excuse destroys or damages any property belonging to another intending to destroy or damage any such property or being reckless as to whether any such property would be destroyed or damaged shall be guilty of an offence'. In terms of *mens rea*, can Derek be convicted of criminal damage?

   (b) The *mens rea* of murder is an intention to cause death or grievous bodily harm. In terms of *mens rea*, can Derek be convicted of murder?

2) Jill and Claire were arguing in a pub one evening over who would get to take Matthew, a man at the other end of the bar, home. The argument escalates and Jill takes her stiletto off, throwing it towards Claire's face. Claire dives out of the way and the stiletto punctures Matthew's face at the other end of the bar, blinding him in the left eye. Her stiletto also breaks several glasses hanging up behind Matthew. Jill is charged with assault occasioning actual bodily harm and criminal damage. She argues that she did not intend (or was reckless) as to Matthew's injury. She also argues that she did not intent (or was reckless) as to causing criminal damage.

   (a) Does it matter that Jill's target victim unforeseeably changed at the last minute? Can she still be charged with Matthew's actual bodily harm?

   (b) Can Jill be convicted of criminal damage?

Chapter 4
Strict liability

Many criminal offences (particularly violent crimes such as assault, grievous bodily harm and murder) require both an *actus reus* and a *mens rea* to secure a conviction. The defendant must have a blameworthy state of mind at the time of his criminal act in order to render him culpable and truly deserving of punishment.

However, there are a handful of common law (and numerous statutory) criminal offences that do not require proof of a mental element for the full offence to be committed. These are known as strict liability offences, and they either require a partial *mens rea*, or no *mens rea* at all.

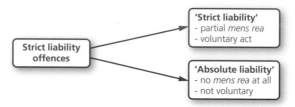

- Strict liability offences appear to contradict the very purpose of the criminal law.
- They punish individuals for simply doing a particular act without a necessary mental element.

Case:	
***Pharmaceutical Society of Great Britain v Storkwain Ltd* (1986)**	Facts: the defendant was charged under s. 58(2) of the Medicines Act 1968, which states: 'no person shall supply specified medicinal products except in accordance with a prescription given by an appropriate medical practitioner.
	Held: despite his lack of knowledge or deception he was found guilty of the offence, as he had supplied medicinal products without a prescription given by an appropriate medical practitioner.

Section 58(2) in *Storkwain* was silent on *mens rea* but other sections of the Medicines Act 1968 specifically referred to mental elements.

As a result, the Lords concluded that s.58(2) was intended to be strict liability.

- The majority of strict liability cases require a voluntary *actus reus* only (as in *Storkwain*).
- However, a small handful of criminal offences do not even require a voluntary *actus reus*.
- These are very rare, but they are known as 'absolute liability' offences.

4.1 Absolute liability offences

- When a criminal offence is labelled as an 'absolute liability' offence, it has no *mens rea* element at all.
- The defendant must simply complete the *actus reus* to be found guilty.
- He may not even know that he has committed the prohibited act – he must simply be found in a particular set of circumstances that constitute the *actus reus*.

- In absolute liability, the defendant will commit the *actus reus* of a criminal offence even if he is unknowingly placed or led into that situation by another person – *Larsonneur* (1933).

Case:	
***Winzar v Chief Constable of Kent* (1983)**	Facts: the defendant was taken to a hospital but he was simply drunk. The police put him in the police car, took him to the police station, and charged him with being found drunk in a highway contrary to s.12 of the Licensing Act 1872.
	Goff LJ: 'Looking at the purpose of this particular offence, it is designed to deal with the nuisance which can be caused by persons who are drunk in a public place. This kind of offence is caused quite simply when a person is found drunk in a public place or highway. It is enough for the commission of the offence if (1) a person is in a public place or a highway; (2) he is drunk; and (3) in those circumstances he is perceived to be there and to be drunk.'

- The *Winzar* decision may seem a little unfair because it was the police officers who placed the defendant in their car in the first place.
- However, absolute liability offences are not concerned about state of mind or blameworthiness; they simply require a particular act to be carried out, which was done.

Workpoint

Why do absolute liability offences exist? What is Parliament intending to achieve by creating these offences?

Checkpoint - absolute liability

Task:	Done!
I can split strict liability offences into two groups and I can explain the main difference between the two	
I can explain the outcome in *Pharmaceutical Society of Great Britain v Storkwain Ltd* (1986)	
I can define an absolute liability offence	
I understand why the courts upheld the conviction in *Winzar v Chief Constable of Kent* (1983)	

4.2 Strict liability offences

- Strict liability offences require only a partial *mens rea*.
- As a result, the defendant only intends (or is reckless to) one part of the *actus reus*, but he will be convicted of the entire *actus reus*.
- A good example of how this works in practice can be found in *Prince* (1875) and *Hibbert* (1869).

Case:	*Prince* (1875) LR 2 CCR 154	*Hibbert* (1869) LR 1 CCR 184
Charge:	Section 55 of the Offences Against the Person Act 1861: *'taking an unmarried girl under the age of 16 out of the possession of her father against his will'.*	
Facts:	*Prince* knew that the girl was in the possession of her father but believed her to be 18 years old	*Hibbert* took a 14 year old girl off the street and had sexual intercourse with her
Result:	Convicted	Acquitted

Case:	*Prince* (1875) LR 2 CCR 154	*Hibbert* (1869) LR 1 CCR 184
Reason:	*Prince* intended to remove the girl from her father's possession	*Hibbert* did not know that the girl was in the possession of her father
Liability:	Intent was required for this part of the *actus reus* only. *Prince* met the requirements	Intention was not proved for a specific part of the offence as it was in *Prince*

Workpoint

Looking at the box above, on what grounds can the defendants in *Prince* and *Hibbert* be distinguished? Why was the defendant in *Prince* found guilty?

4.2.1 The defence of 'due diligence'

• In some strict liability offences, a defence known as 'due diligence' may be offered to the defendant.
• This means that if the defendant took steps to *avoid* committing the crime, be will not be convicted.

Definition

Diligence: take reasonable care to avoid an outcome, be careful, take steps to avoid harm.

• If the defence is not available, then a defendant will still be convicted even if he takes all the steps necessary to prevent him from committing the offence – *Callow v Tillstone* (1900).
• Unless it is expressly listed as a defence in the relevant statute, the courts will decide that due diligence is not available.

Case:	
***Harrow LBC v Shah and Shah* (1999)**	The defendants owned a newsagent. A lottery ticket was sold to a 13 year old by a member of staff. The owners were charged under s.13(1)(c) of the National Lottery Act 1993. The defendants told their staff not to sell tickets to children under 16, to ask for proof of age, to refer to the defendants if still not sure, and rules were clearly displayed in the shop window and staff were frequently reminded.

Case:	
***Harrow LBC v Shah and Shah* (1999)**	Held: only section 13(1)(a) contained a due diligence defence; s.13(1)(c) did not. The defendants were convicted because the offence did not require a *mens rea*.

- The defence of due diligence is the only defence available to strict liability offences.

4.2.2 No defence of 'mistake'

- The defence of mistake is available in criminal law when a defendant commits a criminal offence under a mistaken belief.
- This defence ensures that those who made a genuine mistake as to the facts are not convicted of a criminal offence.
- However, mistake is not available in strict liability offences – *Cundy v Le Cocq* (1884).
- Judges will decide whether an offence is strict liability and whether mistake is therefore available as a defence – *Sherras v De Rutzen* (1895).

Research Point

The defendants in *Cundy* and *Sherras* were charged under the Licensing Act 1872 with different outcomes. Look up the case of *Sherras v De Rutzen* [1895] 1 QB 918. Why was strict liability rejected in this case?

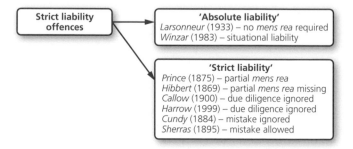

Workpoint

If the defences of mistake and due diligence were made widely available for strict liability offences, what effect would this have on the criminal law?

Checkpoint - strict liability

Task:	Done!
I can define a strict liability offence	
I can distinguish *Prince* (1875) from the case of *Hibbert* (1869)	
I understand why the courts upheld the conviction in *Callow v Tillstone* (1900)	
I can define the defence of due diligence	
I can explain how due diligence is relevant to the case of *Harrow LBC v Shah and Shah* (1999)	
I know why the defence of mistake is an issue in strict liability	
I can distinguish *Cundy v Le Cocq* (1884) from the case of *Sherras v De Rutzen* (1895)	

4.3 Common law strict liability offences

- These days, most strict liability offences are passed by Parliament with clear directions as to whether the defence of due diligence is available or not.
- There are actually very few strict liability offences in common law, except for the three listed below:

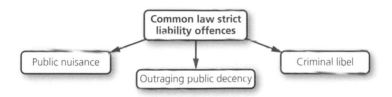

4.3.1 Public nuisance and libel

- The old offence of blasphemous libel was raised in the *Lemon* (1979) case.
- Lord Russell concluded that intent was not necessary because publication is a deliberate action.

4.3.2 Outraging public decency

- This common law offence was held to be an offence of strict liability in *Gibson and Sylveire* (1991).
- It does not have to be proved that the defendant intended (or was reckless) as to his conduct outraging public decency.

Checkpoint - common law strict liability offences	
Task:	**Done!**
I can list a common law strict liability offence with a case authority	

4.4 Statutory strict liability offences

- Many strict liability offences are actually statutory, and most are regulatory in nature.

- In old Acts of Parliament, it is not often clear whether an offence is strict liability or not.
- Parliament has been vague in the past as to whether some statutory criminal offences actually have any *mens rea* at all.
- It is therefore up to the courts to decide through *judicial interpretation* whether a particular paragraph, section or Act contains a strict liability offence.

4.4.1 Judicial interpretation of statutes for strict liability purposes

- There many different factors that a judge can consider when interpreting an Act of Parliament to find strict liability:

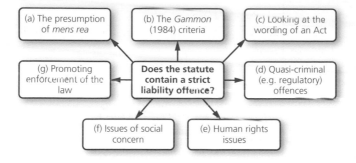

4.4.2 The presumption of *mens rea*

- If the statute clearly states that no *mens rea* is required, then the courts will interpret the offence as one of strict liability.
- When faced with an ambiguous statute, the courts will always start with the assumption that a *mens rea* is required – *Sweet v Parsley* (1969).

Case:	
***Sweet v Parsley* (1969)**	Lord Reid: 'There has for centuries been a presumption that Parliament did not intend to make criminals of persons who were in no way blameworthy in what they did. That means that, whenever a section is silent as to *mens rea*, there is a presumption that, in order to give effect to the will of Parliament, we must read in words appropriate to require *mens rea*.'

- Clear words that an offence requires a *mens rea* will include the following:

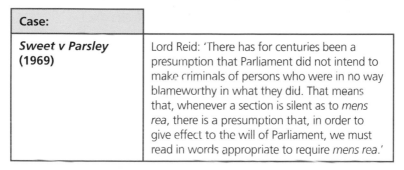

- When a presumption is made, the courts must decide whether the presumption stands (i.e. they can find evidence for it), or the presumption falls (i.e. it really is a strict liability offence).

4.4.3 The *Gammon* criteria

- The significant case in the interpretation of statutes is *Gammon* (1984).
- Lord Scarman laid down criteria for displacing the presumption of *mens rea*.
- The presumption of *mens rea* will stand unless specific criteria are met.

Case:	
Gammon (Hong Kong) Ltd v Attorney-General of Hong Kong (1984)	Lord Scarman: 'Although there is a presumption that *mens rea* is required, this can be displaced by a clear or necessary implication in the statute. A displacement of the presumption is "necessary" when the statute is concerned with social or public safety issues, and even then the presumption will stand unless a strict liability approach will promote the object of the statute. The presumption is particularly strong in "truly criminal" offences.'

Workpoint

Lord Scarman's guidance in *Gammon* on displacing the presumption of *mens rea* can be split up into four criteria. List them.

4.4.4 Looking at the wording of an Act

• In addition to the *Gammon* criteria, judges will examine the whole section or other sections within the statute.
• This will help them decide whether Parliament intended for a *mens rea* to be presumed.

Case:	
Sweet v Parsley (1969)	Lord Reid: 'In the absence of a clear intention in the Act that an offence is intended to be an absolute offence, it is necessary to go outside the Act and examine all relevant circumstances in order to establish that this must have been the intention of Parliament.'

• In a more recent example of broad statutory interpretation, the Insolvency Act 1986 was examined in *Muhamad* (2002).
• The majority of the Act referred to a *mens rea* whereas s.362(1)(a) did not, so it was held to be a strict liability offence.

Workpoint

The National Lottery Act 1993 is provided below. Section 13 was examined in *Harrow LBC v Shah and Shah* (1999).

(a) Can you see any evidence of a *mens rea* in section 13?
(b) Which paragraphs are strict liability paragraphs?
(c) Can you see any evidence of a defence to strict liability?

(d) What does section 13(1)(a) tell the courts about section 13(1)(c)?

(e) Why did the court in *Harrow* interpret section 13(1)(c) as a strict liability offence?

The National Lottery Act 1993.

'13(1) If any requirement or restriction imposed by regulations made under section 12 is contravened in relation to the promotion of a lottery that forms part of the National Lottery,

(a) the promoter of the lottery shall be guilty of an offence, except if the contravention occurred without the consent or connivance of the promoter and the promoter exercised all due diligence to prevent such a contravention;

(b) any director, manager, secretary or other similar officer of the promoter, or any person purporting to act in such a capacity, shall be guilty of an offence if he consented to or connived at the contravention or if the contravention was attributable to any neglect on his part;

(c) any other person who was a party to the contravention shall be guilty of an offence.'

4.4.5 Quasi-criminal offences

- According to the *Gammon* case, *mens rea* is more likely to be presumed if the offence is 'truly criminal'.
- Criminal offences can be split into two groups: violent and regulatory.

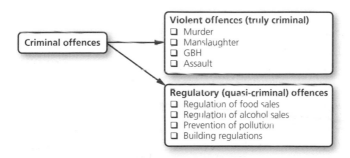

- Violent offences are very serious and often result in harm, injury or death to a victim.
- There is a stronger presumption of *mens rea* in 'truly criminal' offences because the defendant is malicious.

- Regulatory offences are statutory requirements that can be breached through reckless, ignorant or even accidental behaviour.
- These are known as 'quasi-criminal' offences and there is a lesser presumption of *mens rea*.

Case:	
Alphacell Ltd v Woodward **(1972)**	Lord Salmon: 'The offences created by the Rivers (Prevention of Pollution) Act 1951 seem to me to be prototypes of offences which are "not criminal in any real sense, but are acts which in the public interest are prohibited under penalty". I can see no valid reason for reading the word "intentionally", "knowingly" or "negligently" into section 2(1)(a).'

- If a criminal offence carries a significant penalty, or is very serious, it is more likely to be a 'truly criminal' offence.
- In *B v DPP* (2000), section 1(1) of the Indecency with Children Act 1960 was held to be a very serious offence, and so a *mens rea* was required.
- However, in *Howells* (1977), a heavy sentence did not deter the judges from finding strict liability.

Research Point

Look up the case *Howells* [1977] QB 614. How did the Court of Appeal justify finding strict liability despite s.1(1)(a) of the Firearms Act 1968 being a 'truly criminal' offence?

Checkpoint - statutory strict liability offences (1)

Task:	Done!
I can list three areas of law in which statutory strict liability offences can be found	
I can describe five of the seven issues that courts will examine when deciding whether a statutory offence is one of strict liability	
I can list the four criteria as set out in *Gammon (Hong Kong) Ltd v Attorney-General of Hong Kong* (1984)	
I can distinguish 'quasi-criminal' from 'truly criminal' offences and give two examples of each	
I can explain why different conclusions were met in *B v DPP* (2000) and *Howells* (1977)	

4.4.6 Human rights issues

- When a person is imprisoned for committing a strict liability offence, the issue of human rights is raised.
- This is because a strict liability offence does not require a blameworthy state of mind, meaning that inadvertent (i.e. blameless) individuals are sent to prison.
- The most relevant articles of the European Convention of Human Rights are articles 5 and 6:

> *Article 5(1):*
>
> *'Everyone has the right to liberty and security of person. No one shall be deprived of his liberty save as in the following cases and in accordance with a procedure prescribed by law (a) the lawful detention of a person after conviction by a competent court.'*

- Article 5 is not breached if the 'procedure' (i.e. the strict liability offence) is 'prescribed by law' (i.e. a real offence) and carried out by a 'competent court'.

> *Article 6(2):*
>
> *'Everyone charged with a criminal offence shall be presumed innocent until proved guilty according to law.'*

- Article 6 is not breached if the prosecution successfully prove that the defendant is guilty, whether this be a 'truly criminal' offence or a 'strict liability' offence.
- A balance must be struck between the general interest of the community and the protection of the rights of the individual – *DPP ex parte Kebilene* (1999).
- However, article 6(2) does not say anything about what the mental elements of an offence should be, and so strict liability crimes do not breach this article – *R v G* (2008).

Workpoint

Human rights will generally not support a defendant if he is convicted of a strict liability offence (as long as the procedure is prescribed by law in a competent court and the prosecution finds him guilty).

(a) Is it fair to impose a custodial sentence for a strict liability offence? Give reasons for your answer.
(b) Is the defendant truly 'blameworthy'? Give reasons for your answer.

4.4.7 Issues of social concern

• The presumption of *mens rea* can be rebutted if an issue of social concern arises.

Case:	
Sweet v Parsley (1969)	Lord Diplock: 'Where the subject matter of a statute [involves] potential danger to public health, safety or morals, the court may feel driven to infer an intention to impose a higher duty of care on those who choose to participate, and place on them an obligation to take whatever measure may be necessary to prevent the prohibited act.'

• The presumption of *mens rea* can be rebutted in offences which involve public health, safety or morals.
• If an offence is deemed 'truly criminal', the presumption of *mens rea* will be balanced against these issues.

Case:	
***Blake* (1997)**	Hirst J: 'Since throughout the history of s.1(1) of the Wireless Telegraphy Act 1949, an offender has potentially been subject to a term of imprisonment, the offence is "truly criminal" in character, and the presumption in favour of *mens rea* is particularly strong. However, the purpose behind making the unlicensed transmissions a serious criminal offence must have been one of social concern in the interests of public safety. Interference with transmissions [of] vital [emergency] public services poses a grave risk to wide sections of the public. The imposition of an absolute offence must surely encourage greater vigilance on the part of those establishing or using a [radio] station. In these circumstances we are satisfied that s.1(1) does create an absolute offence.'

Workpoint

On what grounds did Hirst J in *Blake* justify making a 'truly criminal' offence an offence of strict liability?

4.4.8 Promoting enforcement of the law

- The presumption of *mens rea* can be rebutted if strict liability will promote the object (i.e. 'purpose') of the statute.
- Strict liability offences encourage greater vigilance (i.e. 'awareness') on the part of ordinary people to prevent the commission of the crime.
- If, however, strict liability will not have this effect, then *mens rea* will be presumed – *Lim Chin Aik v The Queen* (1963).

Workpoint

Imagine that the new strict liability offence below is proposed:

The Student Act 2012

Section 1: It shall be an offence for any full-time or part-time student enrolled in higher education to plagiarise the work of another student or academic.

Section 2: The maximum penalty is not to exceed five days in jail and £2,000 fine.

(a) What is the *actus reus* of this new offence?
(b) What is the *mens rea* of this offence?
(c) Would you (or other students) be deterred from committing this offence?

Checkpoint - statutory strict liability offences (2)

Task:	Done!
In relation to issues of social concern, I can recite Lord Diplock's main criteria in the leading case of *Sweet v Parsley* (1969)	

4.5 Recent cases

- Strict liability has continued to be an issue for the courts in recent times.
- *B v DPP* (2000) s.1(1) of the Indecency with Children Act 1960 was silent on the mental element, so Lord Nicholls reviewed the following issues.

Issue:	Lord Nicholls response:
Presumption of *mens rea*	The rule in *Sweet and Parsley* is good law and the courts should always start with a presumption of *mens rea*
Lack of *mens rea* words	The relevant section in the 1960 Act did not refer to a *mens rea* and Parliament had expressed no other intentions
Necessary implication	Any implication (i.e. 'suggestion') of strict liability should be compellingly clear. Such an implication may be found in 'the language used, the nature of the offence, the mischief sought to be prevented and other circumstances'
Severity of punishment	The sentence was one of imprisonment. Severe stigma would also follow the offender. This re-enforced the presumption of *mens rea*
Purpose of the section	Even though the 1960 Act was meant to protect children, this did not make strict liability a necessary implication
Evidential problems	It might be hard to prove that the defendant made a mistake as to the victim's age, but this does not mean that the offence should automatically be one of strict liability
Effective-ness of strict liability	There is no general agreement that strict liability is necessary to protect children in sexual matters
Effect of *Prince*	The prosecution in *B v DPP* argued that the law had been settled since *Prince* (i.e. mistake was no defence in strict liability). Lord Nicholls disagreed – *Prince* had attracted significant criticism
Law reform	It was a shame that Parliament had not heeded the advice from the Law Commission over the years to be clearer when drafting statutes

Lord Nicholls' conclusion

- There was nothing in s.1(1) of the Indecency with Children Act 1960 to displace the presumption of *mens rea*.
- This modern approach shows the reluctance of criminal courts to declare that a 'truly criminal' offence is one of strict liability.
- The law in *B v DPP* was later applied in *Kumar* (2004).

Workpoint

On a separate piece of paper, draw a big mind map of Lord Nicholls' nine new criteria for interpreting statutes for strict liability.

Does the statute contain a strict liability offence?	
The presumption of *mens rea*	*Sweet v Parsley* (1969)
The *Gammon* (1984) criteria	*Gammon* (1984)
Looking at the wording of an Act	*Muhamad* (2002)
Quasi-criminal (i.e. regulatory) offences	*Alphacell* (1972) *B v DPP* (2000) *Howells* (1977)
Human rights issues	*Kebilene* (1999) *R v G* (2008)
Issues of social concern	*Blake* (1997)
Promoting enforcement of the law	*Lim Chin Aik* (1963)
Recent cases	*B v DPP* (2000)

4.6 Justification for strict liability

- Strict liability offences are controversial because they do not require a blameworthy state of mind.
- To receive a custodial sentence for simply being in the wrong place at the wrong time is particularly hard to justify.
- Protecting public safety appears to be the biggest justification for strict liability offences.

Benefits of strict liability offences:	
1	Strict liability offences are easier to enforce
2	They do not require a *mens rea*
3	Individuals are more likely to plead guilty
4	Parliament can provide a defence if they feel it is appropriate
5	An individual's lack of blame can be taken into account when sentencing
6	Improvement notices and prohibition notices are likely to be served to business in the first instance

Workpoint

Now add your own examples of benefits of strict liability offences.

Negatives of strict liability offences:	
1	There is no evidence to suggest that strict liability offences lead to a higher standard of care (e.g. businesses).
2	If people realise they are going to be prosecuted for an act anyway, why take precautions against it?
3	Strict liability crimes impose guilt upon individuals who are not 'guilty' in the traditional sense.
4	Individuals who take all possible care will still be punished unless a clear defence of due diligence is allowed.
5	It is not clear how strict liability offences persuade people not to commit crimes.
6	Imprisoning individuals when they are not truly blameworthy is contrary to human rights (even though the case law in the UK seems to disagree).

Workpoint

What negative affects do strict liability offences have on individuals trying to run their own businesses (e.g. food, alcohol, companies, health and safety etc.)?

4.7 Proposals for reform

- It is Parliament's responsibility to state whether a *mens rea* is required for a statutory offence or whether it is a strict liability offence.
- It is also Parliament's responsibility to state whether or not a defence is available in instances of strict or absolute liability.

Research Point

The Law Commission has suggested that all strict liability crimes should be treated as crimes of negligence. Look up its Report: *The Mental Element in Crime* (1978) (Law Com No. 89).

(a) How would this reform radically change strict liability offences?
(b) How would this reform radically change the criminal law and society behaviour in general?

- Breaches of regulatory law are easier to deal with (particularly when dealing with businesses and companies):
  1. Fixed monetary penalties;
  2. A requirement that steps must be taken to prevent the offence from happening again;
  3. A restoration order to allow the correct position to be restored;
  4. A stop notice to allow the defendant to correct the situation.

Checkpoint - statutory strict liability offences (3)

Task:	Done!
I can list seven of the nine issues that Lord Nicholls considered in *B v DPP* (2000) before deciding that *mens rea* was to be presumed	
I can list three advantages and three disadvantages to imposing strict liability offences upon individuals and/or businesses	
I can define the Law Commission's 1978 suggestions for the reform of strict liability offences	

Potential exam questions:

1) Critically discuss the factors taken into account by courts when deciding whether a statute has created a strict liability offence.
2) Distinguish absolute from strict liability offences.

Chapter 5
Parties to a crime

The criminal law can become complex when more than one person commits the same crime. For example, what if a group of friends agree to break into a property and one of them commits murder? Since they were all working together, are they all guilty of murder?

- This chapter will examine the ways in which a person can join and/or assist an offender.
- This area of law can therefore be split into two areas: joint enterprise and secondary parties.

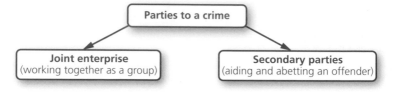

5.1 Joint enterprise

- When a joint enterprise occurs in criminal law, more than one person has committed the same criminal offence.
- They worked together to bring about the result, whether it was pre-planned days in advance, or simply unfolded on the spur of the moment (e.g. in a street fight).

> **Definition**
>
> Joint enterprise: working together, group work, shared effort, equal participation.

Case:	
Stewart and Schofield (1995)	Held: A joint enterprise means taking part in the execution of a crime. A person who is a mere aider or abettor is a secondary party to the commission of whatever crime it is that the principal has committed.

- According to *Stewart and Schofield*, a person who aids or abets an offender is a secondary party.
- A person who takes part in the execution of the crime is part of a joint enterprise to commit that crime.
- Most criminal offences can be committed by a joint enterprise (see below):

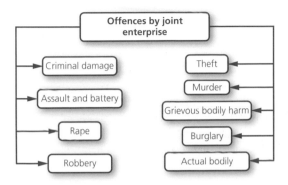

Workpoint

Jack and Freddy planned to burgle a house belonging to the local MP. They collected sharp weapons in advance and went to the house. Kelly was waiting for them. She provided Jack and Freddy with a sawn-off shotgun to use as protection. Jack and Freddy broke in while Kelly waited outside and watched for witnesses. Jack and Freddy managed to steal £600 worth of valuables.

There is a joint enterprise and a secondary party in the above scenario. Who belongs to which category and why?

- Typically, all the members of a joint enterprise possess the same *actus reus* and *mens rea*, making them all equally responsible.
- Problems arise where one member of the joint enterprise does an act that was not pre-planned.

5.1.1 The 'contemplation' principle

- Joint enterprise is a controversial area of law.
- We convict an individual of murder when, technically, he did not commit the *actus reus* (e.g. the act of killing).
- The law has justified this controversial doctrine by applying the following three principles from *English* (1997):

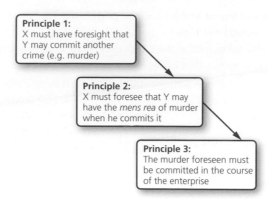

Principle 1:
X must have foresight that
Y may commit another
crime (e.g. murder)

Principle 2:
X must foresee that Y may
have the *mens rea* of murder
when he commits it

Principle 3:
The murder foreseen must
be committed in the course
of the enterprise

- X must foresee (i.e. contemplate) that Y will not only commit another crime but that Y may have the *mens rea* of that crime (i.e. it is not just an accident).
- If X can satisfy these criteria, this means that X will be just as blameworthy as Y.
- X must contemplate that Y will commit murder *within* the course of the enterprise.
- If Y returns to the scene later and commits murder, only Y will be charged with murder.

Case:	
English **(1997)**	When two parties embark on a joint enterprise to commit a crime and one party (X) foresees that in the course of the enterprise the other party (Y) may commit, with the requisite *mens rea*, an act constituting another crime, X is liable for that crime if committed by Y in the course of the enterprise.

- What if X foresaw that Y might intend *actual bodily harm*, but Y actually intended to *kill*?
- Could X escape liability for murder as part of a joint enterprise because he foresaw a slightly different kind of *mens rea* to the one that Y possessed?
- The answer is: all the members of a joint enterprise must foresee what each other *might do*, as opposed to what they will *specifically intend*.

Case:	
***Rahman and others* (2008)**	It would border on speculation to judge what a particular defendant foresaw as to intention. It is safer to focus on the defendant's foresight of what an associate might do.

• A 'weapon change' will not absolve the members of the joint enterprise from liability for the additional criminal act as long as they can foresee the *mens rea* of the perpetrator.

Case:	
English **(1997)**	If the weapon used by the primary party is different to, but as dangerous as, the weapon which the secondary party contemplated he might use, the secondary party should not escape liability for murder because of the difference in the weapon.

Workpoint

Jack and Freddy are disturbed by a family member who is startled to see two burglars. Jack feels threatened when he mistakes her walking stick for a shotgun. He shoots her, killing her. Both Jack and Freddy are charged with burglary and murder as part of a joint enterprise. Should Freddy face a murder charge too? Give reasons for your answer.

English was a significant case in this area and confirmed a string of other cases and principles, including the following:

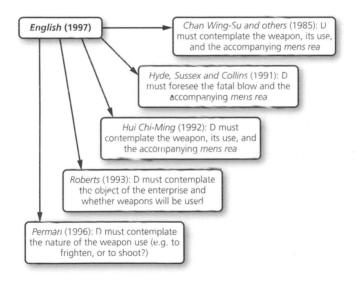

When *Uddin* (1998) reached the Court of Appeal, Beldam LJ took the opportunity to encapsulate the 'contemplation principle' in joint enterprise into seven basic principles:

• All participants are guilty of murder unless one participant's actions are an entirely different type to those foreseen by the others	• All participants are guilty of murder unless the character of the weapon used and its ability to cause death is entirely different to that foreseen by the others
• All participants are guilty of murder if all weapons can be regarded as equally likely to inflict fatal injury	• If one participant does use an entirely different action, the others are not parties to murder but can be charged with other offences (e.g. GBH)
• All participants are guilty of murder if, when a foreseen weapon is produced, they continue to participate in the attack	• All participants are guilty of murder if no one knows which participant used the weapon but its use in the attack was foreseen
• It is not enough that all participants share the same *actus reus* and *mens rea*: all participants must foresee the weapon and the accompanying *mens rea* during its use	**Conclusion:** the 'contemplation principle' applies to the offence of murder, the weapon, its use, and its accompanying *mens rea*

Case:	
O'Flaherty and others (2004)	Courts were keen to avoid the creation of a complex doctrine as to whether one weapon (for instance a knife) differs in character from another (for example a hammer) and which weapons are more likely to inflict fatal injury.

5.1.2 The 'fundamentally different' rule

• If the act committed by a participant is 'fundamentally different' to what the other participants had contemplated, then only the participant who committed that act will be answerable in law for it.

Case:	
Rafferty (2007)	Facts: three defendants attacked the victim. One participant left to use a cash machine. The other two participants dragged the victim into the sea and he drowned.
	Held: the absent participant did not intend to kill and had not contemplated that the other participants would do so because it was a fundamentally different act, so his murder conviction was quashed.

5.1.3 Remoteness

- A participant in a joint enterprise must foresee that one of the other participants may commit a criminal offence.
- The criminal offence committed must be highly probable in the eyes of the other participants.

Case:	
Chan Wing-Su and others (1985)	What has to be brought home to the jury is that occasionally a risk may have occurred to an accused's mind but may genuinely have been dismissed by him as altogether negligible.

Checkpoint - joint enterprise

Item on checklist:	Done!
I can define a 'joint enterprise'	
I can distinguish a principal offender from a secondary party according to the rule in *Stewart and Schofield* (1995)	
I can list at least five crimes that can be committed as part of a joint enterprise	
I can recite the three-part contemplation principle as established in *English* (1997)	
I can explain in simple terms the principles that were laid down in *Uddin* (1998)	
I can give an example of a 'fundamentally different' act	
I can explain what is meant be 'remoteness'	

5.2 Secondary parties

- Many people have heard of the phrase 'aiding and abetting' an offender but are not quite sure what it entails.
- It means helping an offender in some way.

- If found guilty of aiding and abetting an offender, the secondary party will receive the same punishment as the principal offender.

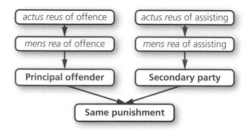

5.2.1 Principal parties

- The principal party carries out the *actus reus* of the criminal offence (with the accompanying *mens rea*).
- He either acts alone, or as part of a joint enterprise with other principal offenders.
- Principal parties sometimes enlist secondary parties to help them out.

Case:	
Giannetto (1997)	Facts: a woman had been killed by either her husband or a hit man enlisted by her husband.
	Held: provided the husband had the *actus reus* and *mens rea* for murder, he was a principal offender and it did not matter that he had enlisted a hit man to do the killing for him.

Martin and Suzanne plan to kidnap Emma from her parents. They enlist 'Mr X' to help them. 'Mr X' knows Emma's family well and can advise Martin and Suzanne on security matters. 'Mr X' drives Martin and Suzanne to Emma's house and provides a crowbar for breaking-in. Martin and Suzanne break in and kidnap Emma. 'Mr X' drives them away from the scene.

Who are principal offenders and who are secondary offenders? Give reasons for your answer.

- If it is impossible to identify who is the principal offender and who is the secondary party, both parties may be acquitted.

Case:	
Lane and Lane (1986)	Facts: a child died while in the care of her parents. Each parent was present and absent during the time of death.
	Held: it could not be proved that one was a principal and one was an accessory. Both were acquitted of manslaughter.

5.3 Aiding, abetting, counselling and procuring

- A secondary party may assist a principal offender in four ways:

(1) Aiding
Helping or assisting the principal prior to or during his commission of the *actus reus* through supply etc.

(2) Abetting
Encouraging the principal at the time of the offence through shouting etc.

(3) Counselling
Encouraging the principal prior to the offence through advising, suggesting or instigating etc.

(4) Procuring
A causal contribution by the secondary party or a causal connection between him and the principal

- It is not entirely clear what aid, abet, counsel or procure mean, but the Lords have encouraged judges to give them their 'ordinary meaning if possible' – *Attorney-General's Reference (No. 1 of 1975)* (1975).

- Secondary parties who help principal offenders will be charged under section 8 of the Accessories and Abettors Act 1861:

> *'Whosoever shall aid, abet, counsel or procure the commission of any indictable offence is liable to be tried, indicted and punished as a principal offender.'*

- Notice how a secondary party found to aid, abet, counsel or procure an indictable (i.e. 'serious') offence will be tried, indicted and punished as a principal offender.

5.3.1 Aiding

- To aid a principal offender is to provide some assistance before and during the commission of the *actus reus* of the crime.
- Although more than mere knowledge is required, the secondary party does not have to be at the scene of the crime to be convicted of aiding.
- Living together does not provide assistance; assistance requires more than mere knowledge – *Bland* (1988).

5.3.2 Abetting

- Abetting requires any involvement from mere encouragement upwards, but being present at the scene is essential.

Case:	
Coney and others (1882)	A man may unwittingly encourage another by his presence, by misinterpreted words, or gestures, or by his silence, or he may encourage intentionally by expressions, gestures or actions intended to signify approval. In the latter case he aids and abets; in the former he does not.

- Abetting can be a silent presence if it encourages the principal.
- Mere encouragement would suffice – *Giannetto* (1996).
- A secret intention to join in is not enough – *Allan* (1965).
- Merely watching an attack is not enough – *Clarkson and others* (1971).
- Voluntary presence in a crowd can abet an offender – *Wilcox v Jeffrey* (1951).

5.3.3 Abetting by omission

- You can abet a principal offender by omission, but only if specific criteria are in place:
  1. D has knowledge of the actions of the principal;
  2. D has the duty or the right to control the principal;
  3. D deliberately does nothing.

Case:	
Du Cros v Lambourne (1907)	If a principal offender drives carelessly and the secondary party is in the passenger seat, the presence in the vehicle plus the right to tell the driver what to do amounts to abetting by omission (if the secondary party does nothing).
Tuck v Robson (1970)	A pub landlord abetted the 'consumption of liquor on his premises after closing time' under the Licensing Act 1964 when he failed to ensure that the drinkers finished and left.

5.3.4 Counselling

- Counselling must be given its ordinary meaning, but this can be quite a wide definition.

> **Definition**
>
> Counsel: advise, solicit, direct, guide, help, support.

Case:	
Calhaem (1985)	There must be contact between parties and a connection between counselling and the offence committed. Equally, the act done must be done within the scope of the advice and not, for example, accidentally.
Luffman (2008)	Facts: D constantly pressured Z to kill the victim. Z kept changing his mind. He went to the victim's house to fake the killing and carried it out. Held: constant pressure from D amounted to counselling despite Z acting of his own accord.

5.3.5 Procuring

- Procuring can mean 'causing' and this can include an act or a word that causes a criminal act to be committed.

Case:	
Attorney-General's Reference (No. 1 of 1975) (1975)	To procure means to produce by endeavour. You procure a thing by setting out to see that it happens and taking the appropriate steps to produce that happening.

Millward (1994)	Facts: a farmer gave his employee a badly-maintained tractor and trailer to drive, which became detached on a public road and killed a bystander.
	Held: the farmer was found to have procured causing death by reckless driving. He had not 'endeavoured' the result but he had 'caused' it.

Workpoint

Alan and Barry, who are both 15, set out to attack Jenny. On the way, they meet Mike, who wants to attack Jenny also. Mike tells Alan and Barry that Jenny is in the shopping centre before leaving them. In the centre, Alan and Barry meet Stanley, who provides them with a baseball bat to attack Jenny with. As Stanley leaves, Barry receives a text message from Mike who departed earlier, telling Barry to aim for Jenny's head. Alan and Barry find and attack Jenny with the baseball bat, inflicting grievous bodily harm. In terms of *actus reus* only, who are the principal offenders, and who has aided, abetted, counselled and procured this offence? Give reasons for your answer.

5.3.6 Innocent agents

• An innocent agent commits the criminal offence but is not blameworthy because they are merely acting for someone else.
• If a principal offender is found not liable for whatever reason, the secondary party may still be convicted.
• To ensure this, the *actus reus* must still be carried out by the principal.

Case:	
Cogan and Leak (1976)	Facts: L terrorised his wife into having sex with C. The wife did not consent, resulting in rape.
	Held: L's rape conviction was upheld on the basis that he had caused the crime to happen, but he could have also committed the offence as a principle offender through the doctrine of 'innocent agent'.
Bourne (1952)	Facts: D forced his wife to perform sexual acts with a dog. She was under duress.
	Held: D aided and abetted the offence even though his wife could not be convicted.

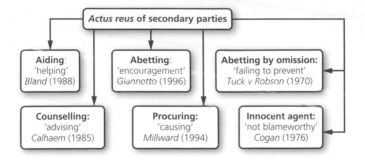

5.4 The *mens rea* of secondary parties

- When aiding, abetting, counselling or procuring a principal offender, the secondary party must possess the following mental components:
  1. *Intention* to aid, abet, counsel or procure the principal offender;
  2. *Knowledge* of the *circumstances* that make up the criminal offence;
  3. *Knowledge* of the principal offender's *mens rea* at the time of the offence.

5.4.1 Intention

- The secondary party must intend to assist the principal offender.
- Mistakes, accidents, recklessness, negligence and complete ignorance will not suffice.

> **Definition**
>
> Intention: desire, foresight, virtually certain consequence, purpose, goal, objective.

> **Workpoint**
>
> Why do you think the secondary party must specifically *intend* to assist the principal offender?

Case:	
***National Coal Board v Gamble* (1959)**	An indifference to the result of the crime does not of itself negate abetting. If one man deliberately sells to another man a gun to be used for murdering a third, he may be indifferent about whether the third man lives or dies, but he can still be an aider or abettor.

Gillick (1986)	Facts: Mrs Gillick was seeking a declaration that a doctor aided and abetted underage sex when he gave her under-age daughter contraceptives.
	Held: the act of aiding or abetting was not illegal because it was necessary for the physical, mental and emotional health of the girl. Clinical judgment negated the doctor's guilty mind, and a guilty mind is an essential ingredient to aiding and abetting.

Workpoint

Traditionally, motive is not relevant to criminal law, only *mens rea*. However, *Gillick* (1986) appears to state that a good intention may be a defence to aiding and abetting. What is the difference between the doctor in *Gillick* who was only interested in the best interests of his patient, and a hit man who is only interested in money?

5.4.2 Knowledge of circumstances

- The secondary party must have knowledge of the circumstances that constitute the offence.
- For example, he must know why the principal offender wants the gun and that he intends to kill another person.
- Exactly how much must the secondary party know before he is said to have 'knowledge' of the offence?
- The law has developed a 'contemplation principle' for secondary parties similar to that for a joint enterprise.
- The secondary party must at least know the essential matters which constitute the offence but he need not actually know that an offence has been committed – *Youden and others* (1950).

Case:	
Bainbridge (1960)	It is not necessary to prove that the secondary party had knowledge of the precise crime or the particular crime. However, he must know more than 'some illegal venture'. A middle ground is required.
DPP of Northern Ireland v Maxwell (1978)	A man will be convicted of aiding and abetting an offence which is *within his contemplation*.

5.4.3 Knowledge of the principal's *mens rea*

- The 'contemplation principle' also requires a secondary party to foresee the principal's *mens rea* at the time of the offence in order to be convicted of aiding and assisting that particular offence – *English* (1997).
- A secondary party will be convicted of murder if he merely foresaw that the principal offender would commit murder with intent to do so.
- The rules in *English* do not breach the European Convention on Human Rights in relation to a right to a fair trial (article 6) – *Concannon* (2001).

Both principal and accessory found guilty of murder:	Principal departed from plan so accessory not guilty:
Chan Wing-Siu (1985)	*English* (1997)
Hyde, Sussex and Collins (1981)	*Uddin* (1998)
Hui Chi-Ming (1992)	*Rafferty* (2007)
Rahman and others (2008)	*Anderson and Morris* (1966)
	Lovesey and Peterson (1970)

Workpoint

Is it fair to convict a secondary party of murder when he did not commit the *actus reus* or possess the *mens rea* for murder himself? Give reasons for your answer.

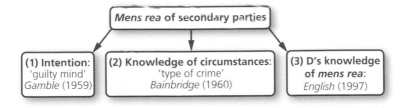

Checkpoint - secondary parties

Item on checklist:	Done!
I can list six ways in which a secondary party can help a principal offender	
I can define a principal party	
I can distinguish between aiding, abetting, counselling and procuring	
I can describe an innocent agent using a practical example	
I can explain what a secondary party must know in terms of circumstances	
I can explain what a secondary party must contemplate in terms of the principal offender's *mens rea*	

5.5 Liability for different offences

• An accessory or a joint enterprise participant can be charged with a separate or lower offence than everybody else.

• This may happen when the accessory or participant contemplates the nature of the principal's act but only some of the harm caused – *Reid* (1975).

• He will be convicted of the separate/lower offence – *Day and Roberts* (2001).

Case:	
***Stewart and Schofield* (1995)**	If joint enterprise can no longer form the basis for liability, other offences may be substituted. Just because the principal's *mens rea* alters unexpectedly does not mean that the other parties are not guilty of other offences.
***Gilmour* (2000)**	Facts: D drove E to a house where E threw in a petrol bomb, killing three occupants. Both were convicted of murder but D's conviction was substituted for manslaughter.
	Held: D was not aware of the size of the bomb or E's intention to cause serious harm, but he did contemplate the act done and that some harm would result. Lower degree of offence was suitable.

- To convict an accessory or participant of a separate or lower offence, the criminal act done by the principal must still be within the scope of the joint enterprise.

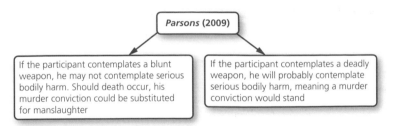

Parsons (2009)

If the participant contemplates a blunt weapon, he may not contemplate serious bodily harm. Should death occur, his murder conviction could be substituted for manslaughter

If the participant contemplates a deadly weapon, he will probably contemplate serious bodily harm, meaning a murder conviction would stand

Workpoint

D and E agree to break into a local newsagent late at night. E has collected two baseball bats to break the windows and a black bag for the money and goods they will steal. They break into the newsagent and the owner comes down to investigate. E hits the owner hard over the head with a hammer that was lying on the floor of the newsagent. The owner dies of his injuries the next day.

(a) What did D foresee that E would do?
(b) What weapon did D foresee that E would use?
(c) What harm or damage did D foresee that might occur?
(d) Is E's act within the scope of the joint enterprise?
(e) What offence(s) will D and E be charged with?

Checkpoint - liability for different offences

Item on checklist:	Done!
I know that an accessory can be convicted of a lesser offence than the principal offender	
I can explain what the accessory/participant must contemplate in terms of what the principal might do in order to be convicted of a lesser offence	
I can explain what the accessory/participant must contemplate in terms of what weapon the principal might use	
I can explain the two-part test as laid down in *Parsons* (2009)	

5.6 Withdrawal from participation

- If an accessory or a participant in a joint enterprise wishes to withdraw from the venture, he may do so and escape liability for the full offence.
- The accessory or participant may still be liable for other offences up to that point.
- The method of withdrawal depends on whether the criminal act is pre-planned or spontaneous.

Definition

Withdrawal: removal, pulling out, departure, leaving, abandonment.

- Repentance without action is not enough (i.e. thoughts will not suffice).
- Words without action is not enough (i.e. don't just 'say' you want to leave).

Case:	
Whitefield (1984)	Dunn LJ: 'Serve unequivocal notice upon the other party to the common unlawful cause that if he proceeds upon it he does so without the further aid and assistance of those who withdraw.'
Eldredge v United States (1932)	McDermott J: 'A declared intent to withdraw from a conspiracy to dynamite a building is not enough, if the fuse has been set, he must step on the fuse.'

- Something 'vastly different and vastly more effective' is required than jumping out of a window and running away – *Becerra and Cooper* (1975).
- Failing to turn up on the day does not constitute 'effective' withdrawal from a joint enterprise.
- Communication must be 'unequivocal' (i.e. plain and clear) – *Rook* (1993).
- Stating an intention to withdraw and then moving away if the criminal act has already commenced is not enough – *Baker* (1994).

Workpoint

John and Michael enter a local chip shop looking for a fight. They both carry knives with them for protection and have used them in the past. John and Michael identify a local gang waiting quietly for their chips and immediately start a fight. The disturbance spills out into the street. John's attention is diverted by Wayne, a frightening man whom he met in prison, running towards him. How can John now effectively and unequivocally communicate his withdrawal from the pre-planned joint enterprise with Michael?

- If the criminal act is spontaneous (i.e. not pre-planned), walking away will suffice as 'effective communication' of withdrawal – *Mitchell and King* (1998).
- Leaving the scene of a street fight will be an effective withdrawal – *O'Flaherty and others* (2004).
- A mere 'lull' in a violent attack does not constitute a withdrawal, a participant must have demonstrably withdrawn – *Mitchell* (2008).

Checkpoint - withdrawal from participation

Item on checklist:	Done!
I can define 'withdrawal' in terms of a joint enterprise	
I can describe the actions or words that will constitute a withdrawal from a pre-planned criminal act using a legal authority as support	
I can define 'vastly effective' in terms of withdrawal from a joint enterprise	
I can describe the actions or words that will constitute a withdrawal from spontaneous criminal activity using a legal authority as support	
I can define 'unequivocal communication' in terms of withdrawal from a joint enterprise	

5.7 Assisting an offender after the commission of the offence

- A secondary party may assist an offender *after* a criminal act has taken place. This may include:
  1. Hiding weapons;
  2. Hiding the offender;

3. Misleading the police or others;
4. Lying to protect the offender;
5. Covering up or destroying evidence.

See section 4(1) of the Criminal Law Act 1967:

> '*Where a person has committed an arrestable offence, any other person who, knowing or believing him to be guilty of the offence or of some other arrestable offence, does without lawful authority or reasonable excuse any act with intent to impede his apprehension or prosecution shall be guilty of an offence.*'

Workpoint

There are defences listed in section 4(1) above. In what instances do you foresee a person may commit this crime and use one of these defences?

5.8 Reform

• The Law Commission has suggested the following reforms.

Participation in Crime (2007) Law Com No. 305	
• Abolish aiding, abetting, counselling and procuring under the Accessories and Abettors Act 1861	• Create a new offence of 'Assisting or Encouraging' (i.e. encouraging can include threats or pressure)
• A defendant can 'fail to take reasonable steps' to prevent the crime from happening under the new offence	• The participant must intend the 'conduct element' of the main offence
• The doctrine of 'innocent agency' should be retained	• For joint enterprise liability, the other participants must intend or believe that the principal offender will commit the main offence
• The participants will not be liable under joint enterprise rules if the main offence fell outside the scope of the enterprise	• A secondary party should negate (i.e. cancel) the effect of their assistance if they wish to withdraw

• There should be a defence available if the participant or secondary party tried to prevent the commission of the main offence	• There should be a defence where a category of persons were being protected by the commission of the offence

• The Ministry of Justice has proposed additional offences in their Report: *Murder, Manslaughter and Infanticide: Proposals for Reform of the Law* (2008):

1. Assisting and encouraging murder;
2. Assisting and encouraging manslaughter;
3. Joint enterprise encapsulated into statutory form.

• New statutory offence based on *English* (1997):

1. The participant must foresee that a victim *might* be killed by a fellow participant with the required intention to do so; or
2. The participant must foresee that serious injury *might* be caused; and
3. The criminal act was still within the scope of the joint enterprise;
4. Absence will not shake off liability (*Rook* 1993).

Workpoint

Jot down a scenario that could be applied to the Ministry of Justice's new statutory offence (above).

Potential exam questions:

1) Explain the 'contemplation principle' in joint enterprise.
2) Compare 'principal offenders' to 'secondary parties'.
3) Distinguish 'aiding', 'abetting', 'counselling' and 'procuring'.
4) Discuss the *mens rea* requirement for secondary parties.
5) Define 'effective withdrawal' in joint liability using legal authorities to illustrate your answer.

Chapter 6
Capacity

In criminal law, a defendant must be mentally capable of committing a criminal offence. In practical terms, a defendant who lacks capacity is unable to form the required *mens rea* (unless, of course, the offence is one of strict liability).

- Only those who are blameworthy should be punished in crime.

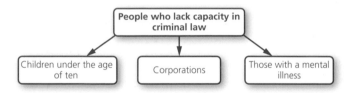

- Children under 10 are believed to be incapable of committing wrong and are therefore not culpable when committing a criminal offence.
- Mentally ill individuals are sometimes unable to form the required *mens rea* of an offence.
- Corporations do not have a 'mind' from which a *mens rea* can be formed.

Workpoint

Why is capacity important in criminal law?

6.1 Children

- It is widely thought that children under 10 do not understand the consequences of their actions. As a result, it would be unfair to punish them.

Doli incapax: incapable of wrong.

- The age of criminal responsibility is set to 10 years old by section 50 of the Children and Young Persons Act 1933:

> 'It shall be conclusively presumed that no child under the age of ten years can be guilty of any offence.'

- The Latin phrase *doli incapax* supports the idea that children are incapable of committing a criminal offence.
- Children who do commit a crime will not be charged, convicted or punished.
- This rule is applied even if the child forms both the *actus reus* and *mens rea* of the offence (e.g. theft).
- Adults using children to commit crime will be liable as principal offenders.

Research Point

In 2003 the Parliamentary Joint Committee on Human Rights criticised the age of criminal liability in their Tenth Report of Session 2002-03, HL1/High Court. Look up paragraphs 35 to 38 and make notes on the main arguments.

- Children under 10 years old who commit crime may be dealt with using family law provisions instead.

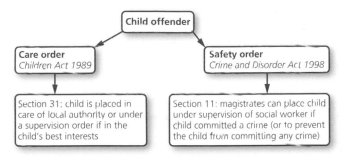

6.1.1 Children aged over 10

- In criminal law, there are three different age groups.
- Children aged between 10 and 21 are placed into one of the following categories:

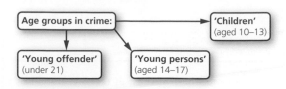

- The presumption of *doli incapax* used to apply to children aged 10–13 but it could be rebutted by the prosecution.
- The prosecution were allowed to rebut *doli incapax* between the ages of 10–13 if they could show evidence that the child knew that his actions were seriously wrong.
- The application of a rebuttable *doli incapax* to children aged 10–13 has since been written off as outdated.

Case:	
C v DPP (1995)	Facts: a boy aged 12 was tampering with a motorbike. He ran away when challenged. The prosecution wished to rebut his *doli incapax* and alleged that his running away proved that he knew his actions were seriously wrong.
	Held: running away may depict mere naughtiness. However, the presumption of *doli incapax* between the ages of 10–13 (even though it was rebuttable) was out of date and contrary to common sense and it was up to Parliament to abolish it.

- The government abolished the rebuttable *doli incapax* to children aged 10–13 when they passed s.34 of the Crime and Disorder Act 1998.

Research Point

Professor Walker in 'The End of an Old Song' (1999) 149 *New Law Journal* 64 put forward the view that simply because the 'presumption' of *doli incapax* had been abolished for children aged 10–13, it did not mean that the defence had been completely abolished for these children. Perhaps, for example, children aged 10–13 could provide evidence to prove that they were *doli incapax*? Look up Professor Walker's article and list the main points of his argument.

- In *JTB* (2009), the House of Lords decided that the presumption of *doli incapax* for children aged 10–13 had been completely abolished.
- They reached this decision after reading two Parliamentary documents:

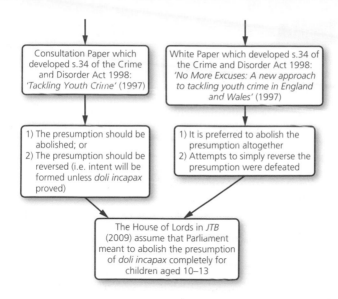

* Children aged 10 and above must meet the same criteria as adult defendants (i.e. *actus reus* and *mens rea* of the offence).
* The presumption that children aged between 10–13 could not commit rape was also abolished by s.1 of the Sexual Offences Act 1993.

6.1.2 Children on trial

* Children are tried in a Youth Court unless the offence is extremely serious.
* Sentences are aimed at reforming behaviour rather than punishing the child.

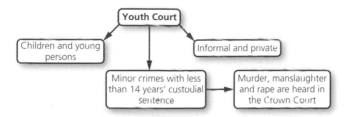

* *T v UK* (1999) confirmed that a trial at Crown Court must be made accessible to a child.
* If a child cannot participate effectively in a Crown Court trial, it may be a breach of article 6 of the European Convention on Human Rights (i.e. right to a fair trial).

Craig, who is 12, has caused significant criminal damage through fire. He is charged with arson under s.1(3) of the Criminal Damage Act 1971 which carries a maximum sentence of life imprisonment.

(1) Which group of youth offenders is Craig placed into?
(2) Is Craig presumed to be 'incapable of wrong'?
(3) Where will he be tried and why?

Checkpoint - children

Item on checklist:	Done!
I can explain why capacity is important in criminal law	
I can locate the law which establishes the current age of criminal responsibility	
I can define *doli incapax*	
I can list the two family law provisions which may be used to aid children under 10 years old who commit a criminal offence	
I can define the three different age groups that young offenders are placed into	
I can explain the effect of *C v DPP* (1995) on the doctrine of *doli incapax*	
I understand why children are tried in a Youth Court	
I can suggest ways in which a Crown Court trial could be made more accessible to a child	

6.2 Vicarious liability

- In the law of tort, a person may be liable for the actions of another. This is known as vicarious liability. An employer, for example, will be liable for the actions of an employee if that employee is acting within his employment contract at the time.

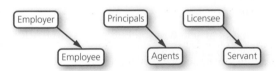

- In criminal law, it is rare to see vicarious liability.

Case:	
Huggins (1730)	Raymond CJ: 'In criminal cases the principal is not answerable for the act of the deputy as he is in civil cases; they must each answer for their own acts and stand or fall by their own behaviour.'

- However, some statutory offences may impose vicarious liability upon a person or a corporation.
- Parliament may do this by including the terms 'person, himself, his servant or agent' into a statutory offence.
- In common law, the offences of public nuisance and criminal libel may also attract vicarious liability.

Workpoint

Why might Parliament wish to impose vicarious liability upon a corporation for a statutory offence?

- If vicarious liability is not clear, judges have other tools at hand in order to ascertain whether Parliament intended liability to be vicarious.

6.2.1 Extending the meaning of words

- Words such as 'sell' or 'permit' in a statute may point to an employer being vicariously liable for his employee if the latter wrongly sells or permits something.

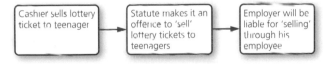

- A *mens rea* is not required in offences like these, so an employer will simply be *acting* through his employee and that will suffice for the offence.
- The employee must, however, be working within the course of his employment at the time of the criminal act.
- An 'authorised act' could therefore include 'selling' goods in a shop or 'supplying' food to a buyer.

Case:	
Adams v Camfoni (1929)	If the employee is not authorised to do the criminal act, then his employer cannot be vicariously liable for him
Coppen v Moore (No. 2) (1898)	If the employee is carrying out an authorised act, the employer will be vicariously liable for him even if the employee wasn't doing the act in quite the right way
Harrow LBC v Shah and Shah (1999)	If the employee is carrying out an authorised act, the employer will be vicariously liable for him even if the employer takes steps to ensure that the law has not been broken

6.2.2 Delegation principle

• If *mens rea* is required, the *actus reus* and *mens rea* of the employee can be transferred up to the employer. This is the delegation principle.

Full responsibility ← Employer's shoulders ← Employee's shoulders

• However, in order to do this, the employer must have delegated responsibility down to the employee in the first place.
• This rule was defined in *Allen v Whitehead* (1930) and confirmed later in *Linnett v Metropolitan Police Commissioner* (1946).

Case:	
Allen v Whitehead (1930)	Facts: an owner of a cafe was charged under s.44 of the Metropolitan Police Act 1839 with allowing prostitutes to meet and remain on his premises. He put notices up and warned the manager of the cafe. However, the manager allowed the prostitutes to stay.
	Held: the acts and knowledge of the manager were imputed to the owner, even though the owner was rarely present and took steps against commission. Ignorance was no defence for the owner – he had delegated the responsibility to the manager and that was enough.

• Any responsibility that has been delegated to the employee must be *complete*. Partial delegation will not allow vicarious responsibility.

Case:	
Vane v Yiannopoullos (1964)	Facts: The defendant (a licensee) was charged with knowingly selling intoxicating liquor to a person he was not entitled to under s.22 of the Licensing Act 1961 when a waitress did so on his premises. The defendant had simply given instructions.
	Held: The licensee was not vicariously liable for her actions.

- The rule in *Vane* suggests that only when an employer or licensee is *away* from the premises can responsibility be fully delegated to the staff who are left.
- *Howker v Robinson* (1972): the employer, licensee or principal does not have to be away from the premises at the time in order to fully delegate responsibility.
- *Bradshaw v Ewart-James* (1983): a master on board a ship is still in control of the ship, so any delegation will be partial.

Workpoint

Mr Sawyer owned and managed his own woodwork shop, Mickey worked there on weekends. One weekend, Mr Sawyer had to attend a family occasion and told Mickey to manage the shop until he got back. When Mickey asked what exactly he had to do, Mr Sawyer said 'See to the customers, answer the phone and sign for the deliveries'. When alone, Mickey sold a chainsaw to a teenager. He was charged with selling a dangerous weapon to a minor.

Can Mr Sawyer be vicariously liable for Mickey's criminal act under the delegation principle? Give reasons for your answer.

6.2.3 Reasons for vicarious liability

- It is very difficult to enforce regulatory offences against individual employees.
- It is almost impossible to prove which employee committed the criminal offence.
- Big companies who enjoy healthy profits should take responsibility for bad practice.
- The threat of vicarious liability forces employers to tighten practices.
- Imposing liability upon the employer, principal or licensee ensures that standards will remain high.
- Employers are more likely to train staff and control them appropriately.
- Licensees are less likely to delegate their significant duties onto less-experienced staff.

6.2.4 Criticisms of vicarious liability

- The defendant (i.e. the employer) is punished for the actions of another.
- The defendant may not have been present at the scene.
- The defendant may not have any knowledge of the circumstances surrounding the offence.
- Many of the statutory offences which allow for vicarious liability include the word 'knowingly' even though some defendants have no knowledge at all.
- The doctrine of vicarious liability is judge-made, meaning that vicarious liability may be implied where Parliament has excluded it from the statute.

Checkpoint - vicarious liability

Item on checklist:	Done!
I can define 'vicarious liability'	
I can locate where vicarious liability may be found in criminal law	
I can describe the two rules that judges use to ascertain whether a statutory offence allows for vicarious liability	
I can define an 'authorised act'	
I can define the 'delegation principle' as defined by *Allen v Whitehead* (1930)	
I can explain the rules surrounding partial delegation of responsibility	
I can list four reasons why vicarious liability is an effective weapon against failing standards in business	
I can list four disadvantages to using vicarious liability to prosecute individuals	

6.3 Corporate liability

- A corporation is a legal person all on its own. A corporation can be punished for committing criminal offences too. There are two ways in which corporations can be distinguished from persons in criminal law:
  1. Finding the required *mens rea* is notoriously difficult;
  2. A corporation can only be fined.

Definition

Corporation: A non-human body or entity with a separate legal personality from its human members (according to *Salomon v Salomon* (1897)).

- A corporation can be liable in criminal law and in civil law.
- According to the Interpretation Act 1978, the word 'person' in a statute includes a body of persons, corporated or unincorporated.

Workpoint

Why is it important that corporations – and not just the people working inside them – can be punished for criminal offences?

- There are three ways in which a corporation can be found liable for a crime:

6.3.1 The principle of identification

- If the offence committed by the corporation requires a *mens rea*, there must be a person within the company who can be identified as having the *mens rea* of the corporation.

Definition

Principle of identification: a person must be identified within the company structure who is the 'directing mind and will' of the company (*Lennard's Carrying Co v Asiatic Petroleum* (1915)).

- The identification principle was established by three cases:
  1. *DPP v Kent and Sussex Contractors Ltd* (1944);
  2. *ICR Haulage Ltd* (1944);
  3. *Moore v I Bresler Ltd* (1944).
- In each case, a senior member of management was identified as the directing mind and will of the company.
- In *DPP v Kent*, the transport manager's intent to deceive was the intent of the company.
- In *ICR Haulage*, the managing director's intention to defraud was taken to be the intent of the company.
- In *Moore*, a branch sales manager was taken to be the directing mind and will of the company when he made false returns with an intent to deceive.
- In the case of *HL Bolton v TJ Graham* (1956), Lord Denning suggested that a corporation was like a human body, and that the directors and managers who ran the company were the brains of the company.

Case:	
HL Bolton Co Ltd v TJ Graham & Sons Ltd (1956)	Denning LJ: 'A company may in many ways be likened to a human body. It has a brain and a nerve centre which controls what it does. Some of the people in the company are mere servants and agents who are nothing more than hands to do the work and cannot be said to represent the mind or will. Others are directors and managers who represent the directing mind and will of the company and control what it does. The state of mind of these managers is the state of mind of the company.'

- In practical terms, managers will be the nerve centre of a company and employees will be the hands.
- The employees play no role in how a company works; they simply carry out the physical tasks.
- It is the managers who control the company. Their *mens rea* is the *mens rea* of the company.

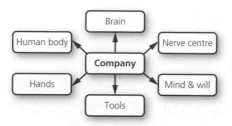

- It is often very difficult to locate the 'nerve centre' of a company.
- If a mere store manager plays a 'directing' role, can his *mens rea* be attributed to the company?

> ## Research Point
>
> In *Tesco Supermarkets Ltd v Nattrass* [1972] AC 153, washing powder was advertised at a reduced price. A shopper tried to buy a full-priced pack at the reduced price and was turned away. Tesco were prosecuted under the Trade Descriptions Act 1968. Tesco claimed a defence: that 'another person' was to blame. The spotlight appeared to be on the store manager: was he 'another person' or was he part of Tesco's directing mind?

- In the *Tesco* case, Lord Denning's ideas in *Bolton* were examined in detail.
- According to Lord Reid in *Tesco*, a store manager was not quite what Lord Denning had envisioned as 'a directing mind'.

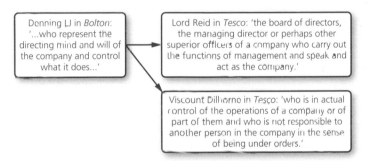

Denning LJ in *Bolton*: '...who represent the directing mind and will of the company and control what it does...'

Lord Reid in *Tesco*: 'the board of directors, the managing director or perhaps other superior officers of a company who carry out the functions of management and speak and act as the company.'

Viscount Dilhorne in *Tesco*: 'who is in actual control of the operations of a company or of part of them and who is not responsible to another person in the company in the sense of being under orders.'

- The decision in *Tesco* means that only individuals in senior positions will be presumed to be the 'controlling mind' of a corporation.
- The further up this individual is in the company, the less likely it is that he has the required *mens rea*.

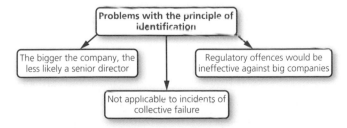

Problems with the principle of identification

The bigger the company, the less likely a senior director

Regulatory offences would be ineffective against big companies

Not applicable to incidents of collective failure

- Several cases have highlighted the disadvantages to the principle of identification.

Case:	
Armstrong v Strain (1952)	It does not apply to *groups* of employees. Devlin J: 'you cannot add an innocent state of mind to an innocent state of mind and get as a result a dishonest state of mind.'
P&O European Ferries Ltd (1991)	The principle of identification does not work when the combined innocent actions of several employees lead to disaster but, individually, no one developed a *mens rea*.
Tesco v Brent LBC (1993)	The divisional court admitted that it was impracticable to suppose that a director of a large company had the required *mens rea*. The cashier had reasonable grounds to believe that the customer was under 18, and that was enough to make the company liable.
Meridian Global Funds Management Asia Ltd v Securities Commission (1995)	The 'directing mind and will' test should be replaced by 'the rules of attribution'. Every company will have a constitution: who has been attributed the power of the company? The constitution (or the relevant statute) must be interpreted carefully.

- Lord Hoffman in *Meridian* suggested 'the rules of attribution' to locate the directing mind and will of a company (i.e. who is power allocated to?)
- However, some company constitutions simply allocate power to a 'board of directors' rather than an individual.

Research Point

Look up the article: Jefferson, M. 'Corporate Liability in the 1990s' (2000) 64 *Journal of Criminal Law* 106. How does the principle of identification change as the cases continue through the decade?

6.3.2 Vicarious liability

- As explained earlier, vicarious liability is where one person is liable for the acts of another. This doctrine can apply to corporations too. This was first recognised in *Great North of England Railway Co* (1846).

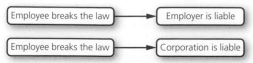

Case:	
Coppen v Moore (No. 2) (1898)	A sales assistant sold ham described as 'Scotch ham' against her employer's instructions. The corporation was vicariously liable under trade description law. It was the company that 'sold' the ham even though the transaction was carried out by an assistant.
National Rivers Authority v Alfred McAlpine Homes (1994)	Facts: employees polluted a river. Held: to make the law an effective weapon in environmental protection, a company must be criminally liable for the acts and omissions of its servant or agents during activities being done for the company.

Research Point

In *HM Coroner for East Kent ex parte Spooner* (1989) 88 Cr App R 10, Lord Bingham distinguished vicarious liability from the principle of identification. How did he do this and how might a company be found liable under each doctrine?

6.3.3 Breach of statutory duty

- Statutory offences can make corporations liable in criminal law.
- This will be particularly true if an 'occupier' is mentioned in the statute and the corporation is an occupier of premises.
- The corporation will be liable for anything that happens on its premises.
- The Health and Safety at Work Act 1974 is an important statute in this area.
- It provides an alternative when common law offences (particularly those which require a *mens rea*) do not succeed.
- Statutory breaches also apply to unincorporated bodies if they have an 'owner' or 'occupier' status (*Clerk to the Croydon Justices ex parte Chief Constable of Kent* (1989)).

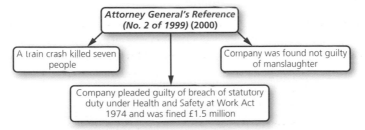

Research Point

Look up the case *Attorney General's Reference (No. 2 of 1999)* [2000] 3 All ER 187. Why did the charge of manslaughter fail?

6.3.4 Exceptions to corporate liability

- A corporation cannot be found liable in criminal law for every offence.
- If a criminal offence has a mandatory life sentence, a corporation cannot be punished.
- If the criminal offence requires a physical act by a person (e.g. rape), a corporation cannot perform the *actus reus*.

- Just because a corporation cannot be liable for particular *actus reuses*, does not mean that the corporation can escape liability altogether.
- The corporation may be a secondary party to such an offence.

Case:	
Robert Millar Contractors Ltd (1971)	Facts: a managing director sent a lorry on a long journey knowing it had a defective tyre. Six people were killed.
	Held: the driver was convicted of causing death by dangerous driving and the managing director and the company were convicted of counselling and procuring those offences.

Checkpoint - corporate liability

Item on checklist:	Done!
I can define a corporation according to *Salomon v Salomon* (1897)	
I can list the three ways by which a corporation can be found liable for a crime	
I can define the identification principle	
I can list the three cases that helped to establish the identification principle	

Checkpoint - continued

Item on checklist:	Done!
I can describe Lord Denning's identification theory as put forward in *HL Bolton Co Ltd v TJ Graham & Sons Ltd* (1956)	
I can explain the effect of *Tesco Supermarkets Ltd v Nattrass* (1972) on Lord Denning's principle in *Bolton*	
I can list three problems with the principle of identification	
I can explain how *Meridian Global Funds Management Asia Ltd v Securities Commission* (1995) interpreted Lord Denning in *Bolton*	
I can explain how a corporation can be liable for a criminal act through the doctrine of vicarious liability	
I can explain why the Health and Safety at Work Act 1974 is important in the area of corporate liability	
I can list two exceptions to corporate liability.	

6.4 Corporate manslaughter

- Since 1991 it has been established that a corporation can be liable for manslaughter.
- Case law developed this area of law until a new Act was passed in 2007.

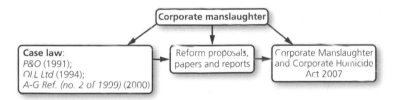

6.4.1 Case law

- The first major case in this area occurred in 1991 when a ferry sank because of careless omissions on the parts of crew members.

Case:	
***P&O European Ferries (Dover) Ltd* (1991)**	Facts: a car ferry sailed with its inner and outer bow doors still open and 192 people were killed. Held: the Sheen Inquiry was launched. The immediate cause was the Chief Officer's failure to ensure that the doors were closed, but the general management structure was sloppy too.

- The Sheen Report (Department of Transport), Report of the Court, No. 8074, (1987), paragraph 14.1:

> 'Board of Directors did not appreciate their responsibility for the safe management of their ships. They did not apply their minds to the question: what orders should be given for the safety of our ships? The directors did not have any proper comprehension of what their duties were.
>
> From the top to the bottom the body corporate was infected with the disease of sloppiness. The failure on the part of the shore management to give proper and clear directions was a contributory cause of the disaster.'

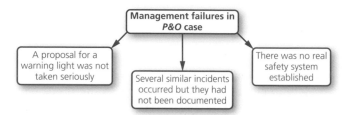

Management failures in P&O case

- A proposal for a warning light was not taken seriously
- Several similar incidents occurred but they had not been documented
- There was no real safety system established

- The trial judge in *P&O* ruled that a corporation could be charged with manslaughter through the principle of identification.
- The old definition of homicide which required a 'human being' was formulated before corporations existed.
- If a 'directing mind or will' could be identified within the corporation, then the corporation could be indicted for manslaughter.

Research Point

Look up the case *P&O European Ferries [Dover] Ltd* (1991) 93 Cr App R 72. Why was the manslaughter charge in *P&O* eventually dismissed by the judge?

6.4.1.1 OLL Ltd *(1994)*

- One of the first documented convictions for corporate manslaughter is *OLL Ltd, The Independent*, 9 December, 1994.
- Four teenagers died in a canoeing tragedy because of risks taken by the small leisure company.
- The small company was run by one man, making it easy to locate the 'directing mind and will' of the company.

- His gross negligence was attributed to the company and he and his company were convicted of gross negligence manslaughter.

6.4.1.2 Attorney-General's Reference (No. 2 of 1999) (2000)

- Two trains collided, killing seven people.
- The safety devices on the train were switched off and the driver failed to notice the warning signals.
- The train driver was not the 'directing mind or will' of the company.
- No person could be identified as having the guilty mind required for a gross negligence manslaughter conviction.
- The Court of Appeal confirmed that a corporation cannot be convicted of gross negligence manslaughter unless there was evidence of a guilty mind in an identified individual.

6.4.2 Reform

- The *P&O* case led the Law Commission to consider reforming the law on corporate manslaughter.
- There were several high-profile disasters around the same time:

  1. The Herald of Free Enterprise disaster (*P&O* case) in which 192 people were killed;
  2. The King's Cross fire in 1987 in which 31 people were killed;
  3. The Clapham rail crash in 1988 in which 31 people were killed;
  4. The Southall rail crash in 1997 in which 7 people were killed.

- The Law Commission published a report: *Legislating the Criminal Code: Involuntary Manslaughter* (Law Com No. 237) (1996).

Proposal:	Detail:
1	There should be a special offence of corporate killing based on gross carelessness
2	The offence would be committed when the corporation's conduct fell far below that which is reasonably expected
3	Any death is caused by a 'management failure' (i.e. the activities that are organised fail to ensure the health and safety of those employed or affected
4	The management failure would be the legal cause of death, even if the death occurred at the hands of an individual
5	Individuals within the company could still be charged with manslaughter alongside the company itself

• Following the 1996 Report by the Law Commission, the Government issued a consultation paper: *Reforming the Law on Involuntary Manslaughter: The Government's Proposals.*

• In 2007, the Corporate Manslaughter and Corporate Homicide Act was passed.

6.4.3 The Corporate Manslaughter and Corporate Homicide Act 2007

• The new offence of corporate manslaughter is set out below:

> '1(1) An organisation to which this section applies is guilty of an offence if the way in which any of its activities are managed:
>
> (a) causes a person's death; and
>
> (b) amounts to gross breach of a relevant duty of care owed by the organisation to the deceased.
>
> 1(3) An organisation is guilty of an offence under this section only if the way in which its activities are managed or organised by its senior management is a substantial element in the breach referred to in subsection (1).'

Workpoint

What are the key words in sections 1(1) and 1(3) above (i.e. any *actus reus*, any relevant circumstances or criteria)?

• Notice how 'organisations' are liable under the 2007 Act – a much wider scope for liability than simply 'corporations' from the old common law.

• 'Organisations' include:

1. corporations;
2. government departments (e.g. transport, health, defence etc.);
3. police forces and other services;
4. partnerships, trade unions and other associations.

• 'Senior management' includes:

1. those who play significant roles in making decisions;
2. those who actually manage or organise those activities.

• Individuals are not liable under the new offence, and no individual need be identified as the 'directing mind or will' of the organisation.

- The 'duty of care' mentioned in the 2007 Act is the same as that found in the civil law of negligence.
- This is a duty to take reasonable care for the health and safety of those in close proximity.
- Two civil law defences are excluded from the 2007 Act:

Latin phrase:	Rule excluded:
ex turpi causa	*'from his own wrong act'* In civil law there is no duty of care between parties when they are jointly engaged in unlawful conduct
volenti	*'willingly'* In civil law there is no duty of care owed to a person when he accepts the risk of harm

- The 2007 Act rejects these civil defences, meaning that if two parties are engaged in unlawful activity or the victim accepts a risk of harm, a duty of care still exists.
- In the case of *Wacker* (2003), it was confirmed that the civil defence of *ex turpi causa* was not allowed as a criminal defence.
- The judge decides whether a corporation owes the relevant duty of care.

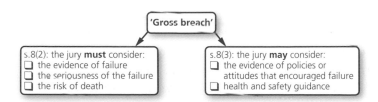

- When deciding whether there was a 'gross breach', a jury *must* consider the factors listed under s.8(2).

- In addition, a jury *may* consider any additional factors listed under s.8(3), and s.8(4) allows a jury to consider anything else that they feel is relevant to the case.

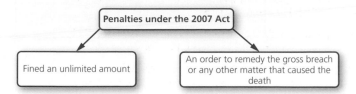

Workpoint

What are the main comparisons between the old common law of corporate manslaughter, and the new statutory offence under the 2007 Act?

6.4.4 Why corporate manslaughter?

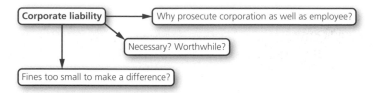

- Reason for liability 1: many corporate deaths have not been caused by individuals but by poor corporate practices.
- Reason for liability 2: health and safety should be a serious issue for corporations and this should be put before profit.
- Reason for liability 3: monopoly companies give the impression of being 'above the law' but statutory offences remind them (and the public) that they are not.
- Criminal offences aimed at corporations help to restore public faith and security in business and trade.
- The courts are able to order the corporation to correct that which went wrong under the 2007 Act.

Checkpoint - corporate manslaughter

Item on checklist:	Done!
I can briefly explain what The Sheen Report said about The Herald of Free Enterprise disaster	
I can explain how *P&O European Ferries (Dover) Ltd* (1991) helped to develop the law of corporate manslaughter	
I can list at least three of the suggestions for reform in the Law Commission's report: *Legislating the Criminal Code: Involuntary Manslaughter* (Law Com No. 237) (1996)	
I can list the main physical components of the new offence of corporate manslaughter under the new 2007 Act	
I can identify three ways in which the 2007 statutory offence of corporate manslaughter can be distinguished from the old common law on corporate manslaughter	
I can define one of the civil defences that are excluded from the 2007 Act	
I can list three advantages to having a corporate manslaughter offence in the United Kingdom	

Potential exam questions:

1) Assess the ways in which incapacitated defendants are dealt with in the criminal court system.
2) Examine the role of vicarious liability in criminal law.
3) Corporations can be indicted for criminal offences the same as adults can:
   (a) explain the ways in which a corporation can be found liable for a criminal offence;
   (b) examine the current law on corporate manslaughter.

Chapter 7
General defences

In criminal law, there are a handful of general defences available to a defendant who admits to committing a crime but argues that he did so with good reason. These general defences are available as a defence to most criminal offences (including murder) and include the following circumstances:

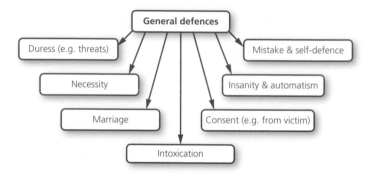

Workpoint

Why is it important that these seven general defences exist in criminal law?

7.1 Duress

- The defendant is admitting that he committed the *actus reus* of an offence.
- He is also admitting that he had the required *mens rea* when carrying out the offence.
- However, the defendant is arguing that he was threatened into committing the crime.
- The threat must include immediate serious injury or death to himself or others.

List at least three potential scenarios where a person may be threatened into committing a criminal offence.

Case:	
Lynch v DPP of Northern Ireland (1975)	Lord Morris: 'It is proper that any rational system of law should take fully into account the standards of honest and reasonable men. For the law to understand not only how the timid but also the stalwart may in a moment of crisis behave is not to make the law weak but to make it just.'

- There are two types of duress.
- The principles for both types of duress are identical.

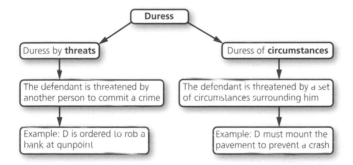

7.1.1 The threat

- The threats must be of death or personal injury – *Hudson and Taylor* (1971).
- A threat to damage or destroy property is insufficient – *M'Growther* (1746).
- The defence of duress draws a clear line between threats to property and threats to the person – *Lynch* (1975).
- Threats to expose a secret sexual orientation are also insufficient – *Singh* (1974).
- A threat of death or serious injury does not need to be the only reason why the defendant committed the offence – *Baker and Wilkins* (1996).

Case:	
Valderrama-Vega (1985)	Facts: the defendant claimed he had imported cocaine because of death threats made by a Mafia-type organisation. He was also heavily in debt and his homosexuality may have been disclosed.
	Held: the Court of Appeal quashed his conviction; the jury had been directed that death threats alone should be the sole reason for committing the crime.

- The threat no longer needs to be directed solely at the defendant.
- Threats towards the defendant's wife and children have been accepted by the courts – *Ortiz* (1986).
- A passenger in a car can be threatened – *Conway* (1988).
- A spouse may threaten to harm herself – *Martin* (1989).

Case:	
Wright (2000)	Kennedy LJ: 'It was both unnecessary and undesirable for the trial judge to trouble the jury with the question of [the victim's] proximity. Some other person, for whose safety D would reasonably regard himself as responsible [will suffice as well as immediate family].'

Workpoint

Darren smuggled heroin into a nightclub and he was caught. He was arrested and charged with various drugs offences. He argued that he needed to deliver the heroin to the ring leader upstairs otherwise his house would be torched at night, when his family are likely to be asleep. Vicky – his wife – also threatened to kill the children if Darren didn't get the money to pay the rent. Can Darren use the defence of duress? Give reasons for your answer.

7.1.2 Imminence of threat and chances to escape

- The threat made towards the defendant must be 'operative' when the offence is committed.
- This means that it is 'active' at the time of the *actus reus* of the offence.

Case:	
Hudson and Taylor (1971)	Facts: the trial judge originally withdrew the defence of duress because the threat of harm could not be immediately put into effect. Held: the threatened injury need not follow instantly but perhaps after an interval.

- A threat may be 'imminent' but not necessarily 'immediate' – *Abdul-Hussain* (1999).
- The threat must follow immediately or almost immediately – *Hasan* (2005).

> ### Workpoint
>
> Revisiting Darren and Vicky's scenario, would a threat to torch their house 'on the next occasion when the whole family are together' be an 'almost immediate' threat? Give reasons for your answer.

- If an opportunity to escape presents itself, the defendant must do so.
- If he does not, his defence of duress may fail.
- A failure to raise the alarm and wreck the whole enterprise may see the defence of duress withdrawn – *Gill* (1963).

Case:	
Pommell (1995)	Kennedy LJ: 'in some cases a delay, especially if unexplained, may be such as to make it clear that any duress must have ceased to operate, in which case the judge would be entitled to conclude that the defence was not open.'

- It is not necessary to seek police protection if this is not possible at the material time – *Hudson and Taylor* (1971).
- The jury must decide whether an opportunity to escape presented itself – *Hudson and Taylor* (1971).
- In deciding whether an opportunity for escape was open, the jury should have regard to:
  1. The defendant's age;
  2. The defendant's circumstances;
  3. Any risks to the defendant.

Would the defence of duress fail in the following circumstances?

(a) The defendant was pinned down while threatened but the police station was across the road.
(b) The person issuing the threats was distracted by a passing group of people.
(c) The defendant was threatened at the airport in Cuba that, when he returned to England, someone else would be waiting for him and he would be killed.

- Even if it is found that the defendant faced an 'immediate' threat, and had no chance to escape or notify the police, the defence of duress will still fail if the defendant commits an offence that was not nominated by the threatening individual.
- Only the nominated offence must be carried out – *Cole* (1994).

7.1.3 Voluntary exposure to threats

- It is not unheard of for a defendant to expose himself to a dangerous situation where he may find himself threatened.
- Criminal organisations, gangs or drug rings all carry the risk of violent threats.
- If a defendant voluntarily chooses to join a dangerous activity, he will not be able to argue duress when he is threatened.

Case:	
Fitzpatrick (1977)	Facts: the defendant pleaded duress to many offences including murder even though he was a voluntary member of the IRA.
	Held: the trial judge stated that: 'if a man chooses to expose himself and still more if he chooses to submit himself to illegal compulsion, duress may not operate even in mitigation of punishment.'
Sharp (1987)	Facts: the defendant was part of an enterprise to rob a post office and he knew of the violent and trigger-happy tenancies of his co-defendants.
	Lord Lane CJ: 'where a person has voluntarily, and with knowledge of its nature, joined a criminal organisation or gang which he knew might bring pressure on him to commit an offence and was an active member when he was put under such pressure, he cannot avail himself of the defence.'

- The defendant does not have to officially join a criminal organisation or a gang.
- The defendant can simply voluntarily associate himself with violent individuals.
- This would also deny him the defence of duress.

Case:	Additional law:
Ali (1995)	The defendants were drug-users who committed robbery because they were indebted to their suppliers. The Court of Appeal would not allow duress where a defendant voluntarily put himself into a position where the threat of violence was likely
Heath (1999)	The defendant was denied duress because he had voluntarily associated himself with the drugs world knowing that debts are collected by intimidation and violence
Harmer (2001)	Voluntary exposure to unlawful violence was enough to deny the defendant of the defence of duress

Workpoint

What if a drug user had not anticipated, when buying drugs, that his supplier would begin to threaten his life? Do you think the rules in *Ali*, *Heath* and *Harmer* are fair? Give reasons for your answer.

- The House of Lords was asked to clarify the law in *Hasan* (2005) and the following three questions were certified to the House of Lords by the Court of Appeal.

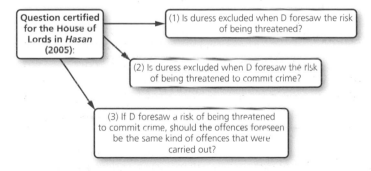

- The Lords decided that question (1) was the correct law.
- The defendant must only foresee (or should have foreseen) that he would be threatened.

• *Heath* (1999) and *Harmer* (2001) were confirmed.

Case:	
Hasan (2005)	Lord Bingham: 'the defence of duress is excluded when as a result of the accused's voluntary association with others engaged in criminal activity he foresaw or ought reasonably to have foreseen the risk of being subjected to any compulsion by threats of violence.'

• If a defendant chooses to mix with 'very bad company' then he should foresee the risk of being threatened.

Case:	
Ali (2008)	Dyson J: 'The core question is whether D voluntarily put himself in the position in which he foresaw or ought reasonably to have foreseen the risk of being subjected to any compulsion by threats of violence.'

• If, however, a defendant joins a non-violent gang and finds himself threatened with violence unexpectedly, he may be able to use duress as a defence to his crime.

Case:	
Shepherd (1987)	Mustill LJ: 'The logic which appears to underlie the law of duress would suggest that if trouble did unexpectedly materialise and if it put the defendant into a dilemma in which a reasonable man might have chosen to act as he did, the concession to human frailty should not be denied to him.'

> ### Research Point
>
> The rule in *Hasan* [2005] UKHL 22 states that duress is not available as a defence when a defendant foresees (or should have foreseen) that he would be threatened. Explain why this development could be viewed as a narrowing of the defence of duress.

7.1.4 Resistance

• If the ordinary man would have been able to resist the threat, it is very unlikely that the defendant will be able to rely on duress as a defence.
• On the issue of resistance, a two-part test has been developed.

```
Graham (2 part test) (1982)
```

| (1) Was D impelled to act as he did because, as a result of what the duressor had said or done, he had good cause to fear death or serious injury?

Answer should be: 'yes' for defence | (2) If so, have the prosecution made the jury sure that a sober person of reasonable firmness, sharing the same characteristics, would not have responded?

Answer should be: 'no' for defence |

- Notice that test (1) is *subjective* (i.e. through the eyes of the defendant) and that test (2) is *objective* (i.e. measured against the reasonable man).
- Notice how the burden remains on the prosecution to prove that a reasonable man would have resisted.
- If they fail to prove this, the defence is available to the defendant.
- The *Graham* test was approved in *Howe and Bannister* (1987).

Test (1):
☐ A physical attack made three months after the crime took place may still be put to the jury as evidence – *Nethercott* (2001)
☐ The threat does not need to be real for the defendant to act upon it – *Cairns* (1999)
☐ The defendant's **honest belief** in the existence of the threat is what matters – *Safi* (2003)
☐ The defendant's honest belief must be **reasonable** – *Hasan* (2005)
☐ The defendant's honest belief must give him 'good cause' to fear death or serious injury

Lord Bingham in *Hasan* (2005): 'it is of course essential that the defendant should genuinely, that is actually, believe in the efficacy of the threat by which he claims to have been compelled. But there is no warrant for relaxing the requirement that the belief must be reasonable as well as genuine.'

Workpoint

X threatened to 'slice up' D and his children if D did not break into a house and retrieve money for an unpaid drug deal. X did not really intend to slice D up, but X knew that D was very afraid of him because X had broken D's nose before. D wishes to plead duress after being charged with burglary. Has D satisfied test (1)? Apply each criteria at a time.

Test (2):
- ❑ If the reasonable man would have resisted, the defence of duress is **unavailable**
- ❑ A defendant's 'grossly elevated neurotic state' cannot be attributed to the reasonable man – *Hegarty* (1994)
- ❑ Vulnerability will not be attributed to the reasonable man – *Horne* (1994)
- ❑ Age, sex, pregnancy, physical disability and recognised psychiatric conditions can be attributed to the reasonable man – *Bowen* (1996)

Lord Lane CJ in *Graham* (1982): 'as a matter of public policy, it seems to us essential to limit the defence of duress by means of an objective criterion formulated in terms of reasonableness.'

Workpoint

Referring back to X and D, would it make any difference if D was suffering from depression and anxiety caused by his medication? Does D satisfy test (2) with these characteristics? If so, has it been easier to answer test (2) in D's favour when ailments such as depression are included?

7.1.5 The scope of duress

- Duress has been applied widely in criminal law. It is a defence to many criminal offences.

Case:	Duress applied to:
Evans and Gardiner (1976)	Manslaughter
Cairns (1999)	Grievous bodily harm with intent
Crutchley (1831)	Criminal damage
Gill (1963)	Theft
Attorney-General v Whelan (1934)	Handling stolen goods
Bowen (1996)	Obtaining property by deception
Hudson and Taylor (1971)	Perjury
Valderrama-Vega (1985)	Drugs offences
Pommell (1995)	Firearms offences
Willer (1986) *Conway* (1988) *Martin* (1989)	Driving offences

Case:	Duress applied to:
Abdul-Hussain (1999) *Safi and others* (2003)	Hijacking
Safi and others (2003)	Kidnapping
Shayler (2001)	Breaching the Official Secrets Act

- You may notice that murder is not included in the table above.
- It has long been established that duress is not a defence to murder.

Case:	
Dudley and Stephens (1884)	Facts: D and S were shipwrecked in a boat with another man and a cabin boy. After days without food and water, the men killed the boy (who was the weakest) and ate him. They were rescued four days later and charged with murder.
	Held: killing a member of their group would not necessarily guarantee their survival. They were sentenced to hang but this was commuted to six months in prison.

- The Lords in *Howe and Bannister* (1987) discussed the applicability of duress to murder.
- They decided that *Dudley and Stephens* was good authority that duress was not available as a defence to murder.

Case:	
Howe and Bannister (1987)	Facts: an older man (Murphy), a younger man, and the two defendants (Howe and Bannister) killed two victims on the Derbyshire moors. The defendants (H&B) pleaded duress because Murphy had a violent history and a criminal record and was likely to carry out his threats against them.
	Held: the defence of duress still failed, in the Court of Appeal and the House of Lords.

- The Lords listed nine reasons why duress should not be available for a murder charge:
  1. The ordinary man, when asked to take a life, may be expected to lay down his own;

2. It would be unjust and inhumane to withdraw legal protection from the innocent victim and offer a cloak of protection to the cowards;
3. Someone who takes the life of an innocent cannot argue it is the lesser of two evils;
4. Even though the Law Commission suggested in 1977 that duress be a defence to murder, Parliament ignored the suggestion;
5. Hard cases could be dealt with in other ways;
6. To recognise the defence would be to overrule *Dudley and Stephens*, which recognised the sanctity of life;
7. No man has the 'right' to take an innocent life even at the price of his own or another's;
8. As a defence it would be too easy to raise and very difficult for the prosecution to disprove;
9. It is for Parliament to decide whether duress should be a defence to murder in law.

Workpoint

Look again at reasons 3 and 4 above. Could it ever be argued that killing an innocent person is the lesser of two evils (i.e. could it save an even greater harm)? Additionally, just because Parliament has not acted on the Law Commission's proposals, does this mean that the idea was rejected?

• Even if the defendant is very young (e.g. a young teenager) the courts have still not been convinced that duress should apply to murder.
• This is despite the fact that a young teenager is probably very susceptible to threats.

Case:	
Wilson (2007)	Lord Phillips CJ: 'Our criminal law holds that a 13-year-old boy is responsible for his actions and the rule that duress provides no defence to a charge of murder applies however susceptible D may be to the duress.'

Workpoint

If the victim in *Wilson* had actually survived his attack and Wilson was instead charged with grievous bodily harm, do you think duress would have succeeded? How easy would it be to apply the *Graham* criteria?

• In *Gotts* (1991) it was confirmed that duress is also not available for charges of attempted murder.

- Lord Jauncey could 'see no justification in logic, morality or law in affording to an attempted murderer the defence which is withheld from a murderer'.

7.1.6 Duress of circumstances

- You may recall that the difference between duress of threats and duress of circumstances is that with the latter, the defendant feels pressures to commit a crime as a result of circumstances around him, or his environment. A good example is a driver mounting a pavement in his car and injuring pedestrians in order to prevent a much more serious crash.
- Sometimes duress of circumstances is referred to as the defence of 'necessity' (i.e. circumstances make it necessary to break the law).
- Duress of circumstances has only been recognised as a defence on its own within the last 25 years through a chain of case law.

Case:	Facts:	Held:
Willer (1986)	D drove his car onto the pavement to escape a gang of violent youths	He was wholly driven by circumstances and would not have acted that way without the threat
Conway (1988)	D was driving recklessly to escape a violent gang	Duress of circumstances allowed despite the gang actually being police officers
Martin (1989)	D was driving while disqualified because his wife threatened to kill herself	Duress of circumstances allowed
DPP v Bell (1992)	D was driving with excess alcohol to get away from a gang who were pursuing him	Duress of circumstances allowed
DPP v Davis (1994)	D was driving with excess alcohol to get away from a violent gang	Duress of circumstances allowed

- It was in *Conway* (1988) that Woolf LJ laid down the ingredients for the new defence of duress of circumstances.

Case:	
Conway (1988)	Woolf LJ: '...the facts establish "duress of circumstances" where [D] was constrained to act by circumstances to drive as he did to avoid death or serious bodily injury to himself or some other person. This approach does no more than recognise that duress is an example of necessity. Whether "duress of circumstances" is called "duress" or "necessity" does not matter.'

- It was confirmed in *Pommell* (1995) that duress of circumstances had general application and was not limited to driving offences.

Workpoint

Write out Woolf LJ's two-part test for duress of circumstances from *Conway*.

- It is just as important in duress of circumstances that the defendant had no opportunity to escape, that the defendant had an honest belief in the circumstances.
- In *Re A (Children) (Conjoined Twins)* (2000) the defence of necessity (sometimes interchangeable with duress of circumstances) was used to justify killing one of the conjoined twins to save the other. This was a rare case.

7.1.7 Reform of duress

- The short history here has been interesting.

Proposal:	Suggestion:
A New Homicide Act? (2005) Law Commission	Duress should be a partial defence to murder (i.e. dropping the charge to manslaughter)
Murder, Manslaughter and Infanticide (2006) Law Commission	Duress should be a full defence to both murder and attempted murder
Murder, Manslaughter and Infanticide: Proposals for Reform of the Law (2008) Ministry of Justice	Makes no reference to Law Commission's proposals

Checkpoint - duress

Item on checklist:	Done!
I can split the defence of 'duress' into two types and I can define each type	
I can explain what kind of 'threat' is required in duress by threats	
I can cite a legal authority to explain whether a 'chance to escape' will hinder the application of duress	
I can explain the rules relating to 'voluntary exposure to threats' as laid down by *Hasan* (2005)	
I can briefly describe the two-part test as laid down by *Graham* (1982) in relation to resistance to threats	
I can list five reasons why duress is not available as a defence to murder	
I can repeat the two-part test in *Conway* (1988) that formulates the 'duress of circumstances' defence	

7.2 Necessity

- As explained above, necessity is sometimes interchangeable with duress of circumstances.
- The case of *Re A (Children) (Conjoined Twins)* (2000) may have changed this, distinguishing necessity from duress of circumstances.

Case:	
Re A (Children) (Conjoined Twins) (2000)	Facts: Mary and Jodie were conjoined twins. Mary was dependent on Jodie. They had six months to live unless separated. Mary would die, but Jodie would live a normal life. The hospital authority applied for a declaration that the surgery was lawful, but the Court of Appeal said it would have been murder. House of Lords: the doctrine of necessity justified the act of murder.

- Brooke LJ in *Re A* described the criteria required for the defence of necessity.
- It is slightly different to that of duress of circumstances.

```
                          ┌──────────────────────┐
                          │  Are duress and      │
                          │  necessity the       │
                          │  same thing?         │
                          └──────────────────────┘
```

Defence: Necessity (Brooke LJ:)	Defence: Duress of circumstances
• The act is needed to avoid inevitable evil • No more should be done than necessary for the purpose to be achieved • The evil inflicted should be in proportion to the evil avoided	• The defendant acts in response to a threat • The threat of serious injury or death is honestly and reasonably believed • There is no reasonable opportunity to escape the threat

- As you can see, the criteria for both defences are distinguishable.
- It should be noted, however, that *Re A* was a very rare case.
- Similarly, because the case was decided in the Civil Division of the Court of Appeal, it is only *persuasive* on criminal courts.

Workpoint

Let us imagine that the House of Lords in a later case affirmed the decision in *Re A* that necessity is now a defence to murder. Using Brooke LJ's three criteria, in the diagram above can you think of two scenarios in which the defence of necessity would justify the killing of an innocent person?

Case:	
Quayle & others (2005)	Facts: the defendants were charged with using cannabis but they argued that it was necessary for the severe pain they were experiencing. Held: any benefits gained by the defendants were outweighed by the public interest in keeping drug-use illegal. Mance LJ: 'The law has to draw a line at some point in the criteria which it accepts as sufficient to satisfy the defence of duress or necessity. The legal defences of duress by threats and necessity by circumstances should in our view be confined to cases where there is an imminent danger of physical injury.'

- Mance LJ in *Quayle* does not refer to the specific criteria as set out by Brooke LJ in *Re A* for the defence of necessity.
- Mance LJ also refers to necessity as 'necessity of circumstances', thus interchanging necessity with duress.

- *Quayle* was followed by *Altham* (2006) which had very similar facts, sending a signal that the approach in *Quayle* was the correct one (i.e. that necessity and duress of circumstances are the same thing).

Checkpoint - necessity

Item on checklist:	Done!
I can explain the facts and decision of *Re A (Children) (Conjoined Twins)* (2000)	
I can recite Brooke LJ's three-part test for necessity in *Re A* (2000)	
I can distinguish necessity from duress of circumstances in light of *Re A* (2000)	

7.3 Mistake

- In criminal law, an individual is allowed to make a genuine mistake.
- This is a full defence, as it renders any offence that they committed 'an accident'.
- There are two types of mistake:

7.3.1 Mistake of fact

- If a defendant mistakes the facts before him, it is unlikely that he had the required *mens rea*.
- The mistake of fact must, of course, be honestly made.

Case:	
***DPP v Morgan* (1976)**	Lord Hailsham: 'Either the prosecution proves that [D] had the requisite intent, or it does not. In the latter, it fails. Since honest belief clearly negates intent, the reasonableness or otherwise of that belief can only be evidence that the belief/intent was held.'

- The judgment in *Morgan* states two things:

- *Morgan* was applied to indecent assault in *Kimber* (1983).
- *Morgan's* application to rape has been overruled by the Sexual Offences Act 2003.
- However, *Morgan* remains applicable to the rest of criminal law, including incidents of mistaken self-defence.

Case:	
Williams (1987)	Lord Lane CJ: 'The question is, does it make any difference if the mistake of [D] was an unreasonable mistake? If the belief was in fact held, its unreasonableness, so far as guilt or innocence is concerned, is neither here nor there. It is irrelevant.'

- *Morgan* and *Williams* were confirmed by the self-defence case of *Beckford* (1988).
- The judgments in *Morgan*, *Williams* and *Beckford* together confirm two things:

Workpoint

Jill was walking home one night in the dark. She thought someone was following her. She stopped to let the other person walk past but no one was there. As she turned into her street, her best friend Ashley (who had missed Jill's party) jumped out at her and yelled 'surprise!' with a birthday present. Jill kicked Ashley in the head and kicked the object out of her hand before running home. Jill is charged with grievous bodily harm. Can she use the defence of mistake? Give reasons for your answer.

7.3.2 Intoxicated mistakes

- If a defendant makes an intoxicated mistake, different rules apply (see further below).

7.3.3 Mistakes of law

- Mistakes of law are treated very differently to mistakes of fact.
- Ignorance of the law is no excuse.
- In other words, it is no defence to argue: 'I didn't know it was illegal'.

Workpoint

Why do you think Parliament and the courts have taken a strict approach to mistakes of law?

- As far back as *Esop* (1836), it was established that foreign individuals who commit an offence in England – thinking the act is perfectly legal – will be prosecuted.
- The defendant must, of course, have both the *actus reus* and *mens rea* of the offence charged.

Checkpoint - mistake

Item on checklist:	Done!
I can identify two types of mistake in law	
I can define the current test for mistakes of fact in criminal law, as established by the cases of *Morgan*, *Williams* and *Beckford*	
I can explain what a mistake of law is and how it is dealt with in criminal law	

7.4 Self-defence

- Self-defence is a full defence in criminal law to many crimes including murder.
- A defendant may defend himself or another.
- Self-defence is a common law defence, but is has been clarified by section 3 of the Criminal Law Act 1967:

> 'Section 3(1): A person may use such force as is reasonable in the circumstances in the prevention of crime, or in effecting or assisting in the lawful arrest of offenders or suspected offenders or of persons unlawfully at large.'

- Section 3 of the 1967 Act goes on to say that it replaces some of the common law rules.
- The courts have since used both statute and common law together – *Cousins* (1982).
- Any evidence of self-defence must be left to a jury – *DPP v Bailey* (1995).
- If the issue of self-defence is merely a 'fanciful and speculative matter' then the judge will withdraw it from the jury – *Johnson* (1994).
- Self-defence is commonly used as a defence against charges of murder and non-fatal offences.
- However, self-defence can be raised as a defence to reckless driving – *Renouf* (1986).
- Self-defence has also been used as a defence to dangerous driving – *Symonds* (1998).

Workpoint

Write the two-part test that is laid down by section 3 of the 1967 Act (above).

7.4.1 Is force necessary?

- When a defendant uses force in self-defence, there are certain criteria that have to be met.
- Any force used must be necessary from the **defendant's** perspective.

'Force'

| The force must be necessary | The **defendant** must believe it is necessary | The defendant may be **genuinely** mistaken as to the force required |

- It does not matter that the defendant was mistaken as to the necessity of the force.
- There is no requirement that the defendant's belief should be reasonable.
- Many of the cases and rules described above for the defence of mistake are found in self-defence too.

Case:	
***Rashford* (2005)**	Dyson LJ: 'it is common ground that a person only acts in self-defence if in all the circumstances he honestly believes that it is necessary for him to defend himself and if the amount of force that he uses is reasonable.'

Workpoint

Describe two scenarios in which a defendant might unreasonably believe he has to use force to defend himself. One is listed for you.

- Kerri is walking through a shopping centre when a mobile phone salesman approaches her. He is reaching into his jacket for a mobile phone but Kerry does not know this. The shopping centre has a history of stabbings. She punches him in the chest to stop him from withdrawing a knife and is charged with common law assault.

- A pre-emptive strike is acceptable – *Beckford* (1988).
- Issuing threats of violence to deter the attacker may constitute self-defence – *DPP v Bailey* (1995) and *Cousins* (1982).
- A defendant does not have to express a reluctance to fight before defending himself – *Bird* (1985).
- A defendant may make preparations to defend himself – *Attorney-General's Reference (No. 2 of 1983)* (1984).

Case:	
Attorney-General's Reference (No. 2 of 1983) (1984)	Lord Lane CJ: 'D is not left in the paradoxical position of being able to justify acts carried out in self-defence but not acts immediately preparatory to it. A person may still arm himself for his own protection.'

7.4.2 The reasonableness of force

- Any force used must be 'reasonable' from the jury's perspective.
- This is technically an objective test – was the force reasonable in the circumstances?
- However, the jury must consider the defendant's experience when answering this question, adding a little subjectivity to the test.
- In *Shannon* (1980) a conviction for murder was quashed when the trial judge failed to remind the jury to consider the defendant's point of view.
- In *Whyte* (1987) Lord Lane CJ commented that it was 'necessary and desirable' for the jury to consider the defendant's point of view.

Case:	
Palmer (1971)	Lord Morris: 'If a jury thought that in a moment of unexpected anguish a person attacked had only done what he honestly and instinctively thought was necessary that would be most potent evidence that only reasonable defensive action had been taken.'

> **Research Point**
>
> Collins LJ provided a concise summary of the law in *Owino* [1996] 2 Cr App R 128. Locate the judgment and write his short summary.

7.4.3 Anthony Martin

- In the famous case of Tony Martin, the farmer from Norfolk, two burglars were shot on entering Martin's farmhouse. Martin was charged with murder and grievous bodily harm and he pleaded self-defence. This was rejected. He put forward evidence that he suffered from a paranoid personality disorder and depression. His murder conviction was substituted for manslaughter (through the defence of diminished responsibility).
- This case ignited the public debate on just how much force a landowner can use when burglars enter his property.

> **Research Point**
>
> Locate Tony Martin's case – *Martin* [2001] EWCA Crim 2245; [2002] 2 WLR 1 – and find out: (a) why his plea of self-defence was rejected, and (b) whether a defendant's psychiatric condition can be used to argue that they perceived a greater danger.

- Following *Martin*, it was established that paranoid schizophrenia would not be put to the jury in self-defence cases – *Canns* (2005).
- The jury should continue to set the standard for reasonable force regardless of individual psychiatric ailments.

7.4.4 Intoxicated self-defence

- As noted above, a defendant can make an honest mistake as to the need for force when defending himself but the jury will deliberate its reasonableness.
- This is not the same for intoxicated self-defence.
- If the honest mistake is caused by *voluntary* intoxication, the defence of self-defence will fail.

Case:	
O'Grady (1987)	Where the jury is satisfied that the mistake as to force or necessity was caused by intoxication, the defence must fail.

- O'*Grady* (1987) was confirmed by O'*Connor* (1991).
- In *Hatton* (2005) it was confirmed that an intoxicated self-defence will not be available to charges of murder.

Workpoint

Why have the courts taken a much stricter view of intoxicated self-defence? Who are they trying to protect?

7.4.5 The Criminal Justice and Immigration Act 2008

- In an unusual move, Parliament has codified the common law rules of self-defence in a new statute without making any amendments. A statutory definition of self-defence therefore exists in section 76 of the Criminal Justice and Immigration Act 2008. It does not add to the law, but it does provide clarity.

7.4.6 Excessive force

- A defendant cannot use excessive force when defending himself.
- Excessive force will see the defence of self-defence being withdrawn from the jury.

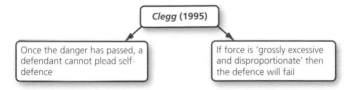

Clegg (1995)

Once the danger has passed, a defendant cannot plead self-defence

If force is 'grossly excessive and disproportionate' then the defence will fail

Workpoint

How would you define 'reasonable force'? Is killing an attacker in self-defence ever reasonable?

Checkpoint - self-defence

Item on checklist:	Done!
I can define the two-part test for self-defence according to section 3 of the Criminal Law Act 1967	
I understand that the defendant can make an honest mistake as to the force required, and that the jury will deliberate its reasonableness	
I can cite legal authority to confirm that a defendant may make preparations to defend himself	
I can cite two legal authorities to confirm that the defendant must believe that the force used in self-defence was reasonable	
I can explain the rule in *O'Grady* (1987)	
I can describe how *Clegg* (1995) added to the law of self-defence	

7.5 Consent

- In criminal law, consent is a defence to many crimes.
- The defendant will typically argue that his victim consented to the harm that was inflicted.
- The burden of proving lack of consent rests with the prosecution – *Donovan* (1934).

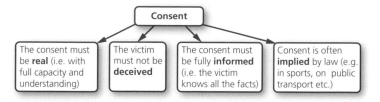

Consent

The consent must be **real** (i.e. with full capacity and understanding)

The victim must not be **deceived**

The consent must be fully **informed** (i.e. the victim knows all the facts)

Consent is often **implied** by law (e.g. in sports, on public transport etc.)

Workpoint

List the reasons why people would consent to harm being inflicted upon them.

7.5.1 Consent must be real

- Consent will be invalid if the victim lacks capacity – *Howard* (1965).
- The victim must be able to understand the act consented to – *Burrell v Harmer* (1967).

7.5.2 The victim must not be deceived

- A victim must not be 'tricked' into consenting.
- A victim can be 'tricked' by being misinformed about the nature or quality of the act.

Earlier cases:	Outcome:
Clarence (1888)	Consent to sex was not invalid simply because an unknown disease was being transmitted. If consent was invalid, the outcome would have been rape
Bolduc v Bird (1967)	If a medical assistant turns out not to be qualified, this does not alter the 'nature and quality' of the act. Consent valid
Mobilio (1991)	If a doctor is performing a medical examination for sexual gratification as opposed to medical reasons, the 'nature and quality' of the act remains the same. Consent valid
Richardson (1998)	The 'nature and quality' of an act does not change simply because a dentist is no longer qualified to practise

- The idea of 'nature and quality' was explored in detail in *Tabassum* (2000).
- The terms 'nature' and 'quality' can be distinguished from each other.
- The victim may be deceived as to only one of the terms.

Case:	
Tabassum (2000)	Facts: the defendant examined the breasts of three women. He was not medically qualified. He claimed he was trying to help the women and that he had no sexual motives.
	Held: his convictions for indecent assault were upheld. The women were consenting for medical purposes, meaning that they had been deceived as to the 'quality' of the act. There was no consent.

- The victims in *Tabassum* were deceived as to the quality of the act, and a victim must consent to both the nature *and* the quality of the act.
- *Tabassum* throws doubt upon the earlier 'nature and quality' cases mentioned above, particularly those involving medical examinations.

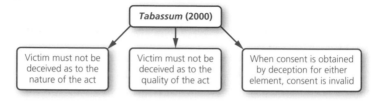

Tabassum (2000)

| Victim must not be deceived as to the nature of the act | Victim must not be deceived as to the quality of the act | When consent is obtained by deception for either element, consent is invalid |

Workpoint

Jenny went for an eye examination at a stall that had opened up at her local shopping centre. The stall said 'eye doctor'. Jenny had her eyes examined by a man in a white lab coat and he told her that she would benefit from laser eye surgery. Jenny made an appointment with a proper clinic. When she got there, she said that she had received a proper examination from one of their eye doctors, but the receptionist informed her that the stalls were for promotional purposes only, and that she had been examined by a sales representative. Jenny was furious. Did she consent to the act? Give reasons for your answer.

7.5.3 Consent must be fully informed

- A victim must have all the facts at hand before consenting.
- An uninformed consent means that the victim is not aware of the details.
- The case of *Clarence* (1888) on the previous page has been overruled by *Dica* (2004).
- A victim no longer consents to infected intercourse unless she is informed of the infection and consents thereafter.

Case:	
Dica (2004)	Facts: the defendant was diagnosed with HIV in 1995. He slept with two women who were unaware of his disease. He was charged with recklessly causing grievous bodily harm. The trial judge directed the jury that *Clarence* may be ignored and consent is no defence because of the seriousness of the disease. Held: (i) the trial judge shouldn't have withdrawn consent from the jury so the defendant was given a re-trial; (ii) a victim may consent to the risk of HIV once fully informed, but otherwise it's biological GBH (5.20).

- The defendant in *Dica* was properly convicted at his re-trial (*Dica* [2005] EWCA Crim 2304).
- *Dica* (2004) was confirmed in *Konzani* (2005) which had very similar facts.
- The rule in *Dica* is not limited to HIV – it is applicable to any serious disease.

> **Research Point**
>
> According to the judgment in *Dica*, a victim who is not informed of her partner's infection is not consenting to sex. Does the act of intercourse turn into rape? Or, is the victim simply not consenting to the infection? Find the case of *B* [2006] EWCA Crim 2945 and make notes on what Latham LJ said about this issue.

- It follows on from *Dica*, *Konzani* and *B* that the defendant must know of his disease.
- This means he has the *mens rea* of recklessness (i.e. he sees a risk and goes ahead anyway).
- If a defendant is not aware of his disease, he will not have the *mens rea* of grievous bodily harm (5.20) – *Williams* (2003).

7.5.4 Consent may be implied by law

- The law implies consent in certain situations.
- The law also limits consent in certain situations.

Workpoint

Why might the law limit a person's right to consent to harm?

- The rules of consent vary according to the type of harm or the area of law.
- In *Brown* (1994) a 'line of consent' was drawn between battery and actual bodily harm.
- It was also made clear when individuals can go too far.
- *Brown* also listed 'lawful' exceptions to the rule, where consent is allowed despite a high risk of injury.
- Consent is allowed in sports, during surgery, during ritual circumcision, tattooing and ear-piercing.

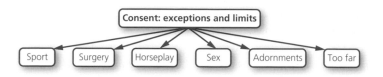

7.5.4.1 Sport

- Boxing and wrestling are lawful as long as they are played within the rules.
- 'Prize fights' are conducted outside the rules and are unlawful – *Coney* (1882).
- 'Off the ball' incidents (i.e. unprovoked violence) are unlawful during sport – *Billinghurst* (1978).
- Where an unlawful act occurs in sport, it shall be judged independently of the rules as an unlawful act in itself – *Bradshaw* (1878) and *Moore* (1898).
- The Canadian case of *Ciccarelli* (1989) was referred to by Lord Mustill in *Brown*.
- The criteria below from *Ciccarelli* may help a court to decide whether an unlawful act during a game went beyond the scope of implied consent:

  1. What is the nature of the game played?
  2. Is it an amateur game or a professional league?
  3. What is the nature of the particular act?
  4. What were the surrounding circumstances?
  5. What was the degree of force employed?
  6. What was the risk of injury?
  7. What was the state of mind of the accused?

List five sports where the risk of injury is significant and where the line of implied consent may be blurred.

Case:	
Barnes (2004)	The Court of Appeal established that criminal prosecutions could only be brought in sport where conduct was **sufficiently grave** to be properly categorised as criminal. The jury would need to consider whether the conduct was **obviously late and/or violent** and not simply 'an instinctive reaction, error or misjudgement'.

- The reason for this very high criminal threshold is that sport already has disciplinary procedures in place.
- Sometimes, incidents happen in the 'heat of the moment' and a player may be warned or sent off.
- Sport also allows for civil actions if a player is injured.
- Criminal actions should therefore be reserved for 'sufficiently grave' harm.

7.5.4.2 Surgery

- The patient must consent to the surgery – *Corbett v Corbett* (1971).
- If the surgery is done without just cause or excuse, it is always unlawful even if consented to – *Bravery v Bravery* (1954).

7.5.4.3 Horseplay

- Community life allows for implied consent.
- School boys who throw each other in the air are not committing assault – *Jones and others* (1987).
- The other members of the horseplay must genuinely believe that their friend is consenting – *Aitken and others* (1992).

7.5.4.4 Sex

- An assault during sex will be prosecuted – despite consent – if the harm is intended to cause more than 'transient or trifling' injury – *Boyea* (1992).
- Consent is a defence to lawful intercourse and other lawful playful/ sexual behaviour even if it *unexpectedly* and *accidentally* results in death – *Slingsby* (1995).

7.5.4.5 Adornments

• Consent is a valid defence for tattooing – *Brown* (1994).
• 'Branding' a person's body (e.g. burning initials onto them) is to be considered the same as tattooing even though it is technically an actual bodily harm – *Wilson* (1997).

Research Point

Look up the case of *Wilson* [1996] 3 WLR 125 which concerns a husband branding his wife's body with his initials. On what grounds did the Lords justify quashing his conviction for actual bodily harm? Do you agree with the Lords?

7.5.4.6 Too far

• As seen in *Slingsby* (1995), consent is a defence to unexpected or accidental injury during sex.
• However, the law has taken a dim view of injuries inflicted solely for sexual gratification.
• The Lords are driven by issues of public interest when deciding violent sexual gratification cases.

Case:	
Attorney-General's Reference (No. 6 of 1980) (1981)	Facts: two teenagers decided to have a bare-knuckle fight, resulting in injuries. Lord Lane CJ: 'It is not in the public interest that people should try to cause each other actual bodily harm for no good reason.'

• Sexual gratification does not automatically render the infliction of harm unlawful – *Donovan* (1934).
• It is not in the public interest that people should try to cause actual bodily harm to each other for no good reason – *Brown* (1994).
• The case of *Brown* (1994) established that consent was a valid defence to assault and battery but nothing beyond that, unless it was a qualified legal exception (e.g. sport).
• The *Brown* case therefore allows both assault and battery to be consented to in sexual situations as well as in general everyday life.

Case:	
Brown and others (1994)	Facts: a group of sado-masochistic homosexuals inflicted severe injuries upon each other for sexual gratification. The police found out by accident and they were all charged with various offences including actual and grievous bodily harm. Their defence was that they consented to everything.
	Lord Templeman: 'the violence of sado-masochistic encounters involves the indulgence of cruelty by sadists and the degradation of victims. Such violence is injurious to participants and unpredictably dangerous.'

- The spread of disease was a particular concern for the Lords, although following *Dica* (2004) a fully informed individual can now consent to contracting HIV.
- *Brown* (1994) was directly applied in *Emmett* (1999) to a heterosexual couple engaging in sado-masochistic activities.
- Most of the Lords in *Brown* were persuaded by issues of public morality as raised in the *Wolfenden Report* (1957), which stated that laws relating to homosexual behaviour were designed to:

> '...preserve public order and decency, to protect the citizen from what is offensive or injurious, and to provide sufficient safeguards against exploitation and corruption of others, particularly those who are especially vulnerable because they are young, weak in body or mind, inexperienced, or in a state of dependence.'

- The line of consent drawn in *Brown* (1994) is still valid today:

Consent:
- ☐ Assault
- ☐ Battery

No consent:
- ☐ ABH
- ☐ GBH
- ☐ Murder

Lord Mustill's dissenting thoughts:	
Reason 1:	the risk of infection is greatly reduced by today's medical care
Reason 2:	the risk of things getting out of hand is no reason to criminalise someone's behaviour
Reason 3:	homosexual sex in itself was legal despite the risk of HIV
Reason 4:	the possibility of corrupting the young was already dealt with in existing legislation

7.5.4.7 The European Court

- The *Brown* (1994) case was taken to the European Court of Human Rights under the reference *Laskey v UK* (1997).
- The appellant argued that the UK judgment breached his human rights under article 8(1) of the European Convention.
- Article 8(1) governs a person's right to respect for private and family life.

Research Point

Find the case *Laskey v UK* (1997) 24 EHRR 39. Did the European Court agree that article 8(1) had been breached? If so, how did the Court justify this breach?

Checkpoint - consent

Item on checklist:	Done!
I can list the basic rules of consent in criminal law	
I can describe three situations in which the victim's consent will not be valid	
I can explain the rule in *Tabassum* (2000) in relation to a deceived consent	
As a result of *Dica* (2004) I can explain why a fully informed consent is vital in law	
I can list the instances in which consent is implied by law	
I can list at least four considerations from *Ciccarelli* (1989) that the courts will take into account when deciding whether the implied consent in sport has been withdrawn	

Item on checklist:	Done!
I can explain the legal threshold for pursuing a sporting injury in the criminal law system as a result of *Barnes* (2004)	
I can explain the 'line of consent' that was drawn in *Brown* (1994)	
I can briefly discuss the social, moral and legal reasons behind the *Brown* decision	

- Apart from the general defences such as duress, self-defence and consent, there are some specific defences available that relate to an incapacitated state of mind.

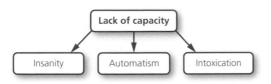

Workpoint

Why is it important to take account of insanity, reflex actions and intoxication in criminal law?

7.6 Insanity

- Insanity is available as a defence to any crime – *Horseferry Road Magistrates' Court ex parte K* (1996).
- Insanity is not available to strict liability crimes (i.e. crimes with no *mens rea*) – *DPP v H* (1997).
- The question of whether insanity can be raised is decided by the judge after reading the evidence – *Dickie* (1984).
- If the judge decides that there is evidence of insanity, he leaves it to the jury to apply – *Walton* (1978).
- Two registered medical practitioners must provide evidence that the defendant meets the legal definition of insanity – s.1 Criminal Procedure (Insanity and Unfitness to Plead) Act 1991.
- A judge has discretion as to how to sentence an insane defendant under s.5 of the Criminal Procedure (Insanity) Act 1964:

  1. A hospital order (with or without a restriction order);
  2. A supervision order;
  3. An order for his absolute discharge.

- These discretionary powers are useful for trivial offences where very little medical treatment is required – *Bromley* (1992).

- A murder conviction still requires indefinite hospitalisation at a high-security hospital (e.g. Broadmoor).

Definition

Special jury verdict: 'not guilty by reason of insanity'.

7.6.1 The definition of insanity

- Even though insanity is a *medical* condition, it has been given a *legal* definition, and it is the legal definition that is applied in law.
- The legal definition of insanity comes from a very old case – M'*Naghten* (1843), which reads as follows:

> 'To establish a defence on the ground of insanity it must be clearly proved that, at the time of the committing of the act, the party accused was labouring under such a defect of reason, from disease of the mind, as not to know the nature and quality of the act he was doing, or, if he did know it, that he did not know he was doing what was wrong.'

Workpoint

The legal definition of insanity above can be broken down into several different parts. List the different elements.

- There is a presumption of sanity in law.
- As a result, it is for the *defence* to prove insanity, but only on a balance of probabilities.
- A 'defect of reason' means that a person must be deprived of his powers of reasoning – *Clarke* (1972).
- A 'defect of reason' does not include momentary lapses of judgment, confusion or forgetfulness – *Clarke* (1972).
- A 'disease of the mind' does not refer to brain functioning (i.e. medical issues) but to mental faculties (i.e. thought processes) – *Kemp* (1957).

Case:	
***Kemp* (1957)**	Devlin J: 'The law is not concerned with the brain but with the mind, in the sense that "mind" is ordinarily used, the mental faculties of reason, memory and understanding. The condition of the brain is irrelevant and so is the question whether the condition is curable or incurable, transitory or permanent.'

• A 'disease of the mind' must come from internal factors – *Quick* (1973).

Case:	
Quick (1973)	Facts: the defendant reacted to his diabetes treatment.
	Held: this was an external cause, not a 'disease of the mind'.
	Lawton LJ: 'The fundamental concept is of a malfunctioning of the mind caused by disease. A malfunctioning of the mind caused by the application to the body of some external factor such as violence, drugs, including anaesthetics, alcohol and hypnotic influences cannot fairly be said to be due to disease.'

Workpoint

Using *Kemp* and *Quick* above, describe a 'disease of the mind' in your own words.

• External factors, such as alcohol or drugs, do not qualify for the defence of insanity.
• Insanity is only concerned with internal factors, which can include medical conditions such as diabetes.

Case:	
Hennessy (1989)	Facts: the defendant was diabetic and had forgotten to take his insulin. While suffering from high blood sugar (hyperglycaemia) he committed several driving offences. He could not remember doing so.
	Held: his condition was caused by diabetes – an internal factor – and therefore the correct defence was insanity.
Sullivan (1984)	Facts: the defendant attacked his neighbour during a post-epileptic seizure.
	Held: an internal cause, correct defence was insanity.
	Lord Diplock: 'it matters not whether the impairment is organic or functional, or permanent or transient. The purpose of the defence of insanity has been to protect society against recurrence of the dangerous conduct, particularly, as in this case, it is recurrent...'

Case:	
***Burgess* (1991)**	Facts: the defendant attacked his friend during a sleepwalking episode. Held: an internal cause, correct defence was insanity. Lord Lane CJ: 'sleepwalking is an abnormality or disorder, albeit transitory, due to an internal factor.'

- The three cases above illustrate that the defence of insanity is only interested in internal malfunctions that cause a defect of reason.
- Diabetics, epileptics and sleepwalkers have been judged as legally insane.
- Such judgments may encourage negative feelings towards sufferers.

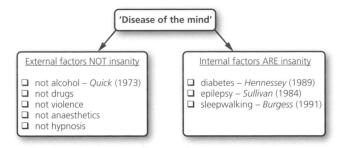

'Disease of the mind'

External factors NOT insanity
- ❑ not alcohol – *Quick* (1973)
- ❑ not drugs
- ❑ not violence
- ❑ not anaesthetics
- ❑ not hypnosis

Internal factors ARE insanity
- ❑ diabetes – *Hennessey* (1989)
- ❑ epilepsy – *Sullivan* (1984)
- ❑ sleepwalking – *Burgess* (1991)

- The *M'Naghten* rules were rejected in the Canadian case of *Parks* (1992), in which sleepwalking was found to be a sleep disorder.
- The *M'Naghten* rules were applied in the Canadian case of *Rabey* (1980), in which post-traumatic stress disorder was found to fit the definition of legal insanity.
- The United Kingdom has considered post-traumatic stress disorder to be automatism – *T* (1990).

Research Point

The Australian case of *Falconer* (1990) 171 CLR 30 examined the internal/external theory in *Quick* (1973). Find Toohey J's decision in *Falconer*. What did he think of the decision in *Quick*?

- The defendant must not understand the 'nature and quality of the act'.
- This must be a result of his defect of reason.

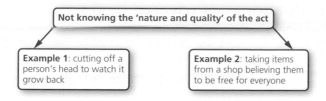

- The defendant must also not realise that his act was 'wrong'.
- This must be a result of his defect of reason.
- 'Wrong' means 'illegal' – M'Naghten (1843) and Windle (1952).
- It does not include 'morally wrong' – Johnson (2007).

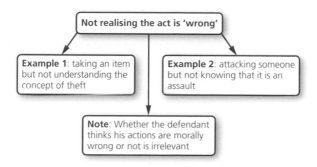

- The High Court of Australia took an alternative view in Stapleton (1952), believing that the 'morality' of the act was more important than its 'legality'.
- This also happened in the Canadian case of Chaulk (1991).

Workpoint

Daniel has a learning disability. He is 15 years old and requires constant supervision because he does not understand acceptable social behaviour. His mother takes him to a sweet shop, where he innocently takes handfuls of sweets. Later on, he takes jeans from a clothes shop and hits the shop assistant, causing bruising. Daniel is charged with theft and assault. Answer the questions below.

(a) Does Daniel have a defect of reason?
(b) If so, has his defect been caused by a disease of the mind?
(c) As a result of his defect, does he understand the nature and quality of his act?
(d) As a result of his defect, does he know that his acts were legally wrong?

7.6.2 Situations not covered by the *M'Naghten* rules

- An irresistible impulse is no longer accepted as grounds for insanity – *Kopsch* (1925).
- It may however be a defence under diminished responsibility – *Byrne* (1960).

7.6.3 Reform

The Law Commission's Draft Criminal Code (1989) proposed to replace the term 'insanity' with 'mental disorder' as follows:

> *'Clause 35(1): A mental disorder verdict shall be returned if the defendant is proved to have committed an offence but it is proved on the balance of probabilities that he was at the time suffering from severe mental illness or severe mental handicap.'*

New term:	Definition under clause 34:
'Mental disorder'	Severe mental illness Arrested or incomplete development of the mind State of automatism Organic or functional Continuing or recurring
'Severe mental illness'	Lasting impairment of intellectual functions Failure of memory, orientation, comprehension or learning Lasting alteration of mood altering judgment Delusional beliefs or jealousy Abnormal perceptions and delusional misinterpretations Disordered thinking preventing reasonable communication
'Severe mental handicap'	A state of arrested or incomplete development of mind Severe impairment of intelligence and social functioning

- Notice how there is much more emphasis on mental illness rather than a 'disease of the mind'.

Workpoint

Examine the two legal definitions of insanity below. What are their main differences? Which one do you think is more appropriate and why?

M'Naghten (1843):

'To establish a defence on the ground of insanity it must be clearly proved that, at the time of the committing of the act, the party accused was labouring under such a defect of reason, from disease of the mind, as not to know the nature and quality of the act he was doing, or, if he did know it, that he did not know he was doing what was wrong.'

Law Commission Clause 35(1):

'A mental disorder verdict shall be returned if the defendant is proved to have committed an offence but it is proved on the balance of probabilities that he was at the time suffering from severe mental illness or severe mental handicap.'

Write down your notes.

Checkpoint - insanity

Item on checklist:	Done!
I can list three mental capacity defences	
I can explain who decides whether insanity can be raised as a defence and what evidence helps towards this decision	
I can explain who decides whether the defendant was insane at the time of his crime	
I can list the penalties available on a verdict of 'not guilty by reason of insanity'	
I can briefly describe the *M'Naghten* (1843) definition of insanity in my own words	
I can define 'disease of the mind' according to *Kemp* (1957)	
I can distinguish between internal and external factors using two legal authorities to support my answer	
I can explain what is meant by 'nature and quality' and 'wrong' in the *M'Naghten* definition of insanity	
I can critically analyse the reforms suggested by the Law Commission and explain why they are a vast improvement on the current outdated law	

7.7 Automatism

- Automatism is another term from the medical world meaning 'automatic'.
- In criminal law, it refers to reflex actions or uncontrollable physical movements.

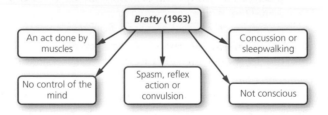

- Automatism is incompatible with *actus reus* in that the movements are involuntary.
- It is also incompatible with *mens rea* in that the defendant has no control.
- Lord Denning in *Bratty* (1963) used the word 'unconscious' but this could be widened to include 'altered', 'clouded' or 'impaired' consciousness.
- If the defendant wishes to raise automatism as a defence, he must provide evidence of it – *Hill v Baxter* (1958).

Case:	
Bratty **(1963)**	Lord Denning: 'When the cause assigned is concussion or sleep walking, there should be some evidence from which it can reasonably be inferred before it should be left to the jury. His mere assertion that he was asleep will not suffice.'

Research Point

Look up Lord Denning's judgment in *Bratty v Attorney-General of Northern Ireland* [1963] AC 386. What kind of evidence does he expect to be put to the jury for concussion or sleepwalking? Where must the evidence come from?

7.7.1 The 'involuntary' requirement

- The defendant must be incapable of exercising control over his bodily movements.
- If he can operate his body to a degree, the defence is not made out – *Isitt* (1978).

Case:	
Isitt (1978)	Lawton LJ: 'is the accused entitled to say, "I am not guilty because my mind was not working in top gear?" It is clear that the appellant's mind was working to some extent, but the fact that his moral inhibitions were not working properly does not mean that the mind was not working at all.'

- If a defendant is driving in the sense of controlling the car and directing its movements, it is not automatism – *Hill v Baxter* (1958).
- The defendant's actions must be 'wholly uncontrolled and uninitiated by any function of conscious will' – *Watmore v Jenkins* (1962).
- The ability to avoid crashing a car and veering away from other traffic or braking violently does not point to full automatism – *Broome v Perkins* (1987).
- Any evidence that the automatism is caused by post-traumatic stress disorder is irrelevant – *Narbrough* (2004).

7.7.2 Self-induced automatism

- If a defendant causes his own automatism, he is responsible for its consequences.
- If automatism is caused by alcohol or drugs then the rules of intoxication will apply (see further below).
- If the defendant is aware that he is about to suffer automatism (e.g. he is feeling drowsy) and he does nothing to alleviate it, it will be considered as self-induced automatism and he will be responsible for the outcome – *Kay v Butterworth* (1945).
- Awareness of the onset of a hypoglycaemic episode is self-induced automatism – *C* (2007).
- When a hypoglycaemic attack causes a total loss of control, this is still self-induced automatism if it could have been prevented – *Clarke* (2009).
- Point to note: Despite the overlap, individuals with diabetes are much more likely to plead automatism than insanity.

Workpoint

What should the following individuals do in order to avoid liability?

(a) David is a long-distance driver and after 8 hours on the road is beginning to feel drowsy. He has a history of jerky movements during sleep.

(b) Suzie realises she has failed to take her diabetes medicine on her way to school.

(c) Laura has just left hospital after nerve treatment. She has been told not to drive, so gets on the bus and assaults the man next to her.

7.7.3 Reflex actions

- A well-known Australian authority states that a reflex action will be no defence if the defendant has put himself in a dangerous position – *Ryan v R* (1967).

Case:	
Ryan v R (1967)	Windeyer J: 'Such phrases as "reflex action" and "automatic reaction" can, if used imprecisely and unscientifically, be like "blackout" – mere excuses. They seem to me to have no real application to the case of a fully conscious man who has put himself in a situation in which he has his finger on the trigger of a loaded rifle levelled at another man.'

- However, an unexpected and innocent reflex action will usually be a full defence, as the defendant will have no *mens rea* for his crime.

7.7.4 Reform

- The Law Commission's Draft Criminal Code (1989) provides a definition of automatism:

> *'Clause 33(1)(a)(i)(ii):*
>
> *automatism is a reflex, spasm or convulsion, or occurs while he is in a condition (whether of sleep, unconsciousness, impaired consciousness or otherwise) depriving him of effective control of his act.'*

Workpoint

What do you think of the scope of the Law Commission's definition? Will it make automatism easier to raise as a defence? In what circumstances?

Item on checklist:	Done!
I can explain what automatism is according to *Bratty* (1963)	
I can use legal authorities to explain what is meant by 'involuntary'	
I can explain why self-induced automatism will fail as a defence and can support my answer with a legal authority	
I can critically examine the Law Commission's proposals for a definition of automatism	

7.8 Intoxication

- The defence of intoxication is applicable to all crimes with a *mens rea*.
- However, there are strict limits to how it can be used.

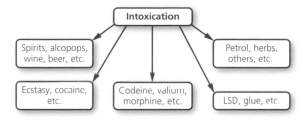

- The method or source of intoxication does not matter – the courts do not distinguish between alcohol and illegal drugs.
- The courts in England have been very strict with intoxicated individuals for social reasons.

Case:	
***Majewski* (1977)**	Lord Simon: 'the public could be legally unprotected from unprovoked violence where such violence was the consequence of drink or drugs having obliterated the capacity of the perpetrator to know what he was doing or what were its consequences.'

- The defendant will typically argue that he 'did not know what he was doing'.
- In legal terms, this will translate as 'could not form the required *mens rea*'.

• The rules of intoxication are as follows:

```
                        ┌─────────────────┐
                        │  Intoxication   │
                        └─────────────────┘
         ┌──────────────────┼──────────────────┐
┌──────────────────┐ ┌──────────────────┐ ┌──────────────────┐
│ It is a full     │ │ The act of       │ │ Involuntary      │
│ defence if the   │ │ getting drunk    │ │ intoxication is  │
│ defendant could  │ │ will constitute  │ │ also no defence  │
│ not form the     │ │ a mens rea of    │ │ if the required  │
│ required         │ │ recklessness     │ │ mens rea was     │
│ intention        │ │ (i.e. no         │ │ still formed     │
│                  │ │ defence)         │ │                  │
└──────────────────┘ └──────────────────┘ └──────────────────┘
```

• If a defendant raises intoxication as a defence, it must be proved that his capacity to form a *mens rea* was non-existent – *Sheehan* (1975).

Case:	
***Sheehan* (1975)**	Held: 'The mere fact that the defendant's mind was affected by drink so that he acted in a way in which he would not have done had he been sober does not assist him at all, provided that the necessary intention was there. A drunken intent is nevertheless an intent.'

7.8.1 Involuntary intoxication

• If a defendant is drugged but forms his own intention, then he has the required *mens rea* for a conviction – *Kingston* (1995).

Case:	
***Kingston* (1995)**	Facts: the defendant committed indecent assault while intoxicated. He did not know that his coffee had been drugged, but he did admit to forming the *mens rea* once drugged.
	Held: despite the involuntary intoxication the defendant formed the required intention on his own, and that will suffice for a conviction. Intoxication was therefore no defence.

• If a defendant becomes involuntarily intoxicated on harmless sleeping pills, evidence must still be provided to prove that they prevented him from forming a *mens rea* – *O'Connell* (1997).
• A defendant's behaviour while voluntarily or involuntarily intoxicated will often reveal whether intention was present or not – *Heard* (2007).
• Simply because an alcoholic drink has a stronger effect than expected does not mean that the defendant was 'involuntarily' intoxicated – *Allen* (1988).

- If an alcoholic drink (e.g. beer) is secretly laced with a much stronger drug (e.g. LSD), the jury may decide that the intoxication was involuntary – *Eatch* (1980).
- The secret addition of LSD to beer was found to be involuntary intoxication in *Ross v Advocate* (1991) (Scotland) and *People v Cruz* (1978) (California).

7.8.2 Non-dangerous or prescription drugs

- When a defendant becomes intoxicated on prescription drugs, it is deemed to be involuntary intoxication – *Majewski* (1977).
- This is because the intoxication is unexpected, unlikely, unforeseeable and not anticipated.

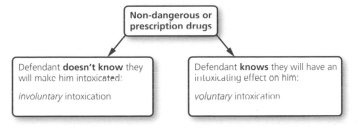

Case:	
***Bailey* (1983)**	Facts: the defendant took his insulin but forgot to eat, making him hypoglycaemic. He committed malicious wounding while in this state.
	Held: a distinction should be drawn between dangerous drugs and medically prescribed drugs. Only if the defendant knew that the drug would cause him to be aggressive or unpredictable could he be said to be reckless and therefore liable.

- Taking morphine to calm a health complaint will be deemed to be involuntary intoxication as long as the defendant did not appreciate the effect it would have – *Burns* (1974).

- Valium tablets – which are designed to calm a patient – will also be deemed to be involuntary intoxication if they cause completely unexpected effects – *Hardie* (1985).

Case:	
Hardie (1985)	Facts: the defendant took his girlfriend's valium and later set fire to the inside of her wardrobe. The trial judge told the jury to ignore the valium and he was convicted of criminal damage.
	Parker LJ: 'There was no evidence that it was known to [D] or even generally known that the taking of valium in the quantity taken would be liable to render a person aggressive or incapable of appreciating risks. The drug is wholly different in kind from drugs which are liable to cause unpredictability or aggressiveness.'

- If the defendant in *Hardie* had **known** of the effect of valium upon him, his act of taking the drug would have been 'reckless'.
- This would have been voluntary intoxication and it would have satisfied the *mens rea* of recklessness for criminal damage.

Case:	Drug:	Offence:	Result:
Burns (1974)	Morphine	-	D did not appreciate effect – conviction quashed
Bailey (1983)	Insulin	Malicious wounding	D did not appreciate effect – conviction quashed
Hardie (1985)	Valium	Criminal damage	D did not appreciate effect – conviction quashed

- It should be remembered that if during the involuntary intoxication of non-dangerous or prescribed drugs, the defendant *develops his own mens rea*, his involuntary intoxication will be no defence – *Kingston* (1995).
- Distinguishing between dangerous and sedative drugs is difficult.
- The jury may consider:

1. The user;
2. The amount taken;
3. How much has been taken before;
4. How the drug is taken;
5. The surroundings or environment in which the drug was taken;
6. What the user hopes will happen;

7. What the user expects will happen;
8. What the user intended to happen.

• Intoxication under duress was held to be involuntary intoxication in *Burrows v State* (1931) (Arizona).

7.8.3 Voluntary intoxication

• When a defendant becomes voluntarily intoxicated, he has *chosen* to consume alcohol or drugs that he knows will alter his ability to think clearly.
• The courts have viewed this as reckless behaviour and it will suffice as the *mens rea* of recklessness – *Majewski* (1977).

Case:	
***Majewski* (1977)**	Lord Elwyn-Jones LC: 'His course of conduct in reducing himself by drugs and drink to that condition in my view supplies the evidence of *mens rea*, of guilty mind certainly sufficient for crimes of basic intent. It is a reckless course of conduct and recklessness is enough to constitute the necessary *mens rea* in assault cases.'
***Bratty* (1963)**	Lord Denning: 'If the drunken man is so drunk that he does not know what he is doing, he has a defence to any charge, such as murder or wounding with intent, in which a specific intent is essential, but he is still liable to be convicted of manslaughter or unlawful wounding for which no specific intent is necessary.'

• In fact, voluntary intoxication will have to be absolutely extreme for the defendant to not even form the 'recklessness' element – *Stubbs* (1988).

- If the *mens rea* required is intention **alone**, then intoxication can provide a defence because intention may be hard to form when intoxicated – *Majewski* (1977).
- Intoxication is therefore a defence to crimes requiring **intent** (i.e. 'specific intent crimes') but not to crimes where **recklessness** will suffice ('basic intent crimes') – *Majewski* (1977).

Definition

Specific intent crimes: criminal offences that specifically require intention for a *mens rea*.

Basic intent crimes: criminal offences in which recklessness will suffice as a *mens rea*.

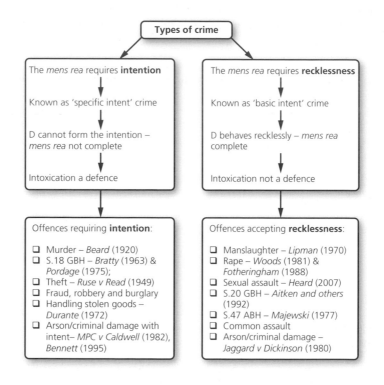

Types of crime

The *mens rea* requires **intention**	The *mens rea* requires **recklessness**
Known as 'specific intent' crime	Known as 'basic intent' crime
D cannot form the intention – *mens rea* not complete	D behaves recklessly – *mens rea* complete
Intoxication a defence	Intoxication not a defence

Offences requiring **intention**:

- ❑ Murder – *Beard* (1920)
- ❑ S.18 GBH – *Bratty* (1963) & *Pordage* (1975);
- ❑ Theft – *Ruse v Read* (1949)
- ❑ Fraud, robbery and burglary
- ❑ Handling stolen goods – *Durante* (1972)
- ❑ Arson/criminal damage with intent– *MPC v Caldwell* (1982), *Bennett* (1995)

Offences accepting **recklessness**:

- ❑ Manslaughter – *Lipman* (1970)
- ❑ Rape – *Woods* (1981) & *Fotheringham* (1988)
- ❑ Sexual assault – *Heard* (2007)
- ❑ S.20 GBH – *Aitken and others* (1992)
- ❑ S.47 ABH – *Majewski* (1977)
- ❑ Common assault
- ❑ Arson/criminal damage – *Jaggard v Dickinson* (1980)

- Intoxication was not always viewed as a mitigating factor to specific intent crimes – at one time it would make a defendant even more culpable.
- However, in *Mead* (1909) it was conceded that intoxication may prevent a defendant from forming the intent to murder.

- This was confirmed in *DPP v Beard* (1920) when Lord Birkenhead accepted that a defendant should not be convicted of a crime if he could not form its *mens rea*.
- As a result, it is sufficient that the defendant does not form the *mens rea* (i.e. intention) while voluntarily intoxicated in order to use intoxication as a defence – *Pordage* (1975) and *Cole* (1993).
- Public policy can determine whether an offence is specific or basic intent – *Heard* (2007).

Research Point

The definition of sexual assault under section 3 of the Sexual Offences Act 2003 is that D must intentionally touch V with a lack of reasonable belief that V was consenting. Look up the judgment of Hughes LJ in *Heard* [2007] EWCA Crim 125. Why was sexual assault held to be a basic intent crime despite the word 'intentionally' in the offence? What did *Majewski* (1977) have to do with the decision?

- It is still not clear which crimes are basic intent, specific intent or strict liability – *Carroll v DPP* (2009).
- If there is evidence that the defendant would not have formed the *mens rea* when sober (e.g. due to illness etc.) then the jury can consider this – *Richardson and Irwin* (1999).

7.8.4 Proving intoxication

- The responsibility is on the defendant to prove not just that he was intoxicated, but that he was intoxicated to such a degree that he couldn't form the required *mens rea*.
- If the trial judge does not think that there is sufficient evidence of this, he will remove intoxication from the jury – *Groark* (1999).

7.8.5 'Dutch courage'

Definition

Dutch courage: drinking alcohol in order to give oneself the confidence to act or commit a crime.

- If a defendant intentionally becomes intoxicated in order to commit a crime, he is deemed to have the intention to commit that crime – *Attorney-General of Northern Ireland v Gallagher* (1963).

Case:	
Gallagher (1963)	Lord Denning: 'If a man, whilst sane and sober, forms an intention to kill and makes preparation for it knowing it is a wrong thing to do, and then gets himself drunk so as to give himself Dutch courage to do the killing, and whilst drunk carries out his intention, he cannot rely on this self-induced drunkenness as a defence to murder, not even as reducing it to manslaughter. The wickedness of his mind before he got drunk is enough to condemn him, coupled with the act which he intended to do and did do.'

- As a result of *Gallagher*, Dutch courage is not a defence to specific intent or basic intent crimes.
- This is because intention is present and recklessness is also present.

Workpoint

The defendant in *Gallagher* argued that when he killed his wife after drinking a bottle of whisky, he could not form the *mens rea* of intention. He was still prosecuted. Why do you think the Court of Appeal rejected his argument? Can you identify a public policy consideration in this decision? What is it?

7.8.6 Intoxication and mental disorders

- If voluntary or involuntary intoxication leads to insanity (as defined under the *M'Naghten* rules), then the defendant will be judged as insane, not intoxicated – *Davis* (1881).
- If voluntary intoxication leads to automatism, it will be considered self-induced and therefore reckless – *Lipman* (1970).
- However, if **involuntary** intoxication leads to automatism, there is no recklessness on the part of the defendant and no criminal liability will follow.
- A 'drunken mistake' is not a defence – the defendant will be judged according to the *Majewski* rules – *Fotheringham* (1988).

7.8.7 Reform

- The Law Commission recently published a report entitled: *Intoxication and Criminal Liability* (Law Com No. 314).
- Several recommendations for reform of the intoxication defence were put forward, some of which are below:

Recommendation:	
(1):	References to 'specific intent' and 'basic intent' should be abolished
(2):	The distinction between voluntary and involuntary intoxication should be retained
(3):	There should be an assumption that D is not intoxicated and the burden is on D to prove that he was (e.g. *Groark* 1999)
(4):	There should be a new rule that if intoxication is proved, there is an assumption that it was voluntary, placing an additional burden on D to prove that it was involuntary
(5):	The distinction between 'dangerous' and 'soporific' drugs should be abolished (over ruling *Hardie* 1985).

Workpoint

In light of the Law Commission's proposals:

(a) What would be the implications of abolishing the rule in *Hardie* (1985)?
(b) Should such a heavy burden of proof be placed onto a defendant's shoulders?

Checkpoint - intoxication

Item on checklist:	Done!
I can list seven intoxicants that may effect a defendant's ability to form a *mens rea*	
I can explain the reason behind the UK's strict approach to intoxicated defendants as described by Lord Simon in *Majewski* (1977)	
I can describe the basic rules of the intoxication defence	
I can explain the rule in *Kingston* (1995) in relation to involuntary intoxication	
I know that a laced drink will be a defence to both specific and basic intent crimes unless the defendant forms his own *mens rea*	
I can explain why intoxication of non-dangerous or prescription drugs is deemed to be involuntary intoxication according to *Bailey* (1983) and *Hardie* (1985)	

Checkpoint - continued

Item on checklist:	Done!
I can list five factors that a jury may consider when distinguishing between dangerous and non-dangerous drugs	
I can explain why voluntary intoxication is not a defence to basic intent crimes and I can provide a legal authority to support my answer	
I can distinguish between specific and basic intent crimes and can give three examples of each	
I can locate the burden of proof when the defence of intoxication is raised	
I can explain the rule in *Attorney-General of Northern Ireland v Gallagher* (1963) in relation to Dutch courage	

Potential exam questions:

1) Evaluate the defence of duress of threats.
2) Describe the criteria applicable to a mistake of fact in law.
3) Explain how self-defence can be used as a general defence in criminal law.
4) Evaluate the general defence of consent.
5) 'The legal definition of insanity leads to a manifest injustice in law.' Discuss this statement with reference to legal authorities.
6) Explain the ways in which the law distinguishes between voluntary and involuntary intoxication and how this affects criminal liability.

Chapter 8
Homicide

The most serious criminal offence is murder. This chapter will examine the criminal offence of murder and the components that make up that crime. It will also explore the special defences to murder, including diminished responsibility, loss of control and involuntary manslaughter.

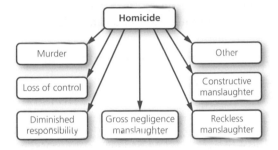

8.1 Murder

- There are several different components to murder, all listed below:

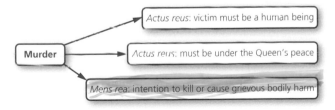

8.1.1 The *actus reus* of murder
- The victim of murder cannot be a foetus – there are other offences for that purpose under the Offences Against the Person Act 1861.

- A baby must be fully expelled from the mother to be a human being in law – *Poulton* (1832).
- A baby must also have a separate existence from its mother – *Enoch* (1833).
- If a baby is stabbed during pregnancy and dies after birth, this is not murder but may be unlawful act manslaughter – *Attorney-General's Reference (No. 3 of 1994)* (1997).
- A dead person cannot be the victim of murder, even if the defendant believes him to be alive.
- Switching a life support machine off is not the *actus reus* of murder; the operating cause of death (e.g. the stab wound) will be – *Malcherek and Steel* (1981).
- A killing which takes place under the Queen's Peace will be prosecuted, but killings during the course of war will not be.
- There was an old rule that if the victim survived for a year and a day after the attack, charges of murder could not be brought – *Dyson* (1908).
- This rule was abolished by s.1 of the Law Reform (Year and a Day Rule) Act 1996.

Workpoint

Why was it important to abolish the year and a day rule in homicide? What effect does this change have on the law of homicide and the defendants who commit murder?

8.1.2 The *mens rea* of murder

- The old term for the *mens rea* of murder is 'malice aforethought'.

Definition

Malice aforethought: an intention to kill or cause grievous bodily harm.

- The defendant must intend to kill or cause grievous bodily harm to satisfy the *mens rea* for murder – *Moloney* (1985).
- This means that the defendant does not have to intend to kill to be charged with murder.
- If direct intention is not present, the jury can ponder whether the defendant foresaw death or serious bodily harm as a virtually certain consequence of his actions (oblique intention) – *Woollin* (1998).
- Grievous bodily harm simply means 'really serious harm' and no elaboration beyond sections 18 and 20 of the Offences Against the Person Act 1861 is required – *DPP v Smith* (1961), *Saunders* (1985), *Janjua* (1998).

- Manslaughter can be considered as an alternative verdict – *Coutts* (2006).

Workpoint

Doug furiously set out to find Peter, who owed him money. Doug banged hard on Peter's front door, shouting 'I'm going to teach you a lesson'. Peter frantically tried to find some money under his floorboards. Doug burst into Peter's house and found Peter upstairs. Peter was still on the floor so Doug kicked Peter in the head really hard shouting 'That will serve you right!' and then left, thinking that Peter was unconscious. Peter had actually suffered severe brain damage and died three months later.

(a) Does Doug have the *actus reus* of murder? Give reasons for your answer.
(b) Does Doug have the *mens rea* for murder? Give reasons for your answer.

8.1.3 Reform

- Clause 54(1) of the Law Commission's Draft Criminal Code (1989) states the following:

> 'A person is guilty of murder if he causes the death of another (a) intending to cause death, or (b) intending to cause serious personal harm and being aware that he may cause death.'

- This definition of murder is simply a codification of the current common law principles.

Checkpoint - murder

Item on checklist:	Done!
I can define the components of the *actus reus* of murder and cite two legal authorities	
I can explain when a person becomes a human being in law with a case authority	
I can describe the old year and a day rule	
I can define the *mens rea* of murder using a case authority	

8.2 Voluntary manslaughter

- Voluntary manslaughter is where the *actus reus* and the *mens rea* of murder is complete.
- However, the defendant argues that he has a good excuse for committing the crime.
- The three defences listed below are special defences only available to a murder charge.

- If used successfully at trial, they will mitigate the murder conviction to one of voluntary manslaughter (see s.2(3) of the Homicide Act 1957).
- This is important because voluntary manslaughter does not apply the mandatory life sentence for killing, allowing judges to use more discretion when sentencing.

8.2.1 Diminished responsibility

Definition

Diminished responsibility: an abnormality of mental functioning which substantially impairs a person's ability to understand, rationalise or exercise self-control.

- The defence of diminished responsibility was introduced into English Law by s.2 of the Homicide Act 1957.
- The definition of diminished responsibility reads similar to that of insanity, but defendants are much more likely to plead the former than the latter.
- It provides a defence in instances when a person cannot, as a result of abnormal mental functioning, take full responsibility for his actions.
- This is even when the killing was premeditated – *Matheson* (1958).
- The defence of diminished responsibility was updated by s.52 of the Coroners and Justice Act 2009.
- This update was a result of the Law Commission's 2006 report entitled *Murder, Manslaughter and Infanticide*, which described the defence as 'badly out of date'.

Old definition under s.2:	New definition under s.2:
'Abnormality of mind'	'Abnormality of mental functioning'
'Condition of arrested or retarded development of mind from any inherent cause or induced by disease or injury'	'Recognised medical condition'
'Substantially impaired mental responsibility'	'Substantially impaired ability to understand the nature of conduct, form a rational judgment or exercise self-control'
-	'Provides an explanation for D's conduct'

- Most of the case law that built up around the old version of s.2 of the Homicide Act 1957 will still be relevant.
- For example, in *Campbell* (1997), it was established that diminished responsibility was not available to a charge of attempted murder.

Workpoint

The reformed definition of diminished responsibility from s.2 of the Homicide Act 1957 is provided below. What do you think are key words to this defence?

2(1) A person ("D") who kills or is a party to the killing of another is not to be convicted of murder if D was suffering from an abnormality of mental functioning which -

(a) *arose from a recognised medical condition;*

(b) *substantially impaired D's ability to do one or more of the things mentioned in subsection (1A), and*

(c) *provides an explanation for D's acts and omissions in doing or being a party to the killing*

(1A) Those things are -

(a) *to understand the nature of D's conduct;*

(b) *to form a rational judgment;*

(c) *to exercise self-control.*

(1B) An abnormality of mental functioning provides an explanation for D's conduct if it causes, or is a significant contributory factor in causing, D to carry out that conduct.

- The four main components of diminished responsibility are as follows:

(1) Must be an 'abnormality of mental functioning'	(2) Must arise from a 'recognised medical condition'
(3) Must have 'substantially impaired' ability to 'understand, rationalise or exercise self-control'	(4) 'Abnormality' must provide an 'explanation' for D's acts and omissions when killing

Workpoint

Which of the following defendants match all four criteria above and could plead diminished responsibility?

(a) Georgia has Downs Syndrome which causes her to black out in 'dark moods of aggression'. She is walking through the park with her mother when she attacks a toddler, killing him.

(b) Linda has post-natal depression. She has been unable to think clearly recently. She intentionally omitted to feed her son over the space of five weeks with the intention to cause him grievous bodily harm.

(c) Marian is an alcoholic and has been for over 20 years. She has nearly died twice because of her condition and has just left hospital following a liver transplant. If she does not drink in the morning, her whole body shakes and she is sick. Her husband refused to buy her more alcohol because they had no money left, so she stabbed him in the chest.

(d) Loraine has been having headaches recently because she is not sleeping through the night. Her impending exams are causing her to lie awake for hours. On the day of the exam, one of her friends teased Loraine about her 'tired and ugly' expression, and Loraine attacked her friend with a sharp compass, causing brain damage and, eventually, death seven months later.

8.2.1.1 'Abnormality of mental functioning'

- The new phrase 'mental functioning' alludes to expert medical opinion.
- The repealed phrase 'abnormality of mind' was interpreted very widely.

Case:	
Byrne (1960)	Lord Parker CJ: An abnormality of mind is 'a state of mind so different from that of ordinary human beings that the reasonable man would term it abnormal'.

- The abnormality does not have to be permanent.
- There is also no requirement that the abnormality should be present since birth – *Gomez* (1964).

Workpoint

What kind of condition or circumstance would you consider to be an 'abnormality of mental functioning'?

8.2.1.2 'Recognised medical condition'

- This is a new addition to the definition of diminished responsibility, replacing the words 'arrested', 'retarded', 'inherent' and 'disease or injury'.
- No further definition of this phrase has been provided, but the old case law provides some clues.

Condition for diminished responsibility:	Case authority:
Adjustment disorder	*Dietschmann* (2003)
Alcohol Dependence Syndrome	*Tandy* (1989) *Wood* (2008)
Asperger's Syndrome	*Jama* (2004)
Battered Woman Syndrome	*Hobson* (1998)
Depression	*Gittens* (1984) *Seers* (1984) *Ahluwalia* (1992) *Swan* (2006)
Epilepsy	*Bailey* (1961) *Campbell* (1997)
Othello Syndrome (extreme jealousy)	*Vinagre* (1979)
Paranoia	*Simcox* (1964)
Pre-menstrual tension & post-natal depression	*Reynolds* (1988)
Psychopathy	*Byrne* (1960) *Hendy* (2006)
Schizophrenia	*Moyle* (2008) *Erskine* (2009) *Khan* (2009)

- If there are several medical conditions, this will strengthen the defence – *Reynolds* (1988).

- If one of the conditions is not a medical condition, it must be discounted.
- Juvenile mental health is included under the term 'recognised medical condition' and will include learning disabilities, autism, etc.

8.2.1.3 'Substantially impair understanding, rational judgement and/or self-control'

- The repealed phrase 'substantially impaired his mental responsibility' was thought to be too vague – the defendant now has to prove that his abnormality substantially impaired one of the three additional factors listed below.

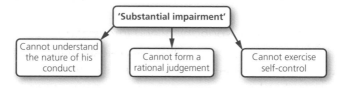

- The word 'substantial' is a jury question – *Byrne* (1960) and *Eifinger* (2001).
- Despite the advances in science, there is no accurate scientific measurement for substantial impairment and so it remains a jury issue – *Khan* (2009).

Case:	
***Lloyd* (1967)**	Ashworth J: 'Substantial does not mean total, the mental responsibility need not be totally impaired. At the other end of the scale substantial does not mean trivial or minimal. Parliament has left it to juries to say on the evidence, was the mental responsibility impaired and if so, was it substantially impaired?'

- The jury have significant freedom when deliberating this criteria.

- Peter Sutcliffe – the Yorkshire Ripper – presented evidence from four psychiatrists that he was suffering from paranoid schizophrenia and the jury still convicted him of murder.

Workpoint

You are a member of the jury and you are watching the trials of Georgia, Linda, Marian and Loraine (in the Workpoint on page 174). Make notes as to whether you believe they have a 'substantial impairment' according to the three-part criteria:

(a) Georgia has Downs Syndrome.
(b) Linda has post-natal depression.
(c) Marian is an alcoholic and has been for over 20 years.
(d) Loraine has been having headaches recently because she is not sleeping through the night.

8.2.1.4 'An explanation for D's acts and omissions'

- This is a new requirement, stating that the substantial abnormality must *cause* the defendant to kill.
- The phrase 'significant contributory factor' means that the defendant's abnormality does not have to be the *sole* cause of the killing.

8.2.1.5 Diminished responsibility and intoxication

- Intoxication on its own is not diminished responsibility because it does not create an abnormality of mind – *Fenton* (1975).
- If the defendant has a recognised medical condition constituting an abnormality of mental functioning but kills while intoxicated, the jury must *ignore* any effect of alcohol or drugs – *Gittens* (1984).
- The jury must consider whether the defendant had an abnormality of mind, 'drink or no drink' – *Egan* (1992).

Case:	
Dietschmann (2003)	Facts: the defendant attacked a stranger while intoxicated. He was suffering from a depressed grief reaction to the death of his girlfriend.
	Lord Hutton: 'Has D satisfied you that, despite the drink, his mental abnormality substantially impaired his mental responsibility for his fatal acts, or has he failed to satisfy you of that? If he has not, the defence of diminished responsibility is not available to him.'

- Brain damage and a psychopathic disorder will be separated from intoxication – *Hendy* (2006).
- An acute stress disorder will be separated from intoxication – *Robson* (2006).
- Depression will be separated from intoxication – *Swan* (2006).

8.2.1.6 Diminished responsibility and alcoholism

- The issue of intoxication is different to that of alcoholism.
- A defendant may argue that his Alcohol Dependence Syndrome constitutes the required 'recognised medical condition'.
- Alcohol Dependence Syndrome will be accepted as diminished responsibility if the defendant had injured his brain through years of abuse or could not resist alcohol at all – *Tandy* (1989) and *Inseal* (1992).

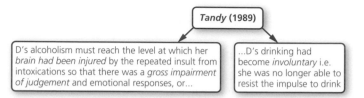

Tandy (1989)

| D's alcoholism must reach the level at which her *brain had been injured* by the repeated insult from intoxications so that there was a *gross impairment of judgement* and emotional responses, or... | ...D's drinking had become *involuntary* i.e. she was no longer able to resist the impulse to drink |

> **Research Point**
>
> The decision in *Tandy* (1989) was heavily criticised for being too strict. Look up the following articles: G.R. Sullivan, 'Intoxicants and Diminished Responsibility' [1994] *Criminal Law Review* 156, and J. Goodliffe, 'Tandy and the Concept of Alcoholism as a Disease' (1990) 53 *Modern Law Review* 809. List the main arguments of both pieces.

- The strict test in *Tandy* was loosened in *Wood* (2008).
- There is no longer a requirement for brain damage as a result of years of abuse.

| (1) Alcohol Dependence Syndrome may constitute an abnormality of mind – the jury will decide. | (2) It is not essential that brain damage has occurred as a result of the years of abuse |

| (3) If the jury decide that ADS is an abnormality of mind, did it 'substantially impair' D's mental responsibility? | (4) The jury should ignore any voluntarily consumed alcohol and only consider alcohol consumed as a result of the ADS |

- The rules in *Wood* were simplified again by Lord Judge CJ in *Stewart* (2009).

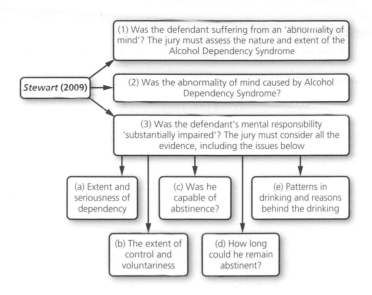

Rule:	Case authority:
Component (1): 'Abnormality of mental functioning'	*Byrne* (1960) *Gomez* (1964)
Component (2): 'Recognised medical condition'	Numerous 1960–2009 cases
Component (3): 'Substantially impair understanding, rational judgment and/or self-control'	*Byrne* (1960) *Lloyd* (1967) *Eifinger* (2001) *Khan* (2009)
Component (4): 'An explanation for D's acts and omissions'	-new-
Intoxication will be ignored when considering diminished responsibility	*Fenton* (1975) *Gittens* (1984) *Egan* (1992) *Dietschmann* (2003) *Hendy* (2006) *Swan* (2006) *Robson* (2006)
Alcohol Dependency Syndrome may constitute diminished responsibility	*Tandy* (1989) *Inseal* (1992) *Wood* (2008) *Stewart* (2009)

8.2.1.7 Procedures of diminished responsibility

• Evidence of diminished responsibility will be put forward when a jury is deciding whether or not a defendant is fit to stand trial for murder – *Antoine* (2001).

• According to s.2(2) of the Homicide Act 1957, the defendant bears the responsibility of proving the defence of diminished responsibility.

• The burden of proof is a balance of probabilities – *Dunbar* (1958).

• If the defendant raises insanity but the prosecution thinks diminished responsibility is more suitable, the prosecution must prove it beyond all reasonable doubt – *Grant* (1960).

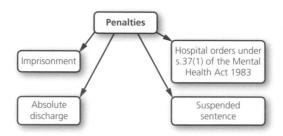

• A defendant may plead guilty through diminished responsibility and simply be sentenced without trial – *Cox* (1968).

• This will only be acceptable on 'clear evidence' that diminished responsibility is met – *Vinagre* (1979).

• A jury is free to disregard the medical evidence as 'not entirely convincing' – *Walton* (1978).

• If a jury rejects the defence of diminished responsibility but the evidence of murder is unsafe, the Court of Appeal may reduce the conviction to manslaughter – *Matheson* (1958) and *Bailey* (1961).

• Even though there is no statutory requirement, the abnormality of mind should be proved by medical evidence – *Byrne* (1960).

• If a medical condition becomes recognised by psychiatrists, murder convictions with evidence of that condition may be quashed – *Hobson* (1998).

• Even though medical evidence is vital, a jury is not bound to accept the evidence and may have to weigh up several different opinions – *Dix* (1982).

Checkpoint - voluntary manslaughter (1): diminished responsibility

Item on checklist:	Done!
I can list three defences that count as 'voluntary manslaughter'	
I can give a brief definition of what diminished responsibility is	
I can describe two changes to the definition of diminished responsibility under s.2 of the Homicide Act 1957 after the 2009 reforms	
I can list the four-part test of diminished responsibility	
I can explain 'abnormality of mental functioning' with the use of a case authority	
I can list at least five 'recognised medical conditions' with case authorities	
With the help of *Lloyd* (1967), I can explain what a jury will consider when deliberating 'substantial impairment'	
I can explain the rule relating to voluntary intoxication and diminished responsibility according to *Dietschmann* (2003)	
I can explain the rule relating to Alcohol Dependency Syndrome and diminished responsibility according to *Steward* (2009)	

8.2.2 Loss of control

> **Definition**
>
> Loss of control: a loss of control due to a qualifying trigger in response to which a person of the same age and sex would have reacted the same.

- Loss of control is a new partial defence to murder under s.54 of the Coroners and Justice Act 2009.
- It replaces the old common law defence of provocation, although the old case law may still apply.
- If used successfully as a defence, the murder conviction will be substituted to one of voluntary manslaughter.

Workpoint

The new defence of loss of control under sections 54 and 55 of the Coroners and Justice Act 2009 is provided below. What do you think are key words to this defence?

'Section 54:

(1) Where a person ("D") kills or is a party to the killing of another ("V"), D is not to be convicted of murder if -

  (a) D's acts and omissions in doing or being a party to the killing resulted from D's loss of self-control;

  (b) the loss of self-control had a qualifying trigger; and

  (c) a person of D's sex and age, with a normal degree of tolerance and self-restraint and in "the circumstances of D", might have reacted in the same or in a similar way to D.

(2) For the purposes of subsection (1)(a), it does not matter whether or not the loss of control was sudden.

(3) In subsection (1)(c) the reference to "the circumstances of D" is a reference to all of D's circumstances other than those whose only relevance to D's conduct is that they bear on D's general capacity for tolerance and self-restraint.

(4) Subsection (1) does not apply if, in doing or being a party to the killing, D acted in a considered desire for revenge.

Section 55:

(2) A loss of self-control had a qualifying trigger if subsection (3), (4) or (5) applies.

(3) This subsection applies if D's loss of self-control was attributable to D's fear of serious violence from V against D or another identified person.

(4) This subsection applies if D's loss of self-control was attributable to a thing or things done or said (or both) which -

  (a) constituted circumstances of an extremely grave character; and

  (b) caused D to have a justifiable sense of being seriously wronged.'

Make a list of the key words for section 54 and a list of key words for section 55.

- There are several components to the loss of control defence which must be met.
- Under s.54(1)(a)(b)(c) a defendant must prove the following three things:

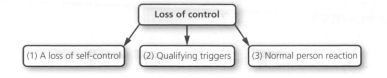

8.2.2.1 A loss of self-control

- This is a vital element to the defence – the defendant must have lost his temper at the time of the killing.
- Under the old provocation defence, the loss of control had to be 'sudden' – *Duffy* (1949).
- There is no longer a 'sudden' requirement, allowing 'slow-burn' reactions to now be considered – s.54(2).
- There must not be any evidence of pre-planning – *Ibrams and Gregory* (1981).
- Pouring petrol over a victim is not a loss of control – *Ahluwalia* (1992).
- Sharpening the murder weapon is not a loss of control – *Thornton (No. 1)* (1992).

Research Point

The Law Commission proposed to remove the loss of self-control element completely to allow for women in abusive relationships to use the defence after a long history of violence. However, the Government disagreed. Look up the following two reports/paragraphs and jot down the argument of the Law Commission and the response from the Government:

Law Commission, *Murder, Manslaughter and Infanticide* (2006), para 5.18; and
Ministry of Justice, *Murder, Manslaughter and Infanticide: Proposals for Reform of the Law* (2008), paras 35–36.

- Whether or not there was a loss of control is a jury question – *Baillie* (1995).
- The need for a loss of control is emphasised by the exclusion of revenge – s.54(4).

8.2.2.2 'Qualifying triggers'

- There are two triggers under the new defence, and either (or both) will suffice.

• One trigger relates to a threat of violence, and another relates to things done or said.

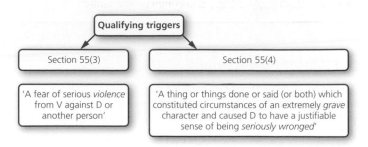

Section 55(3): a fear of violence

• This is similar to the defence of self-defence (Chapter 8) in that the defendant fears an attack and then lashes out.
• The threat must come from the victim, not a third party.
• A defendant may use s.55(3) when violence is threatened against himself or another and this causes him to lose his temper – *Pearson* (1992).
• Domestic abuse cases might use this trigger – *Ahluwalia* (1992) and *Thornton* (1992).
• Gross bullying and terrorising may also come under this trigger – *Ibrams and Gregory* (1981).

Section 55(4): things done or said

• The circumstances must be of a *grave* character and the defendant must feel justifiably *seriously wronged*.
• This new test would no longer allow 'things done' to include a crying baby because this does not equate to grave circumstances – *Doughty* (1986).
• A threat by the local council to demolish your house would also not suffice – *Dryden* (1995).
• Taunts about sexual inadequacy are not grave in nature – *Luc Thiet Thuan* (1997) and *Moses* (2006).
• Being accused of theft will also not qualify under this trigger – *Morgan Smith* (2001).

Consider whether the following old provocation cases would qualify under the s.55(4) trigger. Copy and complete the table.

Case:	Does it qualify under the s.55(4) trigger?
DPP v Camplin (1978): the defendant was raped by the victim and then taunted afterwards, leading him to lose his temper and kill the victim	
Clarke (1991): the defendant was told by his ex-girlfriend that she was pregnant but that she was going to have an abortion. He lost his temper and killed her	
Baillie (1995): the defendant was told by his son that a drug dealer was threatening him. The defendant killed the drug dealer	
Morhall (1996): the defendant was nagged by the victim about his glue-sniffing. He lost his temper and killed the person nagging him	
Mohammed (2005): the defendant, who was a devout Muslim, returned from the mosque to find a young man in his teenage daughter's bedroom. He killed his daughter	

- It remains to be seen how future appeal cases will interpret the s.55(4) trigger.
- Some defendants may feel 'seriously wronged' by the slightest thing, introducing a very wide test.
- However, the word 'justifiable' hints at an external element (i.e. the reasonable man would agree), thus narrowing the test.
- It is not clear whether a mistake would be taken into account (i.e. the defendant misinterpreted a threat of violence).
- The thing done or said does *not* have to come from the victim – it may come from a third party – *Davies* (1975).
- Things done or said can build over a long period of time into an explosive final encounter – *Humphreys* (1995).
- Triggers (a fear of violence **and** things done or said) can be combined under s.55(5).

Case:	
Humphreys (1995)	Both triggers were present in this case: the defendant was threatened with a gang-rape (a serious threat of violence) and then taunted when she attempted to commit suicide.

8.2.2.3 Excluded triggers

• Parliament has introduced tight controls on the qualifying triggers to prevent defendants from cheating.

Workpoint

The excluded triggers under section 55 of the Coroners and Justice Act 2009 are provided below. What do you think are key words?

'Section 55:

(6) In determining whether a loss of self-control had a qualifying trigger -
  (a) D's fear of serious violence is to be disregarded to the extent that it was caused by a thing which D incited to be done or said for the purpose of providing an excuse to use violence;
  (b) a sense of being seriously wronged by a thing done or said is not justifiable if D incited the thing to be done or said for the purpose of providing an excuse to use violence;
  (c) the fact that a thing done or said constituted sexual infidelity is to be disregarded.'

• A defendant cannot use loss of control as a defence if the thing done or said was self-induced – s.55(6)(a) and (b).
• In addition, infidelity is no longer considered as a thing 'done' to cause a loss of self-control.

Workpoint

Removing infidelity from the defence means that 'honour killings' and cheating partners will no longer be an excuse to kill. However, is it a good idea to remove infidelity from jury consideration? Give reasons for your answer.

8.2.2.4 Normal person reaction

• According to s.54(1)(c), a person of the same sex and age with a normal level of self-restraint must have reacted the same as the defendant did – *DPP v Camplin* (1978).

- Apart from age, sex, a normal level of self-restraint and a normal level of tolerance, no other characteristics are relevant – *DPP v Camplin* (1978), *Luc Thiet Thuan* (1997) and *Attorney-General for Jersey v Holley* (2005).
- However, the 'normal person' must be placed *in the circumstances* of the defendant.

Workpoint

Apply the criteria under s.54(1)(c) to the defendants below. Who satisfies the 'normal person' test? Remember, the 'normal person' will be the same age and sex as the defendant and will experience the same circumstances as the defendant but will have a normal level of tolerance and self-restraint.

(a) Terry has Attention Deficit Hyperactivity Disorder. He loses his patience very quickly and is fired from yet another job. He kills his employer.

(b) Loralie has been suffering from severe depression for two years after the death of her husband. On a visit to the cemetery, youths taunt her. She loses her temper and strangles the youngest youth.

(c) Jasper was sexually assaulted as a child. Fred tried to sexually assault him one night when he was walking home from university. Jasper recalls his previous experiences and defends himself using a knife, stabbing Fred through the heart.

- In *Morhall* (1996) an addiction to glue-sniffing was deemed to be a relevant circumstance.
- In *Gregson* (2006) unemployment was a relevant circumstance, and if this leads to depression and epilepsy, these may be relevant circumstances too.
- A history of sexual abuse may be a relevant circumstance – *Hill* (2008).
- However, any relevant circumstances must not influence the defendant's level of tolerance and self-restraint.
- The jury will probably not conclude that a person of 'normal tolerance and self-restraint' would head-butt, strangle and electrocute his ex-girlfriend – *Clarke* (1991).
- A person of 'normal tolerance and self-restraint' would also not repeatedly kick a victim to death who is curled up on the pavement – *Van Dongen* (2005).

8.2.2.5 Procedures of loss of control

- The defence of loss of control is only available to a charge of murder, not attempted murder.
- The defendant must provide 'sufficient evidence' of his defence and the prosecution must disprove it beyond a reasonable doubt – s.54(5).

Checkpoint - voluntary manslaughter (2): loss of control

Item on checklist:	Done!
I can give my own definition of the new 'loss of control' defence from the Coroners and Justice Act 2009	
I can recite the three-part test for loss of control under s.54(1)(a)(b)(c) of the 2009 Act	
I can describe the 'loss of control' element using two case authorities	
I can describe the first 'qualifying trigger' under s.55(3) with a case authority	
I can explain both elements of the second 'qualifying trigger' under s.55(4) with two case authorities	
I can recall an 'excluded trigger' under s.55(6) of the 2009 Act	
I can describe the different components to the 'normal person reaction' under s.54(1)(c)	

8.2.3 Suicide pacts

Definition

Suicide pact: two or more people agree to kill each other, but one remains alive.

- A suicide pact is defined under s.4 of the Homicide Act 1957 as: 'a common agreement between two or more persons having for its object the death of all of them'.
- Whoever remains alive may be found guilty of voluntary manslaughter rather than murder.
- The burden of proof is on the defendant on a balance of probabilities.

8.3 Involuntary manslaughter

- The three offences listed below are available when the *actus reus* of murder is present (i.e. the victim has died) but there is no evidence of the *mens rea* of murder.

- All three forms of involuntary manslaughter are old common law *offences*.
- They are *not defences* to murder like diminished responsibility, loss of control and suicide pacts.

8.3.1 Constructive manslaughter

Constructive manslaughter: unlawful act manslaughter, doing a dangerous act that causes death.

- Often referred to as 'unlawful act manslaughter', constructive manslaughter requires the defendant to do (i.e. 'construct') an unlawful and dangerous act.
- If that act leads to a death he will be charged with constructive manslaughter rather than the original unlawful act (i.e. actual bodily harm).

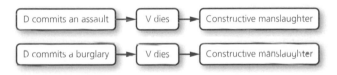

- There are four criteria that must be satisfied for constructive manslaughter.

(1) D must commit an unlawful act

(2) The act must be dangerous

(3) D must have the *mens rea* of the unlawful and dangerous act

(4) That act must have caused death

Workpoint

Jay is driving while over the legal limit for alcohol. He veers onto the pavement and kills a toddler. Has he satisfied all four criteria above to be charged with constructive manslaughter? Give reasons for your answer.

8.3.1.1 An 'unlawful act'

- A civil wrong used to suffice, e.g. trespass to land – *Fenton* (1830).
- A criminal offence is now deemed more appropriate to found a conviction of constructive manslaughter – *Franklin* (1883).
- The *actus reus* and the *mens rea* of the unlawful act must be in place – *Lamb* (1967) and *Jennings* (1990).
- The criminal offence does not necessarily have to be an offence against the person:

Unlawful criminal act:	Case authority:
Assault	*Larkin* (1943) *Lamb* (1967) *Mallet* (1972)
Battery	*Church* (1965) *Mitchell* (1983)
Criminal damage	*DPP v Newbury and Jones* (1977)
Arson	*Goodfellow* (1986) *Willoughby* (2004)
Robbery	*Dawson* (1985)
Burglary	*Watson* (1989)
Administering a noxious substance (s.23 OAPA 1861)	*Cato* (1976)
Affray	*Carey and others* (2009)
Cruelty to a person under 16 (s.1 Children and Young Persons Act 1933)	*Gay* (2006)

- The unlawful act must be an 'act' in the physical sense – an omission will not suffice for constructive manslaughter.

Case:	
Lowe (1973)	Phillimore J: 'If I omit to do something, with the result that [a child] suffers injury to its health which results in its death, we think that a charge of manslaughter should not be an inevitable consequence even if the omission is deliberate.'

8.3.1.2 The act must be 'dangerous'

- In addition to the defendant performing an unlawful act, it must be dangerous – *Church* (1965).

Case:	
Church (1965)	Edmund Davies J: 'for such a verdict inexorably to follow, the unlawful act must be such as all sober and reasonable people would inevitably recognise must subject the other person to, at least, the risk of harm resulting therefrom, albeit not serious harm.'

- Following *Church*, the test became that of the 'sober and reasonable bystander' which was an objective test – *Ball* (1989).
- The very least kind of harm is causing fright by threats – *Reid* (1975).
- Fright or shock must lead to physical harm (e.g. victim may have a weak heart) – *Dawson* (1985).
- The jury was entitled to ascribe to the bystander any previous knowledge that D had about the victim – *Watson* (1989).

Case:	
Ball (1989)	Facts: D burgled the house of an 87 year old man. D verbally abused the victim and left. The victim died of a heart attack 90 minutes later.
	Lord Lane CJ: 'D (and therefore the bystander) during the course of the unlawful act must have become aware of [V]'s frailty and approximate age, and the judge's directions were accordingly correct.'

- In the similar case of *Dawson* (1985) the 'sober and reasonable bystander' would not know of the victim's heart condition.

Workpoint

Kieran and Michael set fire to a pile of newspapers that they found abandoned in their neighbours' back garden. They ran away, leaving the newspapers burning. The toddler who lived there ran out to play and was severely burned by the fire, dying from her injuries a few days later. Applying the criteria listed above, is Kieran and Michael's act 'dangerous'? Give reasons for your answer.

8.3.1.3 D must have the mens rea of the unlawful act

- The defendant must have the *mens rea* of the unlawful act – the injury cannot be a mistake or an accident.
- A strict liability offence (i.e. no *mens rea* requirement) was allowed in *Andrews* (2002).
- The defendant does not have to intend or even foresee death as a consequence of his unlawful act – *DPP v Newbury and Jones* (1977).

Look up the case of *R v Lamb* [1967] 2 QB 981. Why had the defendant not committed an unlawful act?

8.3.1.4 The act 'must have caused death'

- The chain of causation must connect the defendant's unlawful and dangerous act to the death.
- If the defendant does not touch the victim, he may still, by reason of an unlawful and dangerous act, have caused her death – *Mitchell* (1983).
- Causation requires the outcome to be reasonably foreseeable – *Goodfellow* (1986).
- Injecting heroin into the victim will constitute an unlawful and dangerous act that causes the victim's death – *Cato* (1976).
- Self-injection by the victim breaks the chain of causation – *Dalby* (1982), *Dias* (2001) and *Kennedy* (2007).

```
                    Constructive manslaughter
```

(1) D must commit an unlawful act *Fenton* (1830) *Franklin* (1883) *Lamb* (1967) *Jennings* (1990)	(2) The act must be dangerous *Church* (1965) *Ball* (1989) *Reid* (1975) *Dawson* (1985)
(3) D must have the *mens rea* of the unlawful and dangerous act *Andrews* (2002) *DPP v Newbury and Jones* (1977) *R v Lamb* (1967)	(4) That act must have caused death *Mitchell* (1983) *Goodfellow* (1986) *Kennedy* (2007) *Cato* (1976)

Checkpoint - Involuntary manslaughter (1): constructive manslaughter

Item on checklist:	Done!
I can define constructive manslaughter	
I can explain the 'unlawful act' element of constructive manslaughter using five legal authorities	
I can explain what is meant by 'dangerous' using a case authority	
I know that the defendant must have the *mens rea* of the unlawful act	
I can explain why the unlawful act must cause the death for a charge of constructive manslaughter to be brought	

8.3.2 Gross negligence manslaughter

> **Definition**
>
> Gross negligence manslaughter: grossly negligent behaviour that leads to a death.

- Gross negligence manslaughter is a common law offence that originates from the civil law of tort.
- This offence is all about objectivity: the defendant will be judged according to the behaviour or standard of the reasonable man.

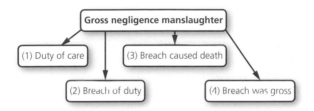

8.3.2.1 Duty of care

- There must be a duty upon the defendant to care for the victim – *Donoghue v Stevenson* (1932).
- This duty may be contractual, professional, familial, assumed or arising out of a dangerous situation.

Case:	
Donoghue v Stevenson (1932)	Lord Atkin: 'You must take reasonable care to avoid acts and omissions which you can reasonably foresee would be likely to injure your neighbour... persons who are so closely and directly affected by my act that I ought reasonably to have them in contemplation.'

- The civil law 'duty of care' criteria laid down by Lord Atkin are to be applied in criminal law cases of gross negligence manslaughter – *Wacker* (2003).
- The jury must decide whether a duty of care existed – *Litchfield* (1998).
- Small factors in combination may give rise to a duty of care – *Willoughby* (2005).
- Failing to contact the emergency services for a half-sibling may give rise to a duty of care – *Evans* (2009).

Workpoint

Apply Lord Atkins' 'duty of care' test to the following scenarios. Would you have a duty of care over these individuals? Give reasons for your answer.

(a) Shelly is your neighbour. She gives you a shopping list every Friday and you buy her shopping for her because she has recently been diagnosed with post-natal depression and needs to stay at home.

(b) Greg is your great-grandson. He is 10 years old and has come to stay with you for the weekend. You only see him once a year.

(c) You are a primary school teacher and are putting together a nativity play. You suspect that the stage is too weak for an adult to stand on, but believe that the children will be fine. On the night of the play, a parent walks onto the stage and falls through it, causing injury.

8.3.2.2 Breach of duty

- Once a duty of care is established by whatever means, the duty must be breached.
- In civil law, a person who falls below a *reasonable* standard of care can be sued for negligence – *Andrews v DPP* (1937) and *Nettleship v Weston* (1971).
- In criminal law, the standard is *gross* negligence – *Adomako* (1995).

8.3.2.3 The breach must cause the death

- A chain of causation must be present between the defendant's grossly negligent conduct and the victim's death.

8.3.2.4 The breach must be gross

- A breach of duty is usually dealt with through civil law.
- Something more is required to justify punishment in criminal law, and it has been described as 'culpable negligence of a grave kind' – *Doherty* (1887).

Case:	
Bateman (1925)	Lord Hewart CJ: 'The negligence of the accused went beyond a mere matter of compensation between subjects and showed such disregard for the life and safety of others as to amount to a crime against the state and conduct deserving punishment.'
Andrews v DPP (1937)	Lord Atkin: 'Simple lack of care as will constitute civil liability is not enough. For purposes of the criminal law there are degrees of negligence, and a very high degree of negligence is required to be proved – the grossest ignorance or the most criminal inattention.'

Case:	
Adomako (1995)	Lord Mackay: 'The essence of the matter, which is supremely a jury question, is whether, having regard to the risk of death involved, the conduct of the defendant was so bad in all the circumstances as to amount in their judgment to a criminal act or omission.'

- The jury may consider the risk of death when deliberating whether the negligence was gross – *Misra and Srivastava* (2004).

Case:	
Misra and Srivastava (2004)	Judge LJ: 'The question for the jury was not whether D's negligence was gross and whether, additionally, it was a crime, but whether his behaviour was grossly negligent and consequently criminal.'

Research Point

Look up the following article: J.Herring and E.Palser, 'The Duty of Care in Gross Negligence Manslaughter' [2007] Crim LR 24. Make notes about the main arguments in this piece.

Checkpoint - Involuntary manslaughter (2): gross negligence manslaughter

Item on checklist:	Done!
I can define gross negligence manslaughter and describe the four required components	
I know what a 'duty of care' entails after reading Lord Atkin's judgment in *Donoghue v Stevenson* (1932)	
I understand that the duty must be breached and this must, in turn, cause the death	
I can explain why the breach of duty must be gross using two case authorities	
I can define the jury question of grossness in light of *Misra and Srivastava* (2004)	

8.3.3 Reckless manslaughter

Reckless manslaughter is not seen very often in criminal law, but it does exist – *Lidar* (2000).

Case:	
Lidar (2000)	The test is whether D was aware of the necessary degree of risk of serious injury to the victim and nevertheless chose to disregard it, or was indifferent to it.

8.3.4 Reform of involuntary manslaughter

- The Law Commission made two suggestions in its paper: *A New Homicide Act for England and Wales?* (2005) (No. 177).

Constructive manslaughter: the defendant should foresee at least a risk of causing harm when performing his unlawful act (as opposed to the 'sober and reasonable man' foreseeing the harm)	**Gross negligence manslaughter**: the defendant's conduct falls far below what would be reasonably expected and the risk of death would be obvious to a reasonable person in his position (the current law)

8.4 Reforming the law of homicide

- In 2005, the Law Commission published a paper entitled: *A New Homicide Act for England and Wales?* (No. 177).
- This was then followed by a Final Report, entitled: *Murder, Manslaughter and Infanticide* (2006) (No. 304).
- A three-tier structure was suggested for the whole of homicide.

1. First degree murder;
2. Second degree murder;
3. Manslaughter.

8.4.1 First degree murder

- The defendant intended to kill or intended serious injury.
- In addition, he was aware of a serious risk of death.

8.4.2 Second degree murder

- The *mens rea* for murder was present but the defendant had a partial defence.
- The partial defences would include loss of control or diminished responsibility.

8.4.3 Manslaughter

- In this category would be gross negligence manslaughter and constructive manslaughter.
- This is because, unlike first and second degree murder, there is no intention to kill, and so the label of 'murder' at any degree would not be appropriate.

Potential exam questions:

1) Define the components of the offence of murder using legal authorities.
2) Analyse the updated law on diminished responsibility.
3) Jane and Freddy took their son, daughter and their two school friends to the countryside for a picnic. They squeezed through a disused security gate and settled in a large meadow next to the power station. Jane and Freddy did not watch the children and the children wondered off to explore the power station. The two friends found a large electric pylon. All four children played under it. All four of them were electrocuted. Jane and Freddy are charged with gross negligence manslaughter. You are one of the jury members. Apply the relevant laws. Are they liable? Give reasons for your answer.

Chapter 9
Non-fatal offences against the person

Non-fatal offences against the person usually require some kind of infliction of force upon the body. The offence charged will depend on the seriousness of the injury inflicted and the mental element of the defendant. Non-fatal offences against the person will be explored in detail in this chapter.

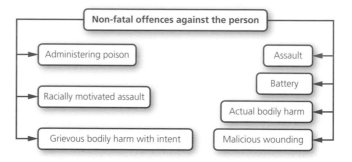

- The offences listed above are very old criminal offences.
- Assault and battery are founded in common law (although the Criminal Justice Act 1988 recognises their existence).
- Actual bodily harm, malicious wounding and grievous bodily harm are statutory offences dating back to 1861.

9.1 Assault

- Assault is a common law offence and is defined by case law.
- However, it is charged under s.39 of the Criminal Justice Act 1988:

> 'Common law assault [and battery] shall be summary offences and a person guilty of either of them shall be liable to a fine not exceeding level 5, to imprisonment for a term not exceeding six months, or both.'

9.1.1 The *actus reus* of assault

- The act of assault was defined by *Collins v Wilcock* (1984).

- The following elements must be in place for an assault to occur.

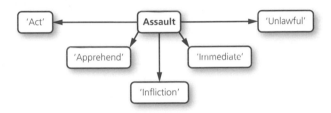

- Contact is not required for an assault.
- A genuine 'apprehension of force' is required – *Lamb* (1967).
- There must be an 'act' to cause this apprehension – *Collins v Wilcock* (1984).
- An omission will not suffice – *Fagan v Metropolitan Police Commissioner* (1969).

- Revealing a gun can constitute an assault – *Lodgon v DPP* (1976).
- Threatening letters can be an assault – *Constanza* (1997).
- Silent telephone calls were also held to be an assault – *Ireland* (1997).
- 'Immediate' can include looking through a window – *Smith v Woking Police* (1983).

Case:	
Ireland (1997)	Facts: the defendant made silent telephone calls to women at night. Lord Steyn: 'He intends by his silence to cause fear and he is so understood. She may fear the possibility of immediate personal violence, [this] will depend on the impact of the caller's potentially menacing call on the victim.'

- An empty threat will not constitute an assault – *Tuberville v Savage* (1669).
- A threat will constitute an assault if in conjunction with a weapon – *Light* (1857).
- The 'act' of assault must be unlawful (i.e. no consent) – *Slingsby* (1995).

Workpoint

Which of the scenarios below are assaults?

(a) Lauren tells Mark that if he doesn't stop flirting with other girls, she is going to leave him.
(b) Chloe tells Joey that she'll hit him over the head with a frying pan if he doesn't cook the bolognaise properly.
(c) John throws his pen at Lucy and she has to duck so that it misses her face.
(d) Kelly reaches to pull a rug out from under Lisa's feet.

9.1.2 The *mens rea* of assault

- The *mens rea* for assault is intention or recklessness as to causing the victim to apprehend the immediate infliction of unlawful personal force – *Venna* (1975).
- The recklessness is subjective (i.e. defendant sees a risk of apprehension of force and goes ahead anyway).
- Intoxicated behaviour will constitute the recklessness – *Majewski* (1977).

Assault	
Case:	**Rule:**
Collins v Wilcock (1984)	*Actus reus* of assault is apprehension of force
Lamb (1967)	'Act' and 'apprehension' required
Fagan v MPC (1969)	Omission will not suffice for an assault

Assault	
Case:	**Rule:**
Lodgon v DPP (1976)	Revealing a gun is an assault
Constanza (1997)	Threatening letters are an assault
Ireland (1997)	Silent telephone calls are an assault
Smith v Woking Police (1983)	Looking through a window is an assault
Tuberville v Savage (1669)	Empty threat is not an assault
Light (1857)	Threat accompanied with weapon is assault
Slingsby (1995)	Consent renders assault lawful
Venna (1975)	*Mens rea* of assault is intention or recklessness
Majewski (1977)	Intoxication will constitute the recklessness

Checkpoint - assault

Item on checklist:	Done!
I can name the statute under which an assault can be charged	
I can define the *actus reus* of assault according to *Collins v Wilcock* (1984)	
I can list three different examples of an *actus reus* of assault using case authorities as support	
I can explain the mental element required for an assault according to *Venna* (1975)	

9.2 Battery

- Battery is also a common law offence defined by case law.
- It is also charged under s.39 of the Criminal Justice Act 1988:

> 'Common law [assault and] battery shall be summary offences and a person guilty of either of them shall be liable to a fine not exceeding level 5, to imprisonment for a term not exceeding six months, or both.'

9.2.1 The *actus reus* of battery

- The act of battery was also defined by *Collins v Wilcock* (1984).

Workpoint

The *actus reus* of battery is below. What are the key words from Lord Goff's definition?

Collins v Wilcock (1984), Goff LJ: 'A battery is the actual infliction of unlawful force on another person.'

- The following elements must be in place for a battery to occur.

- Contact is required for a battery (even if this is indirect) and this can include physical restraint.

Case:	
***Collins v Wilcock* (1984)**	Goff LJ: 'It has long been established that any touching of another person, however slight, may amount to battery. Everybody is protected not only against physical injury but against any form of physical molestation.'

- Touching a victim's skirt was equivalent to touching the victim – *Thomas* (1985).
- The touching must be hostile – *Wilson v Pringle* (1986).
- If the touching was unlawful, it is more likely to be hostile – *Brown* (1993).

Workpoint

Write down a scenario in which you believe a person may experience the actual infliction of unlawful force upon their body by another person.

- The *actus reus* of battery may be a continuing act and the *mens rea* can be formed at any point during that act – *Fagan v MPC* (1969).
- The defendant does not have to touch the victim (i.e. an indirect battery) – *Martin* (1881).

- An indirect battery is treated the same as if the defendant performed a direct battery – *DPP v K* (1990).
- Hitting an adult who then drops a child is an indirect battery of that child (i.e. similar to transferred malice) – *Haystead v CC of Derbyshire* (2000).

Workpoint

Which of the scenarios below are batteries?

(a) Lauren pushes Mark out of the door when she finally dumps him for flirting with other girls.
(b) Chloe does in fact hit Joey over the head with a frying pan because he didn't cook the bolognaise properly.
(c) When Lucy ducks to miss the pen that John threw at her, it hits Abrahim (sitting behind her) in the eye.
(d) Kelly pulls the rug out from under Lisa's feet and Lisa falls over.

9.2.2 Batteries and omissions

- An assault cannot be committed by an omission, but a battery can be.
- There must be a duty to act on the defendant in order for his omission to be liable.

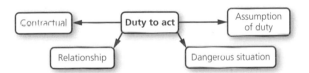

- If a defendant therefore creates a dangerous situation by omitting to do or say something, he is liable for the harm that results – *Miller* (1983).

Case:	
DPP v Santana-Bermudez (2003)	Facts: a policewoman asked the defendant if he had any 'sharps' before searching him. He said 'no'. She was pricked by a needle.
	Kay J: 'Where someone (by an act or word or a combination of the two) creates a danger and thereby exposes another to a reasonable foreseeable risk of injury which materialises, there is an evidential basis for the *actus reus* of a [battery].'

9.2.3 Batteries and consent

- A victim can consent to a battery (and an assault) – *Brown* (1993).
- If consent is provided, the touching is lawful and no crime has been committed – *Slingsby* (1995).
- The victim must consent to both the nature and quality of the touching – *Tabassum* (2000).
- Consent is implied for the 'ordinary jostlings of everyday life' – *Collins v Wilcock* (1984) and *Wilson v Pringle* (1986).
- The police can use reasonable force to arrest a defendant – *Wood (Fraser) v DPP* (2008).

Workpoint

Have batteries been committed below? Give reasons for your answer.

(a) Jane assumed care of her mother-in-law, Peggy. When Jane was out grocery shopping one weekend, Peggy tripped over an internet cable that Jane had left out on the floor. Peggy fell over.

(b) Kate went into a salon to take part in a survey about hairstyles. Jake, a hairdresser, put his fingers through Kate's hair and smelt her hair, which she thought was odd. It transpired that Jake was not a hairdresser and simply took sexual gratification from feeling women's hair.

- When a defendant is charged with 'common law assault' it often means that an assault *and* a battery have occurred at the same time.

9.2.4 The *mens rea* of battery

- The *mens rea* for battery is also intention or recklessness as to the infliction of unlawful force – *Venna* (1975).
- The recklessness is subjective (i.e. defendant sees a risk of inflicting unlawful force and goes ahead anyway).
- Intoxicated behaviour will constitute the recklessness – *Majewski* (1977).

Battery	
Case:	Rule:
Collins v Wilcock (1984)	*Actus reus* of battery is unlawful infliction of force
Thomas (1985)	Touching clothes is touching the victim
Wilson v Pringle (1986)	Touching must be hostile

Battery	
Case:	**Rule:**
Brown (1993)	Unlawful touching is probably hostile
Fagan v MPC (1969)	Battery can be a continuing act
DPP v K (1990)	Indirect battery will suffice
DPP v Santana-Bermudez (2003)	Failing to act can be a battery
Brown (1993)	Victims can consent to battery
Tabassum (2000)	Nature and quality must be consented to
Venna (1975)	*Mens rea* of battery is intention or recklessness
Majewski (1977)	Intoxication will constitute the recklessness

Checkpoint - battery

Item on checklist:	Done!
I can define the *actus reus* of battery according to *Collins v Wilcock* (1984)	
I can list the key elements in the *actus reus* which must be met	
I can give three examples of an *actus reus* of battery using case authorities as support	
I can explain why consent is an important issue to battery	
I can explain the mental element required for an assault according to *Venna* (1975)	

9.3 Actual bodily harm

- When an assault or a battery causes injury, the defendant is charged with actual bodily harm.

- The defendant will be charged with actual bodily harm whether it was an assault or a battery that occasioned the injury.
- Actual bodily harm is an old statutory offence under s.47 of the Offences Against the Person Act 1861:

> *'Whosoever shall be convicted of any assault occasioning actual bodily harm shall be liable to imprisonment for five years.'*

- This offence is widely known as 'a section 47' and is triable either way.
- Definitions as to *actus reus* and *mens rea* are enshrined in subsequent case law.

9.3.1 *Actus reus of* actual bodily harm

- Technically, all that is required is an assault or battery (see section above).
- However, the assault or battery must cause 'any hurt or injury calculated to interfere with the health or comfort of the victim' – *Miller* (1954).

Bruising | Scratching | Grazing | Fractures | Concussion

- Cutting off a person's ponytail can amount to 'bodily' harm – *DPP v Smith (Michael)* (2006).
- Psychiatric injury will also suffice – *Chan Fook* (1994).

Case:	
Chan Fook (1994)	Court of Appeal: 'The body of the victim includes all parts of his body, including his organs, his nervous system and his brain. Bodily injury therefore may include injury to any of those parts of his body responsible for his mental and other faculties.'

- Mere emotions or states of mind such as fear, distress or panic will not suffice as bodily harm – *Chan Fook* (1994).
- Bodily harm will require a recognised psychiatric illness – *Burstow* (1997).
- Years of domestic abuse is not a recognised psychiatric illness – *Dhaliwal* (2006).

Look at the scenarios below. Are they merely batteries, or could Bill be charged with actual bodily harm? Give reasons for your answer.

(a) Bill walked up to John and pushed him out of the way, causing John to fall onto concrete and bruise himself.
(b) Bill snatched a book off Kerry, giving her a paper cut.
(c) Bill forcibly kissed Shola on the cheek when she refused to go out with him.
(d) Bill goes to hit his younger brother Adam over the head with a dinner plate, causing Adam to run into the dinner table and bump his head.

9.3.2 *Mens rea* of actual bodily harm

- Actual bodily harm does not have its own *mens rea* – it simply borrows the *mens rea* of the assault or battery that was inflicted – *Savage* (1991).
- As a result, if a defendant performs the *actus reus* and *mens rea* of battery and it happens to lead to injury, he will have all the elements in place for a charge of actual bodily harm – *Roberts* (1971).

Case:	
Savage and Parmenter (1991)	Lord Acker: 'The verdict of assault occasioning actual bodily harm may be returned upon proof of an assault together with proof of the fact that actual bodily harm was occasioned by the assault. The prosecution are not obliged to prove that the defendant intended to cause some actual bodily harm or was reckless as to whether such harm would be caused.'

Returning to Bill (see the workpoint above), what is the *mens rea* required for each of the scenarios below in order for him to be charged with actual bodily harm?

(a) Bill walked up to John and pushed him out of the way, causing John to fall onto concrete and bruise himself.
(b) Bill snatched a book off Kerry, giving her a paper cut.
(c) Bill goes to hit his younger brother Adam over the head with a dinner plate, causing Adam to run into the dinner table and bump his head.

9.3.3 Consent and actual bodily harm

- A victim can consent to an assault and a battery, but no more – *Brown* (1993).
- However, a victim can consent to serious injuries in law if they fall under a special exception – *Attorney-General's Reference (No. 6 of 1980)* (1981).
- The exceptions include properly conducted games and sports, lawful chastisement or correction, reasonable surgical interference and other dangerous exhibitions.

Research Point

Look up the case *Wilson* [1996] Crim LR 573. Why was the husband charged with actual bodily harm and why did the courts decide not to interfere with the wife's consent?

- In *Barnes* (2005) it was held that only a particularly grave injury in sporting activities will be pursued by the criminal courts.
  1. Conduct beyond what is expected may be criminal;
  2. Players consent to unfortunate accidents;
  3. Intentional infliction of injury is criminal;
  4. Reckless infliction will be criminal if off-the-ball or during a heated moment.
- If a defendant mistakenly believes that the victim consents, this may be a defence – *Jones* (1986) and *Aitken and others* (1992).

Actual bodily harm	
Case:	**Rule:**
Miller (1954)	The assault or battery must cause injury
DPP v Smith (Michael) (2006)	Cutting off a ponytail is 'bodily' harm
Chan Fook (1994)	Psychiatric injury will suffice
Burstow (1997)	Must be a recognised psychiatric condition
Dhaliwal (2006)	Prolonged domestic abuse does not qualify
Savage (1991)	No separate *mens rea* for actual bodily harm
Roberts (1971)	Mental element for battery will suffice
Brown (1993)	Victims cannot consent to actual bodily harm

Actual bodily harm	
Case:	**Rule:**
Attorney-G's Ref (No. 6 of 1980) (1981)	Exceptions exist in law (e.g. surgery & sport)
Barnes (2005)	Sporting exceptions
Jones (1986)	Mistaken belief in consent is relevant

Checkpoint - actual bodily harm

Item on checklist:	Done!
I can cite the statutory location of the criminal offence of actual bodily harm	
I can describe the *actus reus* of actual bodily harm using three legal authorities as support	
I can describe the *mens rea* of actual bodily harm in light of *Savage* (1991)	
I understand that the line of consent drawn in *Brown* (1993) means that a victim cannot consent to an actual bodily harm	
I can explain the sporting exception under *Barnes* (2005)	

9.4 Malicious wounding

- Moderately serious injuries are charged under s.20 of the Offences Against the Person Act 1861.
- This offence is commonly known as 'malicious wounding' and is triable either way with a maximum of five years in jail.

Workpoint

Below is the statutory definition of malicious wounding. What are the key words in the definition, including what you believe are the *actus reus* and *mens rea* of the offence?

'Whosoever shall unlawfully and maliciously wound or inflict any grievous bodily harm upon any other person, either with or without a weapon or instrument, shall be guilty of an offence and shall be liable to imprisonment for not more than five years.'

9.4.1 *Actus reus* of malicious wounding

- The *actus reus* requires an unlawful infliction of either a wound *or* grievous bodily harm.

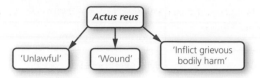

- The word 'inflict' does not require an assault – *Beasley* (1981), *MPC v Wilson* (1984) and *Burstow* (1997).
- A 'wound' must break through all the layers of the skin and does not include internal bleeding – *JCC v Eisenhower* (1983).
- A broken bone will not constitute a wound unless the skin is broken – *Wood* (1830).
- 'Grievous bodily harm' means really serious harm, but does not have to be life-threatening – *DPP v Smith* (1961).
- The jury can be directed as to 'serious harm' – *Saunders* (1985).

Case:	
***Bollom* (2003)**	Facts: a baby suffered bruising and abrasions to her body, arms and legs. This would not be grievous bodily harm to an adult. Held: age, health and other factors relating to the victim can be considered when determining whether the injuries amounted to grievous bodily harm.

- A severe depressive illness caused by a stalker can amount to grievous bodily harm – *Burstow* (1997).

- Biological grievous bodily harm now exists as a result of *Dica* (2004) and the reckless transmission of HIV.

Workpoint

Callum and Jake were play-fighting in secondary school. They were both 15 years old and carried knives to protect themselves. Callum made a comment about Jake's mother and Jake lashed out with his knife. Callum suffered a broken rib and a stab wound to the stomach. Can Jake be charged under section 20 for either injury? Give reasons for your answer.

9.4.2 *Mens rea* of malicious wounding

- Unlike actual bodily harm, malicious wounding does have its own *mens rea*.
- The word 'maliciously' features in s.20 of the OAPA 1861.
- 'Maliciously' has since been defined as intentionally or recklessly – *Cunningham* (1957).

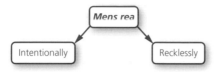

- The defendant must therefore intend or be reckless as to some physical harm, but he does not have to foresee that it will be grievous (i.e. really serious) – *Mowatt* (1967) and *Parmenter* (1992).

Case:	
Mowatt (1967)	Lord Diplock: 'the word "maliciously" does import an awareness that his act may have the consequence of causing some physical harm to some other person... it is quite unnecessary that the accused should have foreseen the gravity described in the section i.e. a wound or serious injury.'

Workpoint

Revisiting Callum and Jake (on the previous page), imagine that you are a jury member hearing Jake's trial. You are satisfied that the *actus reus* has been met. What *mens rea* are you looking for in order to successfully prosecute Jake for malicious wounding (i.e. what must be running through Jake's mind when he lashes out at Callum and causes the stab wound)?

Malicious wounding	
Case:	**Rule:**
Beasley (1981)	'Inflict GBH' does not require an assault
JCC v Eisenhower (1983)	'Wound' must break through the skin
Wood (1830)	A broken bone is not a 'wound'
DPP v Smith (1961)	GBH is 'really serious harm'
Saunders (1985)	Direction on 'serious harm' will suffice

Malicious wounding	
Case:	**Rule:**
Bollom (2003)	Victim characteristics can be considered
Burstow (1997)	A severe depressive illness can be GBH
Dica (2004)	Transmission of HIV is biological GBH
Cunningham (1957)	The *mens rea* is intention or recklessness
Mowatt (1967)	Defendant must foresee *some* harm

Checkpoint - malicious wounding

Item on checklist:	Done!
I can cite the statutory location of the criminal offence of malicious wounding.	
I can draw out the key words from the definition of malicious wounding	
I can define a 'wound' using a legal authority	
I can define 'grievous bodily harm' using three legal authorities	
I can describe the *mens rea* of malicious wounding after *Cunningham* (1957)	
I can explain the influence of *Mowatt* (1967) on the *mens rea* of malicious wounding	

9.5 Grievous bodily harm with intent

- The most serious non-fatal offence against the person is grievous bodily harm with intent.
- It is found under s.18 of the Offences Against the Person Act 1861:

> *'Whosoever shall unlawfully and maliciously by any means whatsoever wound or cause any grievous bodily harm to any person, with intent to do some grievous bodily harm to any person [or with intent to resist or prevent the lawful apprehension or detainer of any person] shall be guilty of an offence.'*

- The main difference between malicious wounding (s.20) and grievous bodily harm (s.18) lies in the *mens rea*.
- This is reflected in the maximum punishments – five years under s.20 and life imprisonment under s.18.
- It is indictable to Crown Court for trial.

9.5.1 *Actus reus* of grievous bodily harm with intent

- The *actus reus* of grievous bodily harm (s.18) is almost the same as malicious wounding (s.20) – it requires a defendant to wound or cause (not 'inflict') grievous bodily harm.

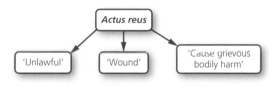

Actus reus case recall for s.20 & s.18...	
Beasley (1981)	'Inflict GBH' does not require an assault
JCC v Eisenhower (1983)	'Wound' must break through the skin
Wood (1830)	A broken bone is not a 'wound'
DPP v Smith (1961)	GBH is 'really serious harm'
Saunders (1985)	Direction on 'serious harm' will suffice
Bollom (2003)	Victim characteristics can be considered
Burstow (1997)	A severe depressive illness can be GBH

9.5.2 *Mens rea* for grievous bodily harm with intent

- The word 'maliciously' refers to intention or recklessness – *Cunningham* (1957).
- However, there is a specific intent to do some grievous bodily harm under s.18.
- Therefore, the word 'maliciously' can be disregarded – *Mowatt* (1967).

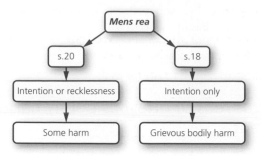

- When it comes to intention, the defendant's foresight of consequences is evidence of intention only, not intention itself – *Moloney* (1985).
- The grievous bodily harm must be a virtual certainty and the defendant must realise that this was the case – *Nedrick* (1986) and *Woollin* (1998).

Checkpoint - grievous bodily harm with intent

Item on checklist:	Done!
I can cite the statutory location of the criminal offence of grievous bodily harm with intent	
I can draw out the key words from the definition of grievous bodily harm with intent	
I can describe two main differences between s.20 (malicious wounding) and s.18 (grievous bodily harm)	

Offence:	*Actus reus:*	*Mens rea:*
Assault	The apprehension of immediate, unlawful force	Intention or recklessness as to the apprehension of force
Battery	Actual infliction of unlawful force	Intention or recklessness as to the actual infliction
s.47 Actual bodily harm	An assault or battery that causes harm or injury	The *mens rea* of assault or battery will suffice
s.20 Malicious wounding	Inflicting wounds or grievous bodily harm	Intention or recklessness as to some harm
s.18 Grievous bodily harm	Causing wounds or grievous bodily harm	Intention as to some grievous bodily harm

9.6 Reform

- The Offences Against the Person Act 1861 is an old statute and suggestions for reform have been constant.

Body:	Reform idea:
Criminal Law Revision Committee	*Offences Against the Person*, 14th Report, Cmnd 7844 (1980)
Law Commission	*Draft Criminal Code* (1989)
Law Commission	*Legislating the Criminal Code: Offences Against the Person and General Principles*, Law Com No. 218, (1993)
Home Office	*Violence: Reforming the Offences Against the Person Act 1861*, Consultation Document, (1998)

Workpoint

The recommendations from the Home Office (1998) are below. Make notes as to which current offence (i.e. assault, battery, s.47, s.20 and s.18) you think the reforms are most similar to and any key words you think are relevant.

Intentional serious injury.

1(1) A person is guilty of an offence if he intentionally causes serious injury to another.
(4) A person guilty of an offence under this section is liable on conviction on indictment to imprisonment for life.

Reckless serious injury

2(1) A person is guilty of an offence if he recklessly causes serious injury to another.
(3) A person guilty of an offence under this section is liable (b) to imprisonment for a term not exceeding 6 months or a fine not exceeding the statutory maximum.

Intentional or reckless injury.

3(1) A person is guilty of an offence if he intentionally or recklessly causes injury to another.
(3) A person guilty of an offence under this section is liable (a) on conviction on indictment to imprisonment for a term not exceeding 5 years; (b) on summary conviction, to imprisonment for a term not exceeding 6 months or a fine not exceeding the statutory maximum.

Assault.

4(1) A person is guilty of an offence if -

(a) he intentionally or recklessly applies force to or causes an impact on the body of another;
(b) he intentionally or recklessly causes the other to believe that any such force or impact is imminent.

(2) No offence is committed if the force or impact is in the circumstances generally acceptable in the ordinary conduct of daily life and the defendant does not know or believe that it is in fact unacceptable to the other person.

9.7 Racially or religiously aggravated assaults

• Actual bodily harm and malicious wounding (under sections 47 and 20 of the OAPA 1861) can be racially or religiously motivated.
• This happens when a defendant attacks a victim simply because they are a member of a particular group.
• Under s.29 of the Crime and Disorder Act 1998, the term of imprisonment will be increased to represent the hostility towards a particular racial or religious group.

Research Point

Look up the case *DPP v Pal* [2000] Crim LR 756. Why was it decided that racial hostility was not shown in this case?

Potential exam question:

Damien and his brother Lee went to Kelly's house to collect money she owed them. The brothers were armed with weapons because Kelly's new boyfriend Spike was a security guard and all four of them had fallen out over the matter. Damien burst into Kelly's house first, followed by Lee. Damien swung at Kelly with his baseball bat but missed. He pinned her against the wall and demanded his money before Spike appeared. Kelly punched Damien in the face and burst open his bottom lip.

Lee ran upstairs to look for the money and ran into Spike. Spike took Lee's hammer off him and threatened to hit Lee with it if he didn't leave. Lee punched Spike in the face giving him a black eye. Spike swung for Lee with the hammer and cracked Lee's head open.

Damien, Lee, Kelly and Spike have all committed non-fatal offences. Notwithstanding any defences they may use, explain in detail the offence(s) that each party will be charged with.

Chapter 10
Sexual offences

Sexual offences have recently undergone a radical reform. The Sexual Offences Act 2003 now governs this area of law and all the relevant offences have been updated.

> ### Research Point
>
> Look up the independent review entitled: *Setting the Boundaries - Reforming the Law on Sex Offenders* which was published in July 2000. Read the opening paragraph. Why was reform in this area of law urgently necessary?

10.1 The old law

- The old law on sexual offences was described as a 'patchwork quilt of provisions' by the *Setting the Boundaries* (2000) review.
- Old common law rules and values were codified in the Sexual Offences Act 1956.
- Social attitudes towards women and lifestyle choices have since moved on.
- Rape was governed by s.1 of the Sexual Offences Act 1956.
- All other forms of sexual contact were charged as indecent assault under sections 14 and 15 of the 1956 Act.
- The *actus reus* of indecent assault was significantly wide.

Indecent assault under the old law:	
McAllister (1997)	Oral sex
Boyea (1992)	Penetration of the vagina with hand
Court (1989)	Spanking
Tabassum (2000)	Stroking a woman's breasts
Price (2003)	Stroking a woman's lower leg

- The test for 'indecency' was vague and simply required a 'right-minded person' to believe the conduct was indecent – *Court* (1989).
- A whole collection of reforms were suggested by the *Setting the Boundaries* (2000) review:

Area of law:	Reform suggestion by (2000) review:
Rape	A new definition to include the mouth and female genitalia
Assault by penetration	A new offence to cover the use of objects
Sentencing	A life sentence should be available to reflect nature of crime
Sexual assault	A new offence to cover all non-penetrative sexual touching

- The Government published their own White Paper entitled: *Protecting the Public - Strengthening Protection against Sex Offenders and Reforming the Law on Sexual Offences* (2002).
- The Sexual Offences Act 2003 entered into force on 1 May 2004.

10.2 Rape

- Rape is the most serious sexual offence.
- It is a statutory offence under s.1 of the Sexual Offences Act 2003.

Definition

Rape: forced sexual intercourse.

- Rape now attracts a maximum sentence of life imprisonment to reflect the seriousness of the crime.

The statutory offence of rape is provided below. What are the key words, the *actus reus* elements and the *mens rea* elements of the offence?

1(1) A person (A) commits an offence if -
(a) he intentionally penetrates the vagina, anus or mouth of another person (B) with his penis;
(b) B does not consent to the penetration, and
(c) A does not reasonably believe that B consents.

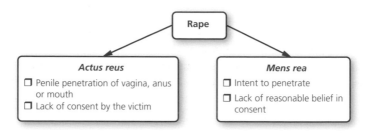

Rape

Actus reus	**Mens rea**
☐ Penile penetration of vagina, anus or mouth ☐ Lack of consent by the victim	☐ Intent to penetrate ☐ Lack of reasonable belief in consent

10.3 The *actus reus* of rape

- The *actus reus* of rape has been expanded to include the mouth of the victim and the courts now take oral rape very seriously – *Ismail* (2005).

10.3.1 Penetration

- Rape under s.1 of the 2003 Act requires penetration by a penis.

Definition

Penetration: a continuing act from entry to withdrawal – s.79(2) of the 2003 Act.

- It follows that only a man can commit this particular offence.
- A woman can, however, be a secondary party to rape by ordering a victim to remove clothes and have intercourse – *DPP v K and C* (1997).
- A defendant commits rape if he penetrates *with* consent and then fails to withdraw when consent is revoked – *Kaitamaki* (1984) and *Cooper and Schaub* (1994).

10.3.2 Lack of consent

• Part of the *actus reus* of rape is a lack of consent by the victim.
• There is no need for the use of force or for the victim to submit (i.e. surrender) to intercourse as a result of threats.

Case:	
***Olugboja* (1982)**	Dunn J: 'It is not necessary for the prosecution to prove that what might otherwise appear to have been consent was in reality merely submission by force, fear or fraud. The jury should be directed that consent, or the absence of it, is to be given its ordinary meaning.'

• A victim must consent by choice and have the freedom and capacity to make that choice – s.74 of the 2003 Act.
• Kidnapping a victim and then having intercourse with her is sufficient evidence that consent was not made by choice – *McFall* (1994).
• Tricking a victim into a relationship is also evidence that her consent was not a free choice – *Jheeta* (2007).

Workpoint

Jack and Jill had been in a sexual relationship for three years. Jill was beginning to doubt whether she loved Jack anymore and they argued about it constantly. Jack came home late one night and Jill decided to finish the relationship. They had a serious argument and Jack said he would seek full custody of their son if Jill didn't perform oral sex on him 'one last time'. She did so, but she later argued that she wasn't consenting and had therefore been raped. Jack argued that he didn't force her and dismissed her accusation as 'rubbish'.

Has Jack performed the *actus reus* of rape? Give reasons for your answer, focusing particularly on the issue of consent (or lack thereof).

10.3.3 Consent to sex and consent to sexually transmitted diseases

• Sexually transmitted diseases and sexual intercourse are treated *separately* by the criminal courts.
• If a victim does not consent to sexual infection, the defendant will be charged with a non-fatal offence such as biological grievous bodily harm – *Dica* (2004).
• However, the victim still consented to the act of intercourse and so it is not rape – *B* (2006).

Case:	
B (2006)	Latham LJ: 'Where one party to sexual activity has a sexually transmissible disease which is not disclosed to the other party, any consent that may have been given to that activity is not thereby vitiated (i.e. cancelled). The act remains a consensual act. However...such consent does not include consent to infection by disease.'

10.3.4 Evidential presumptions about consent

• Section 75 of the 2003 Act makes presumptions about consent.
• The victim is presumed *not* to have consented in certain circumstances.
• It is then up to the defendant to submit evidence to prove otherwise.
• These provisions are known as 'evidential presumptions'.

Workpoint

Section 75 is provided below, which contains presumptions about consent. List any key words.

Section 75(1): If in proceedings for an offence it is proved -
(a) that [D] did the relevant act;
(b) that any of the circumstances in subsection (2) existed; and
(c) that [D] knew that those circumstances existed,

[V] is to be taken not to have consented to the relevant act unless suf-ficient evidence is adduced...and [D] is to be taken not to have reason-ably believed that [V] consented unless sufficient evidence is adduced.

The certain circumstances are provided under s.75(2):

Section 75(2): The circumstances are that -

(a) any person was, at the time of the act or immediately before, using violence against [V] or causing [V] to fear that immediate violence would be used against him;
(b) ...or against another person;
(c) [V] was, and [D] was not, unlawfully detained at the time;
(d) [V] was asleep or otherwise unconscious at the time;
(e) because of [V]'s physical disability, [V] would not have been able at the time of the relevant act to communicate to [D] whether [V] consented;
(f) any person had administered to or caused to be taken by [V], with-out [V]'s consent, a substance which, when it was administered or taken, was capable of causing or enabling [V] to be stupefied or overpowered at the time.

- If one of the criteria above are satisfied, then there is a presumption that the victim did not consent.
- The burden of proof falls to the defendant to prove that the victim did in fact consent.

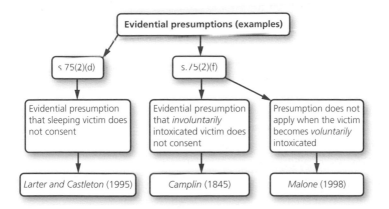

Case:	
Bree (2007)	Sir Igor Judge: 'A drunken consent is still consent. Where [V] has voluntarily consumed even substantial quantities of alcohol, but nevertheless remains capable of choosing whether or not to have intercourse, and in drink agrees to do so, this would not be rape.'

Workpoint

Do you think there could be an evidential presumption in any of the scenarios below that the victim was not consenting? If so, provide the relevant statutory ground for the presumption.

(a) Craig locked the door to the toilets and told Jenny that she could only go if she performed oral sex on him.

(b) Emma was sleepwalking. She walked into David's bedroom. David asked her if she was sleepwalking and she didn't respond. They had intercourse anyway.

(c) Shobia suffered years of domestic abuse at the hands of her husband Jamil. She was petrified that he would beat her up if she refused his advances for intercourse.

(d) Laura had consensual intercourse with her boyfriend Mark after she found out that he had cheated on her with all of her friends at the weekend and was she really angry with him.

(e) Darren spiked Jo's drink and took her home when she appeared to look drowsy. They had intercourse before she passed out.

10.3.5 Conclusive presumptions about consent

- Section 76 of the 2003 Act also makes presumptions about consent.
- The victim is presumed *not* to have consented if she was deceived in some way.
- The defendant is *not* allowed to produce evidence to prove otherwise.
- These provisions are known as 'conclusive presumptions'.

Workpoint

Section 76 is provided below, which contains presumptions about consent. List any key words.

Section 76(1): If in proceedings for an offence it is proved that [D] did the relevant act and that any of the circumstances specified in subsection (2) existed, it is to be conclusively presumed -

(a) that [V] did not consent to the relevant act; and
(b) that [D] did not believe that [V] consented to the relevant act.

(2) The circumstances are that -

(a) [D] intentionally deceived [V] as to the nature or purpose of the relevant act;
(b) [D] intentionally induced [V] to consent to the relevant act by impersonating a person known personally to [V].

- The provisions under s.76 mean that a defendant cannot argue that he had a reasonable belief in consent or provide evidence to prove consent.
- This is because he *intentionally* deceived the victim (i.e. he knew from the beginning that her consent was false).
- The deception must relate to the nature or purpose of the intercourse (e.g. that it will heal an illness etc).
- The defendant is deceptive if he impersonates the victim's husband, fiancé or boyfriend – *Elbekkay* (1995).
- However, if the defendant simply lies about his financial status or professional prospects, the nature and purpose of the intercourse remains unaffected.

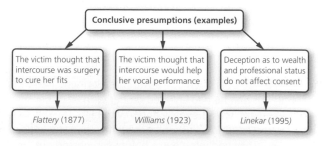

Case:	
Jheeta (2007)	Sir Igor Judge: 'The ambit of s.76 is lir[...] In rape cases, the "act" is vaginal, an[...] Section 76(2)(a) is relevant only to the[...] deliberately deceives [V] about the na[...] one or other form of intercourse. No[...] tions arise merely because...of com[...]

Case: Fothe[...] (198[...]

[...]AL OFFENCES

Workpoint

Why do you think Parliament has included 'evidential presumptions' and 'conclusive presumptions' about consent in the new Sexual Offences Act 2003?

10.4 The *mens rea* of rape: a reasonable belief in consent

- The defendant must intend to penetrate the victim with his penis.
- In addition, he must not have a reasonable belief in her consent.
- Before reform, the defendant was allowed to argue that he had an honest but unreasonable belief in consent.
- It must now be proved that the defendant had a reasonable belief in consent (see table below).

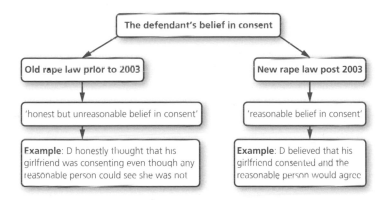

- All the circumstances will be considered including any steps taken by the defendant to ascertain consent – s.1(2).
- If the defendant is intoxicated, the jury will ignore this and simply ask the same question: whether his belief was reasonable – *Woods* (1981).

	Facts: the defendant was drunk and climbed into the marital bed where the babysitter was sleeping. He had intercourse with the babysitter under the genuine belief that she was his wife.
	Trial judge: 'the reasonable grounds are grounds which would be reasonable to a sober man.'
	Watkins LJ: (in agreement) 'in rape, self-induced intoxication is no defence, whether the issue be intention, consent or, as here, mistake as to the identity of the victim.'

Workpoint

Do the following three defendants possess the *mens rea* for rape?

(a) John and Stacey took heroin and had intercourse during one of their 'trips'. John was aware that he was having intercourse but his mind was intercepted by hallucinations. Stacey complained that she was raped the next day.

(b) Amy dressed provocatively and went to visit Stuart. She had a crush on him. She flirted with Stuart and touched him suggestively. He allowed her to perform oral sex on him. Amy later complained that she did not want to perform oral sex and feels used – she simply wanted to be his girlfriend.

(c) Callum and Kim were in their final year at high school. During a lunch break, Callum asked Kim if he could film her performing oral sex on him on his mobile phone. Kim looked unsure and asked him repeatedly what he was going to do and what it entailed before she reluctantly agreed. She looked uncomfortable throughout the act. She later felt violated and went to the police, saying that she was pressured into consenting.

10.5 Rape: marriage

- It was understood that when a woman said her marriage vows, she was consenting to sex with her husband for the rest of her life – *Jones* (1973).
- In *R v R* (1992) it was finally accepted that a wife can refuse intercourse and a husband can now be charged with rape.

Item on checklist:	Done!
I can provide a brief explanation as to why the old law of rape was reformed	
I can recite the statutory definition of rape under the Sexual Offences Act 2003	
I can define 'penetration' under the 2003 Act	
I can explain what 'lack of consent' means in relation to the *actus reus* of rape	
I can give an example of 'lack of consent' with a legal authority	
I can explain the rule in *B* (2006) in relation to consent, rape and disease	
I can explain what is meant by an 'evidential presumption' under s.75 of the 2003 Act	
I can list at least three circumstances under s.75(2) in which the courts will presume a lack of consent	
I can explain what is meant by a 'conclusive presumption' under s.76 of the 2003 Act	
I can give an example of a type of deception that will lead to a conclusive presumption of lack of consent	
I can define the *mens rea* of rape	
I can explain what is meant by 'reasonable belief' in consent and how this can be distinguished from the old law prior to 2003	

10.6 Assault by penetration

- 'Assault by penetration' is a new offence under the Sexual Offences Act 2003.
- It allows for the prosecution of any person who penetrates a victim vaginally or anally by any means whatsoever.

Workpoint

The statutory offence of assault by penetration is provided below. What are the key words, the *actus reus* elements and the *mens rea* elements of the offence?

2(1) A person (A) commits an offence if -

(a) he intentionally penetrates the vagina or anus of another person (B) with a part of his body or anything else;
(b) the penetration is sexual;
(c) B does not consent to the penetration; and
(d) A does not reasonably believe that B consents.

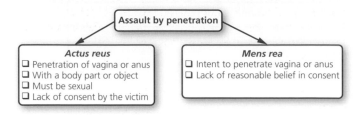

Assault by penetration

Actus reus	*Mens rea*
❑ Penetration of vagina or anus	❑ Intent to penetrate vagina or anus
❑ With a body part or object	❑ Lack of reasonable belief in consent
❑ Must be sexual	
❑ Lack of consent by the victim	

10.6.1 'Sexual'

- The only thing that distinguishes an assault by penetration from an ordinary assault is that the former must be 'sexual' in nature.
- This is difficult to define and both parties may have conflicting accounts.
- The Sexual Offences Act 2003 has attempted to define 'sexual' under s.78:

'Section 78: Penetration, touching or any other activity is sexual if a reasonable person would consider that:

(a) whatever its circumstances or any person's purpose in relation to it, it is because of its nature sexual; or

(b) because of its nature it may be sexual and because of its circumstances or the purpose of any person in relation to it (or both) it is sexual.'

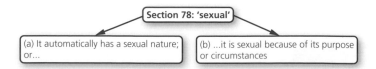

Section 78: 'sexual'

(a) It automatically has a sexual nature; or...

(b) ...it is sexual because of its purpose or circumstances

> ## Workpoint
>
> Three examples of activity are given below. Which ones do you think are 'sexual' under the s.78 definition? Then give your own example of a sexual assault by penetration.
>
> (a) Jane has her smear test. Her vagina is penetrated with a scraping device to gather cervical cells.
> (b) Craig and Shaun are a homosexual couple. Craig inserts three fingers into Shaun's anus during their sexual activities.
> (c) Margaret is suffering from abdominal pain and the doctor needs to examine her colon. He inserts a finger into her anus to feel for abnormalities.

- If a defendant drugs his victim and then penetrates the victim's anus with his finger, this is assault by penetration under s.2 – *Coomber* (2005).
- Attacking a teenage girl in a field and inserting a finger into her anus is sexual because of its nature – *Cunliffe* (2006).
- Assault by penetration under s.2 is viewed as the lesser offence when compared to s.1 (rape) – *Lyddaman* (2006).

Checkpoint - assault by penetration

Item on checklist:	Done!
I can define assault by penetration under s.2 of the Sexual Offences Act 2003	
I can explain what is meant by 'sexual' under s.78 of the 2003 Act	
I can distinguish between a non-sexual assault and an assault by penetration by giving my own example of each	

10.7 Sexual assault

- 'Sexual assault' is a new offence under the 2003 Act which replaces the old offence of indecent assault.

> *'Section 3(1): A person (A) commits an offence if -*
>
> *(a) he intentionally touches another person (B);*
> *(b) the touching is sexual;*
> *(c) B does not consent to the touching; and*
> *(d) A does not reasonably believe that B consents.'*

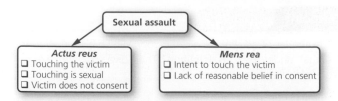

- There are subtle differences between regular assault and sexual assault.
- The *mens rea* for sexual assault is intention to touch the victim.
- 'Touching' is a new concept for criminal law and includes touching any part of the body with anything and through anything – s.79(8).
- The 'sexual' aspect is defined in s.78 (see above).

Workpoint

Recent sexual assault cases are provided below. Do you think the touching in each case makes the assaults 'sexual' under s.78? If so, under which ground? Copy and complete the table:

Sexual assault cases:	Facts:	Automatically sexual?	Sexual purpose or circumstances?
Bamonadio (2005) *Ralston* (2005) *Burns* (2006)	Touching V's breasts		
Elvidge (2005) *Forrester* (2006)	Touching V's private parts		
Turner (2005)	Kissing V's private parts		
W (2005)	Kissing V's face		
Nika (2005)	Pressing D's body against V's buttocks		
Osmani (2006)	Rubbing D's penis against V's body		
Deal (2006)	Sniffing V's hair while stroking her arm		

Sexual assault cases:	Facts:	Automatically sexual?	Sexual purpose or circumstances?
Bounekhla (2006)	Ejaculating onto V's clothes while dancing		
R v H (2005)	Touching V's clothing		

Checkpoint - sexual assault

Item on checklist:	Done!
I can define sexual assault under s.3 of the Sexual Offences Act 2003	
I can explain what is meant by 'touching' under the *actus reus* of sexual assault	
I can give three examples of sexual touching under the s.78 definition of 'sexual'	

10.8 Offences against children under 13

- There are various offences available when the victim of rape, assault by penetration or sexual assault is under 13.
- These are very serious offences and this is reflected in their heavy sentences and stricter liability.

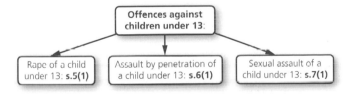

Offences against children under 13:

Rape of a child under 13: **s.5(1)**

Assault by penetration of a child under 13: **s.6(1)**

Sexual assault of a child under 13: **s.7(1)**

10.8.1 Rape of a child under 13

- The rape of a child under 13 is an offence under section 5(1) of the 2003 Act.

- The offence is very similar to rape under s.1 but there are subtle differences in *actus reus* and *mens rea*.

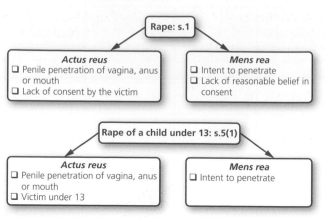

Rape: s.1

Actus reus
❑ Penile penetration of vagina, anus or mouth
❑ Lack of consent by the victim

Mens rea
❑ Intent to penetrate
❑ Lack of reasonable belief in consent

Rape of a child under 13: s.5(1)

Actus reus
❑ Penile penetration of vagina, anus or mouth
❑ Victim under 13

Mens rea
❑ Intent to penetrate

Workpoint

Copy and complete the table below. Make a note of the main differences between rape (s.1) and rape of a child under 13 (s.5).

Differences in *actus reus*:	Differences in *mens rea*:

- The main difference between rape (s.1) and rape of a child under 13 (s.5) is that consent (or lack of it) is not an issue – *R v D* (2006).
- The victim is not allowed to consent and the defendant cannot 'reasonably believe' in consent.
- All that has to be proved is that the defendant intended to penetrate the victim with his penis and that the young victim was in fact penetrated – *R v G* (2008).

Case:	
***Corran and others* (2005)**	Facts: the defendant met the 12 year old victim when she was surrounded by much older friends. They had a sexual relationship lasting several weeks. The defendant genuinely thought the victim to be 16. He was charged with rape of a child under s.5.
	Held: the trial judge said that both V's consent and D's honest belief in her age were completely irrelevant and the Court of Appeal upheld his conviction.

Research Point

Look up the case *R v G* [2008] UKHL 37 which involves a 15 year old boy and a 12 year old girl. What did Lord Hoffman say about the purpose of section 5 in relation to its strict liability?

10.8.2 Assault by penetration of a child under 13

• Under s.6(1), it is an offence to penetrate a child under 13 by any means.

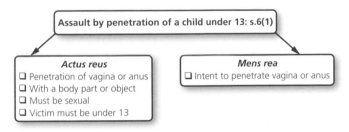

• Liability is again strict in relation to the age of the victim – the defendant cannot argue that he genuinely believed the victim to be older.
• All that has to be proved is that the defendant intended to penetrate the victim with a part of his body or an object, and that the young victim was in fact sexually penetrated.
• Cases brought under s.6(1) include *R v RC* (2005) involving a 12 year old victim, and *R v C* (2006) involving a 5 year old victim.

10.8.3 Sexual assault of a child under 13

• Under s.7(1) it is an offence to commit a sexual assault on a child under 13.

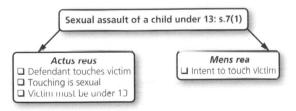

• Liability is strict in relation to the age of the victim.
• All that has to be proved is that the defendant intended to touch the victim and that the young victim was in fact sexually touched.
• Cases brought under s.7(1) include *Vatcher* (2006) involving a 7 year old boy and *Mackney* (2006) involving an 11 year old girl.

- A female defendant kissed two young girls on the lips at a house party in *Davies* (2005).

Alistair ran a small paedophile ring with five other members. The police had been tipped off as to the activities of the group. The police surrounded a children's play centre where Alistair and his members had gathered with three very young children. The police burst in and arrested Alistair, Fred and Martin. Write down what each defendant must do in terms of *actus reus* and *mens rea* to be charged with that offence.

(a) Alistair was charged with assault by penetration of a child under 13 contrary to s.6(1) of the Sexual Offences Act 2003.

(b) Fred was charged with the rape of a child under 13 contrary to s.5(1) of the Sexual Offences Act 2003.

(c) Martin was charged with sexual assault of a child under 13 contrary to s.7(1) of the Sexual Offences Act 2003.

10.8.4 Sexual activity with children over 13

- It is an offence under s.9(1) of the 2003 Act to engage in sexual activity with a child under 16.
- This offence covers a whole range of sexual activity.
- Since specific offences already exist for sexual activity with a child under 13, this offence will typically be relevant when the victim is aged between 13 and 15.

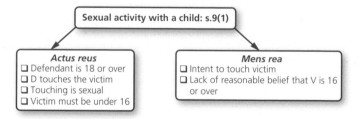

- Liability is not so strict under s.9(1) because the defendant is allowed a reasonable belief that the victim is 16 or over.
- If the touching involves penetration of the victim's vagina, anus or mouth with a penis, body part or object, then the offence is indictable to Crown Court – s.9(2).
- For any other sexual touching, the offence is triable either way – s.9(3).
- For a defendant under 18, he will be charged under s.13(1) which simply means a lesser maximum sentence.

Case under s.9(1):	Nature of offence:
Eitreri (2005)	D, aged 24, had consensual sex with a 13 year old girl
Couch (2005)	D, aged 18, engaged in sexual activities with a 14 year old girl
Gardner (2005)	D penetrated a 14 year old girl's vagina with his fingers
Elliot (2005)	D, aged 35, had consensual sex with a 14 year old girl
Monks (2006)	D performed oral and anal sex on a 15 year old boy
Greaves (2006)	D engaged in sexual activity with two girls aged 12 and 14

- The defendant cannot argue that he reasonably believed the victim to be consenting and s.9(1) is strict liability in this respect – *Gardner* (2005).
- The defendant is only allowed a reasonable belief as to the victim's age.

Workpoint

Cheryl and David had been going out together for 5 months. They had been having intercourse for most of that time. David was 19 and was a university student. Cheryl said that she was 17 and finishing her A-Levels, when in fact she was 15 and finishing her GCSEs. David is charged under s.9(1) with sexual activity with a child. Has he satisfied the *actus reus* and *mens rea* of the offence? Give reasons for your answer.

Checkpoint - offences against children under 13

Item on checklist:	Done!
I can list three specific sexual offences from the 2003 Act that can be committed against a child under 13	
I can distinguish between the statutory requirements of rape contrary to s.1(1) and the rape of a child under 13 contrary to s.5(1)	
I can highlight how the 2003 Act has introduced stricter liability into the offences of rape (s.5), assault by penetration (s.6) and sexual assault (s.7)	
I can give a practical example of when the offence under s.9(1) of the 2003 Act may be used	

10.9 Incest

- The old crime of incest has been updated by the Sexual Offences Act 2003.
- Incest refers to sexual activities between family members.
- Incestuous relationships are sometimes consensual (i.e. both parties have chosen to have intercourse despite their genetic connection).

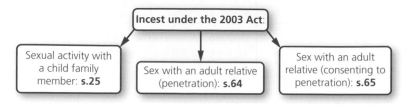

Incest under the 2003 Act:

Sexual activity with a child family member: **s.25**

Sex with an adult relative (penetration): **s.64**

Sex with an adult relative (consenting to penetration): **s.65**

10.9.1 Sexual activity with a child family member

- This offence under s.25 of the 2003 Act covers any kind of sexual activity, from touching to penetration.
- It will often be charged in addition to other offences above (e.g. in cases of child rape within the family).
- Consent is irrelevant – there is no mention of it in the *actus reus* or *mens rea*.
- The first s.25 case was *AT* (2006) and the Court of Appeal said that consent from the victim (aged 13) was a 'limited concept'.

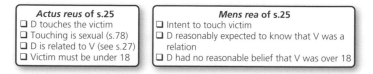

Actus reus of s.25	*Mens rea* of s.25
❑ D touches the victim	❑ Intent to touch victim
❑ Touching is sexual (s.78)	❑ D reasonably expected to know that V was a
❑ D is related to V (see s.27)	relation
❑ Victim must be under 18	❑ D had no reasonable belief that V was over 18

10.9.2 'Family relationships'

- This area of law requires both parties to be 'relatives' as part of the *actus reus*.
- This term has been defined under s.27(2) as a:
  1. Parent;
  2. Grandparent;
  3. Brother or sister;
  4. Half-brother or half-sister;
  5. Aunt or uncle;
  6. Foster parent (past or present).

10.9.3 Sex with an adult relative: penetration

- A person (D) commits an offence under s.64(1) if he penetrates an adult relative (E).
- This offence is applicable to two related adults (e.g. brother and sister) who choose to enter into a sexual relationship.

Actus reus of s.64(1)	*Mens rea* of s.64(1)
❑ D is 16 or over	❑ Intent to penetrate E
❑ D penetrates E's vagina or anus with a body part or object	❑ D reasonably expected to know that V was a relation
❑ D penetrates E's mouth with his penis	
❑ Penetration is sexual (s.78)	
❑ E must be over 18	
❑ D is related to E (s.27)	

10.9.4 Sex with an adult relative: consenting to penetration

- A person commits an offence under s.65(1) if he or she *allows* an adult relative (R) to penetrate him or her.
- This offence will be used in conjunction with s.64(1) (above) to ensure that both adult relatives are criminally liable.
- The 'consenting recipient' is now the defendant (D) under s.65(1).

Actus reus of s.65(1)	*Mens rea* of s.65(1)
❑ R penetrates D's vagina or anus with a body part or object	❑ D reasonably expected to know that R was a relation
❑ R penetrates D's mouth with his penis	
❑ D consents to penetration	
❑ Penetration is sexual (s.78)	
❑ R must be over 18	
❑ R is related to D (s.27)	

Workpoint

Darren and Lorena are brother and sister. They share the same mother, Maria, but they do not share the same father. They were split up when they were five years old have just met up after a 17-year separation. They look very similar and there is an instant sexual attraction. They do not see each other as 'family' and are struggling to remain just friends. They come to you for advice on whether they would be breaking any laws if they began a relationship. You turn to sections 64 and 65 of the Sexual Offences Act 2003.

Advise Darren and Lorena what they must do in terms of *actus reus* and *mens rea* in order to commit a criminal offence.

Checkpoint - incest

Item on checklist:	Done!
I can list three specific sexual offences from the 2003 Act that can be committed against a family member	
I can recite the *mens rea* requirement for a charge under s.25 of sexual activity with a child family member	
I can locate the two provisions under which a consenting adult relative can be prosecuted for engaging in sexual activity with another relative	
I can offer a view as to why Parliament has made consenting to penetration a criminal offence under s.65	

10.10 Miscellaneous offences

- The Sexual Offences Act 2003 is now the one-stop-shop for all sexual offences.
- It contains many other provisions, some of which are listed below:

Provision:	Offence:	Case law:
Section 4	Causing a person to engage in sexual activity	*Devonald* (2008) *Ayeva* (2009)
Section 14	Grooming (i.e. arranging or facilitating)	
Section 15	Meeting a child (i.e. travelling with intention)	
Section 61	Administering a substance with intent	*Spall* (2007)
Section 62	Committing an offence with intent to commit a sexual offence	*Wisniewski* (2004)
Section 63	Trespass with intent to commit a sexual offence	
Section 66	Exposure with intent to cause alarm or distress	
Section 67	Voyeurism (i.e. observing for gratification)	*Bassett* (2008)
Section 69	Intercourse with an animal	
Section 70	Sexual penetration of a corpse	

10.11 Overview

• The main offences are as follows:

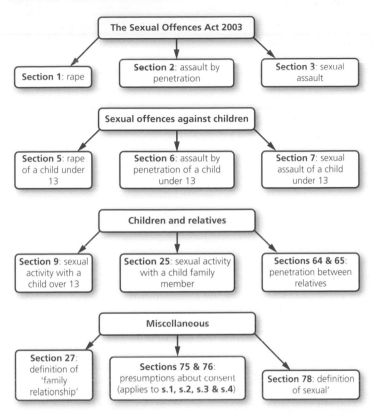

The Sexual Offences Act 2003

Section 1: rape

Section 2: assault by penetration

Section 3: sexual assault

Sexual offences against children

Section 5: rape of a child under 13

Section 6: assault by penetration of a child under 13

Section 7: sexual assault of a child under 13

Children and relatives

Section 9: sexual activity with a child over 13

Section 25: sexual activity with a child family member

Sections 64 & 65: penetration between relatives

Miscellaneous

Section 27: definition of 'family relationship'

Sections 75 & 76: presumptions about consent (applies to **s.1, s.2, s.3 & s.4**)

Section 78: definition of sexual'

Potential exam question:

1) Provide a critical commentary about the new law of rape under s.1 of the Sexual Offences Act 2003.

Chapter 11

Theft

This chapter will explore the offence of theft, which is mainly covered by the Theft Act 1968. This chapter will also explore the types of property that can be stolen. The offence of theft appears simple but contains many components that have become more complex as modern technology has developed.

11.1 The origins of theft

- The Theft Act 1968 created a new and simple code for the law of theft and other property offences.
- The 1968 Act was the result of the Eighth Report of the Criminal Law Revision Committee, *Theft and Related Offences*, Cmnd 2977 (1966).

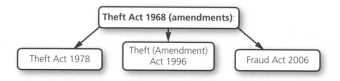

Theft Act 1968 (amendments):

Theft Act 1978 → Theft (Amendment) Act 1996 → Fraud Act 2006

Research Point

Lord Diplock referred to the new Theft Act 1968 in *Treacy v DPP* [1971] 1 All ER 110. Look up the judgment and list his thoughts about it.

11.2 The definition of theft

- Theft is defined by s.1(1) of the Theft Act 1968.

> 'Section 1(1): A person is guilty of theft if he dishonestly appropriates property belonging to another with the intention of permanently depriving the other of it.'

Workpoint

Write what you think are the key *actus reus* and *mens rea* words to theft.

- The definition of theft seems quite short and straightforward, but it is not.
- The physical and mental words within s.1(1) have their own definitions within the Theft Act 1968.
- These definitions (i.e. the definition of 'appropriates') have accumulated their own case law.

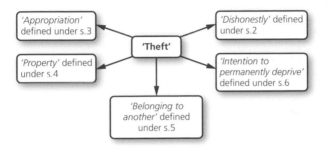

Workpoint

Before looking at each word in detail, apply the basic s.1(1) definition of theft to the following scenario.

Stacey was working in the law library with Lawrence on their land law revision. Lawrence showed Stacey the new land law book he had bought. It was the expensive one that Stacey could not afford. When they packed up to go home later, Stacey put all of her library books in her bag, including Lawrence's land law book. Neither of them noticed until the next day when Lawrence couldn't find his book in his bedroom and Stacey found it in her bag. She read through it and decided to keep it. Has Stacey committed theft according to the basic definition? Give reasons for your answer using some of the key words in the definition.

Checkpoint - basic theft

Item on checklist:	Done!
I can explain where the idea for the Theft Act 1968 came from	
I can list the amendments to the Theft Act 1968	
I can describe the aim behind the Theft Act 1968 as explained by Lord Diplock in *Treacy v DPP* (1971)	
I can apply the physical elements of theft to an everyday scenario	
I can apply the mental elements of theft to an everyday scenario	
I understand that each component of theft has its own definition within the 1968 Act	

11.3 'Appropriation'

- A vital component of the *actus reus* is the appropriation of property.

Definition

Appropriate: take, acquire, obtain, grab, seize, get, steal, rob, pinch.

- Appropriation is the physical act of taking something, whether it be a wallet on a bus or a bank balance.
- Appropriation is defined under s.3(1) of the 1968 Act:

> 'Section 3(1): Any assumption by a person of the rights of an owner amounts to an appropriation, and this includes, where he has come by the property (innocently or not) without stealing it, any later assumption of a right to it by keeping or dealing with it as owner.'

Workpoint

Write your own definition of 'appropriation'.

- Appropriation means assuming (i.e. adopting) the rights of the owner.

- Offering items for sale that belong to another person is appropriation – *Pitham v Hehl* (1977).
- Grabbing a handbag is an appropriation even if it falls to the floor – *Corcoran v Anderton* (1980).
- The defendant does not have to assume *all* of the rights of the owner, any right will suffice – *R v Morris* (1983).

Case:	
Atakpu v Abrahams (1994)	Facts: the defendants obtained cars in Germany and Belgium using false driving licences and passports. They were arrested for theft at Dover.
	Held: the moment of appropriation was in Germany and Belgium. No theft had occurred on English soil. Convictions quashed.

- A theft can still take place if the owner consents to the appropriation – *Gomez* (1993).
- This is because the defendant may use deception to obtain the consent.

Case:	
Lawrence (1972)	Facts: a student got into a taxi. He opened his wallet to the driver and the driver took too much money from it, later arguing that there was no appropriation because he had consent.
	Viscount Dilhorne: 'Parliament by the omission of "without the consent of the owner" has relieved the prosecution of establishing that the taking was without the owner's consent. That is no longer an ingredient of the offence.'

• If consent is induced in any other way, this may also be 'appropriation' under s.3(1).

Case:	
Hinks (2000)	Facts: the victim was of low intelligence and lavished gifts upon the defendant, who accepted a TV and £60,000 from him. The defendant argued that all gifts were genuine and with the victim's consent. Lord Steyn: 'It is immaterial whether the act was done with the victim's consent or authority. The majority of cases do not differentiate between cases of consent induced by fraud and consent given in any other circumstances.'

11.3.1 Appropriation of bank balances

• If a cheque is fake, the property is obtained by deception and thus 'appropriated' by the buyer – *Dobson v General Accident Fire and Life Assurance Corporation* (1990).
• Where the object is a bank balance and the defendant is in another country, the offence takes place where the defendant sends the telex – *Osman* (1989).
• Signing blank cheques does not assume the rights of an owner, but presenting them to the bank to be cashed does – *Ngan* (1998).
• In computer banking, appropriation takes place where the keyboard command manifests into a physical effect.

Case:	
Governor of Brixton Prison ex parte Levin (1997)	Facts: the defendant used a computer in Russia to gain access to bank accounts in America. His actions in Russia had instantaneous effects on computers in America. Held: even though the defendant was 10,000 miles away, he had an effect on computers in America and this was where the appropriation took place. It matters little where the defendant is actually located.

11.3.2 Purchasing and appropriation

• If a consumer *innocently purchases* stolen goods and acquires ownership rights to that item, he is not guilty of theft – *Wheeler* (1990).
• This exception is included within the Theft Act 1968 to protect innocent consumers.
• This does not include instances where someone simply takes an item and then later decides to keep it.

'Section 3(2): Where property or a right or interest in property is or purports to be transferred for value to a person acting in good faith, no later assumption by him of rights which he believed himself to be acquiring shall, by reason of any defect in the transferor's title, amount to theft of the property.'

Workpoint

List the key words from s.3(2).

Authority:	Rule:
s.3(1)	The definition of 'appropriation'
Pitham v Hehl (1977)	Selling items belonging to another is an appropriation of the owner's rights
Corcoran v Anderton (1980)	Grabbing an item is an appropriation
R v Morris (1983)	Assuming any right of the owner is appropriation
Atakpu v Abrahams (1994)	The moment of appropriation is vital to the charge of theft
Gomez (1993)	It doesn't matter whether the victim consents to the appropriation or not
Lawrence (1972)	Deception may be used to obtain consent which leads to appropriation
Hinks (2000)	A genuine gift may be appropriated if the victim is being taken advantage of
Dobson v General Accident (1990)	If a cheque is fake, the property has been obtained by deception and thus appropriated
Osman (1989)	Sending a telex is the moment of appropriation
Ngan (1998)	Presenting a cheque to be cashed is the moment of appropriation
Levin (1997)	The result of a computer command is where appropriation takes place (which could be miles away)
s.3(2) and *Wheeler* (1990)	Innocent purchasers do not appropriate property

Workpoint

Work out whether an appropriation has taken place in any of the scenarios below and give reasons for your answer.

(a) Justin has a big argument with his neighbour Fred, who was due to go on his annual holiday and needed somebody to look after his cat. Fred left his cat with Justin despite the argument. A few days later, Justin advertises the cat for sale in the local newspaper.

(b) Ben has a huge crush on Jennifer, who is twenty years older and married. Ben has little money but lavishes Jennifer with gifts anyway. Ben is at risk of missing his rent payment and Jennifer feels sorry for him, but still accepts a Blu-ray player, diamond earrings and expensive shoes that her husband would never buy for her.

(c) Jerry is a war fanatic and buys old hero medals at auctions. He bought a Victoria Cross from the First World War. The police contact him three weeks later to inform him that it is in fact stolen property and the original owner – the soldier himself – wants it back.

(d) Lewis had concert tickets to see Beyonce. He was in a queue outside the venue when he was approached by Tom, who wanted the ticket. Lewis said he wasn't selling. Tom presented a handful of £50 notes. Lewis counted £600 and handed his ticket over. When he tried to cash the notes two days later, the bank informed Lewis that they were stolen (and marked) notes from a bank raid last month.

(e) Dean set up a false bank account in a UK bank. He was planning to steal money from his colleague's bank account and transfer it into his new account. Dean was dragged away on a family holiday to Majorca but still managed to get internet access and transfer the money from his colleague's account into his. Dean was arrested at Heathrow airport one week later.

Checkpoint - appropriation

Item on checklist:	Done!
I can locate the statutory definition of appropriation and define it in my own words	
I can list four rights of an owner that can be appropriated by another	
I can explain the importance of *Gomez* (1993) and *Lawrence* (1972) in relation to consent and appropriation	

11.4 Property

- The word 'property' appears in the definition of theft under s.1(1) of the Theft Act 1968.
- It is an important part of the *actus reus* and a very flexible term.

Definition

Property: possessions, belongings, goods, assets, materials, goods, land, items.

- Property is most commonly known as land or physical items that can be stolen.
- It is also defined by its own paragraph under s.4(1) of the 1968 Act:

> *'Section 4(1): "Property" includes money and all other property real or personal, including things in action and other intangible property.'*

Workpoint

Write your own definition of 'property'.

- Section 4(1) lists virtually all kinds of property, from real property (e.g. land) to intangible property (e.g. an idea).

- The definition of property is wide because many different types of property exist.
- Personal property is most commonly stolen, including wallets and mobile phones.
- Body parts are also 'property' for the purposes of the 1968 Act if skill has been applied to them – *Kelly and Lindsay* (1998).

Workpoint

Are the following items real property, personal property or a thing in action?

(a) Motor Corporation Ltd signs a fake cheque for a new industrial warehouse.
(b) Polly takes Alan's engraved pen off him and throws it in the river.
(c) Margaret is entitled to access her bank account, but a large corporation has emptied her account and she cannot gain access to anything with her debit card.

11.4.1 Things that cannot be stolen

- There are a small number of things that cannot be stolen.
- These items are listed under the 1968 Act.

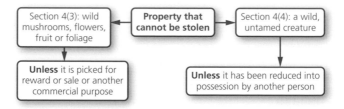

- Under s.4(3), wild plants and fruits cannot be stolen unless for sale.
- Picking blackberries for consumption is not theft, but picking holly to sell at Christmas is theft.
- Under s.4(4), wild creatures (e.g. badgers) are not usually property – *Cresswell v DPP* (2006).
- Wild animals taken into possession by landowners (e.g. a zoo) are property capable of being stolen.

11.4.2 Real property

Definition

Real property: land, property, building, site, field, house, factory.

• A person can steal real property in three circumstances.

Section 4(2) is provided below. List key words and phrases to help you distinguish between subsections (a), (b) and (c).

4(2) A person cannot steal land, or things forming part of land and severed from it by him, except in the following cases -

(a) when he is a trustee or personal representative, or is authorised or as liquidator of a company, to sell or dispose of land belonging to another, and he appropriates the land or anything forming part of it by dealing with it in breach of the confidence reposed in him;

(b) when he is not in possession of the land and appropriates anything forming part of the land by severing it or causing it to be severed or after it has been severed;

(c) when, being in possession under a tenancy, he appropriates the whole or any part of any fixture or structure let to be used with the land.

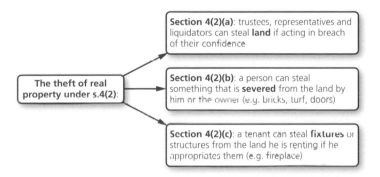

Section 4(2)(a): trustees, representatives and liquidators can steal **land** if acting in breach of their confidence

The theft of real property under s.4(2):

Section 4(2)(b): a person can steal something that is **severed** from the land by him or the owner (e.g. bricks, turf, doors)

Section 4(2)(c): a tenant can steal **fixtures** or structures from the land he is renting if he appropriates them (e.g. fireplace)

If Freddie dismantles his shed on Sunday afternoon and then his neighbour, Barry, steals the shed door on Sunday night, under what section can Barry be charged, if any?

11.4.3 Things in action

• A 'thing in action' is included as property under s.4(1) of the 1968 Act.

Definition

A thing in action: a right to do something, e.g. withdraw money from your own account.

• A person's 'right' to do something can be stolen just the same as their personal property can be stolen.
• A good example is when a defendant causes another person's bank account to be debited – *Kohn* (1979).

11.4.4 Intangible property

• Some forms of property have no physical presence, such as a patent (i.e. an idea with copyright).
• A quota (i.e. allocation of something) can be stolen – *Attorney-General of Hong Kong v Chan Nai-Keung* (1987).
• Knowledge of questions on an examination paper was held **not** to be intangible property capable of being stolen – *Oxford v Moss* (1979).

Can be stolen:	Cannot be stolen:
Money	Wild fungi, flowers, fruit or foliage
Real property and items severed from it	Wild creatures not taken into possession
Personal property	Real property – except under s.4(2)
Things in action and intangible property	Knowledge

Checkpoint - property

Item on checklist:	Done!
I can locate the statutory definition of property and define it in my own words	
I can list four different types of property that can be appropriated by another	
I know which items cannot be stolen under sections 4(2) and 4(3) of the 1968 Act	
I can define 'real' property in my own words	

| I can explain the three circumstances in which real property can be stolen under s.4(2) of the 1968 Act | |
| I can define a 'thing in action' and explain how this entity can be stolen | |

11.5 Belonging to another

- Under the s.1(1) definition of theft, the property must 'belong to another'.
- A very wide definition of this phrase has been provided by s.5(1) of the 1968 Act.

> *'Section 5(1): Property shall be regarded as belonging to any person having possession or control of it, or having in it any proprietary right or interest (not being an equitable interest arising only from an agreement to transfer an interest).'*

- The definition is intentionally very wide so that the prosecution do not have to prove who is the legal owner.

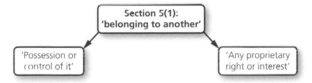

Section 5(1): 'belonging to another'

'Possession or control of it'   'Any proprietary right or interest'

11.5.1 Possession or control

- Under the s.5(1) definition, the victim must have 'possession or control' of the property.

Workpoint

If you hire a car for the day, who has possession and/or control of the car between you and the hire company? Give reasons for your answer.

- Possession or control does not have to be lawful (i.e. items stolen from a shop can then be stolen from the thief).
- A defendant can steal his own property if another person had possession or control of it – *Turner* (1971).

Case:	
Turner (1971)	Facts: the defendant left his car at a garage for repairs. He agreed to pay for the repairs on collection, but he stole the car during the night instead. He argued that it was his own property.
	Held: the garage had possession and control of the car and so the defendant was guilty of stealing his own car from another.

- A car that has been impounded is not possessed or controlled by the company; they simply have a right to enforce a fine – *Meredith* (1973).
- A person may be in possession of an item even if they do not know it is there (e.g. materials left on a person's property overnight) – *Woodman* (1974).

Workpoint

Who has possession and/or control in these instances? Give reasons for your answer.

(a) Kate drives her brother's new BMW into town while he is out. The car is then stolen from a car park in town.

(b) Clay Pigeons Ltd left a pile of clay on its industrial premises over the weekend. The manager thought that all of the clay had been transported abroad on the Friday evening. Craig climbed over the barbed wire and stole the clay.

(c) Libby stole a pair of jeans from a famous high-street store. Her friend Jenny came over that night and stole the jeans off Libby to wear over the weekend.

11.5.2 Proprietary right or interest

- If the victim does not have possession or control over the stolen item, he or she might have some other interest or 'right' to it.
- This may include an equitable interest (e.g. beneficiaries to a trust fund).
- If there are co-owners (e.g. husband and wife own a house), one owner can steal the proprietary interest from the other – *Bonner* (1970).

11.5.3 Lost property

- The courts are reluctant to say that property has been completely abandoned.

- There are very few situations in which a person will be guilty of theft of an item that does not belong to another.
- However, under s.5(2), a person can steal trust property (i.e. trust property does not belong to another but there are trustees who have a right to it) if he acts dishonestly.

11.5.4 Property received under an obligation

- It is not uncommon in law for items or money to be handed over to another person to 'look after' or 'deal with' in a particular way.
- This property will still belong to the original owner according to s.5(3).

> 'Section 5(3): Where a person receives property from or on account of another, and is under an obligation to the other to retain and deal with that property or its proceeds in a particular way, the property shall be regarded as belonging to the other.'

Workpoint

Do the following people have an obligation to deal with the property in a particular way under s.5(3)?

(a) John receives inheritance from his mother, who recently died. It is £12,000 and she wants it all donated to the Dog's Trust.

(b) Kerry is trusted by her employers – Banks Ltd – to pay a big cheque into the company bank account.

(c) Loralie receives a big lump sum from her grandmother to help with her 'university challenges'.

- Under s.5(3) it is important that the defendant was obliged to deal with the property in a particular way and then failed to do so.

Case:	
Hall (1972)	Facts: the defendant was a travel agent who received deposits from clients. He paid the deposits into the firm's general account, but never organised tickets and was unable to return the money. He was charged with theft.

Case:	
Hall (1972)	(continued) Held: his conviction was quashed because he was not under an obligation to deal with the deposits in a particular way.
Klineberg and Marsden (1999)	Facts: the defendants sold timeshare apartments. The customers paid the purchase price on the understanding that it would be held by an independent company until the apartments were ready. The independent company only received £233 and the defendants banked over £500,000.
	Held: they were guilty of theft because they were under an obligation 'to retain and deal with that property or its proceeds in a particular way' and they had not done this.

• Section 5(3) is not limited to companies.

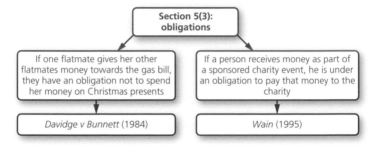

11.5.5 Property received by mistake

• If property is handed over to another person by mistake, the property still belongs to the original owner.
• In addition, section 5(4) places an obligation upon the person to restore (i.e. return) the property to the original owner.

Definition

Restoration: pay back, restore, return.

Workpoint

Section 5(4) is provided on the next page. List any key words in this provision and write your own definition of this provision.

> Section 5(4): Where a person gets property by another's mistake, and is under an obligation to make restoration of the property or its proceeds or of the value thereof, then the property or proceeds shall be regarded as belonging to the person entitled to restoration, and an intention not to make restoration shall be regarded as an intention to deprive that person of the property or proceeds.

- It is not entirely clear when a 'legal obligation' will be imposed upon a defendant to pay the money back.
- If your employer overpays you, you **are** under a legal obligation to make restoration – *Attorney-General's Reference (No. 1 of 1983)* (1985).
- There is **not** a legal obligation to restore overpaid betting transactions – *Gilks* (1972).

Section:	Rule:
5(1)	The definition of 'belonging to another' includes possession, control, or a proprietary right or interest
5(2)	A person can steal trust property if he acts dishonestly
5(3)	Property will belong to the original owner if it is received with an obligation to deal with it in a particular way
5(4)	Property will belong to the original owner if it is mistakenly transferred to another. There may be a legal obligation to restore it

Checkpoint - belonging to another

Item on checklist:	Done!
I can locate the statutory definition of 'belonging to another' and can describe the two ways in which property can belong to another	
I can explain the concepts of 'possession' and 'control' and explain how they can feature separately or together in a scenario	
I can define a proprietary right or interest in property	
I know the difference between 'abandoned' and 'lost' property for the purposes of belonging to another	
I can describe the obligation imposed upon a person under s.5(3) and who the property belongs to in these instances	

Checkpoint - continued

Item on checklist:	Done!
I can provide three legal examples to illustrate how s.5(3) works in practice	
I can explain the purpose of s.5(4) and define the provision in my own words	

11.6 The *mens rea* of theft

- The *mens rea* of theft is not as entrenched in statute as the *actus reus* is.
- Under the s.1(1) definition of theft above, you will have picked out two mental components which must be met:

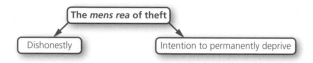

- Motive is not relevant to the *mens rea* of theft.

11.6.1 Dishonesty

- Dishonesty is not defined by the 1968 Act, but s.2(1) gives three examples as to when a defendant is **not** dishonest.

> 'Section 2(1): A person's appropriation of property belonging to another is not to be regarded as dishonest:

(a) if he appropriates the property in the belief that he has in law the right to deprive the other of it	(b) if he appropriates the property in the belief that he would have the other's consent if the other knew	(c) (except were the property came to him as a trustee) if he appropriates the property in the belief that the person to whom the property belongs cannot be discovered by taking reasonable steps

- The word 'belief' is clearly important to dishonesty as it features in s.2(1)(a)(b)(c).

- If the defendant honestly holds one of the beliefs under s.2(1)(a)(b)(c), then he is not dishonest – *Turner* (1971).

Workpoint

Are the following individuals dishonest under the 1968 Act? Give reasons for your answer.

(a) Tamsin was in a hurry to catch the bus to an interview. She went into her older sister's bedroom and looked through the many designer clothes for a cashmere coat. Her older sister had saved for over a year to buy the coat and told Tamsin never to wear it, but Tamsin figured that because she had an interview, her sister would let her wear it.

(b) Greg was at his friend Abdul's house. Abdul showed Greg his sword collection which he brought over from Pakistan. Three days later, Abdul's swords were stolen during a burglary. Greg was walking down Abdul's street the next day and found one of the swords in a bush. Greg wasn't entirely sure who the sword belonged to, but kept it anyway.

(c) Jenny was babysitting and injured her finger. She went into Mr and Mrs Lindsell's kitchen and used two plasters.

(d) Matthew finds a wallet on the Metro. There is no name or address in it, but there is a debit card and £350. He shouts out in the carriage 'Who has lost their wallet?' and no one responds. He decides to keep it

- Even though the defendant is allowed to have an unreasonable (but genuine) belief, the more unreasonable it is, the less likely the jury is to believe it!

Case:	
Small (1987)	Facts: the defendant found a car that had been abandoned for two weeks. The doors were unlocked; the keys were in the ignition; there was no petrol in the tank; the battery and the tyres were flat. He never thought it might be stolen.
	Held: his conviction for theft was quashed because he had an honest belief that the owner could not be found and there was evidence that he believed the car was abandoned.

- If a defendant later agrees to pay for the stolen property, this does not prevent his mental state from being dishonest – s.2(2).
- The jury are expected to know what 'dishonest' behaviour is – *Brutus v Cozens* (1972).

• Dishonesty should be judged by the jury according to the standards of ordinary descent people – *Feely* (1973).

Research Point

Look up the Eighth Report of the Criminal Law Revision Committee, *Theft and Related Offences*, Cmnd 2977 (1966). Why did they choose the word 'dishonestly' when drafting a new offence of theft?

11.6.2 The *Ghosh* case

• It was unclear whether the jury test for dishonesty was subjective or objective.
• The issue was settled in *R v Ghosh* (1982) and the answer is: both.

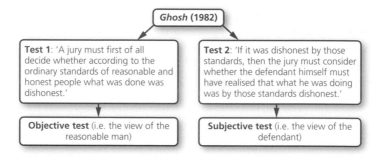

Ghosh (1982)

Test 1: 'A jury must first of all decide whether according to the ordinary standards of reasonable and honest people what was done was dishonest.'

Test 2: 'If it was dishonest by those standards, then the jury must consider whether the defendant himself must have realised that what he was doing was by those standards dishonest.'

Objective test (i.e. the view of the reasonable man)

Subjective test (i.e. the view of the defendant)

Workpoint

The facts of *Ghosh* are below. The *actus reus* of theft is already met. You are a jury member. Apply the two dishonesty tests to decide whether Dr Ghosh is dishonest or not.

Facts: the defendant was a doctor acting as a consultant in a hospital. He claimed fees for an operation he had not carried out. He said that he was not dishonest as he was owed the same amount for consult-ation fees.

You should structure your answer as follows:

Application of the objective test

Application of the subjective test

Your conclusion.

- The Court of Appeal made it clear in *Ghosh* that a defendant could not argue that even though he knew he was dishonest, he was convinced that his actions were morally right.
- The *Ghosh* test has since been recognised as a two-stage test – *DPP v Gohill and another* (2007).

Research Point

The *Ghosh* test has attracted criticism. Find the article: Griew, E. 'Dishonesty: the objections to Feely and Ghosh' [1985] Crim LR 341. Professor Griew lists some significant problems with the *Ghosh* test in this article. List three of them.

11.6.3 Intention to permanently deprive

- In addition to dishonesty, the defendant must intend to permanently deprive the victim of their item.
- Borrowing something with the intention of returning it later is not theft.
- If money is taken but replaced later, there is still an intention to permanently deprive the owner of the original banknotes – *Velumyl* (1989).
- Section 6 of the 1968 Act provides some guidance on the phrase.

'Section 6(1): A person appropriating property belonging to another without meaning the other permanently to lose the thing is nevertheless to be regarded as having the intention to permanently deprive the other of it if:

...his intention is to treat the thing as his own to dispose of regardless of the other's rights

...a borrowing or lending of it may amount to so treating it if the borrowing or lending is for a period and in circumstances making it equivalent to an outright taking or disposal

Workpoint

Now write your own example of each.

- The dictionary definition of 'dispose of' was used in *Cahill* (1993).
- The definition widened to include 'dealing with' in *DPP v Lavender* (1994).
- Treating an item as your own to dispose of will suffice – *Marshall* (1998).

Case:	
R v Raphael (2008)	Facts: the defendants stole the victim's car and demanded £500 for its return. It was eventually found in a street.
	Judge J: 'The express language of section 6 includes an intention on the part of the taker to "treat the thing as his own to dispose of regardless of the other's rights". To make its return subject to a condition inconsistent with his right to possession of his own property [is a good example].'

- According to s.6(1), borrowing or lending may reveal an intention to permanently deprive depending on the period or circumstances.

Case:	
Lloyd (1985)	Facts: a film had been taken, copied, and the original returned, undamaged.
	Lord Lane CJ: 'S.6(1) is intended to make clear that a mere borrowing is never enough to constitute the guilty mind unless the intention is to return the thing in such a changed state that it can truly be said that all its goodness or virtue has gone.'

- Picking a bag up, rummaging through it, finding nothing to steal and then replacing it is not an intention to permanently deprive – *Easom* (1971).
- If a defendant parts with the stolen property knowing that there is a risk he will not get it back, he is treating the property as his own to dispose of – s.6(2).

Workpoint

Carla snatches Mike's pay-as-you-go card when he is not looking. She tops her phone up using his card by £8.00. She returns his card with only 3p left on it, which is practically useless. Does Carla have the intention to permanently deprive? Give reasons for your answer.

Item on checklist:	Done!
I can identify the *mens rea* of theft in the s.1(1) definition of theft	
I can list the three circumstances under s.2(1)(a)(b)(c) in which a defendant is not dishonest for the purposes of the 1968 Act	
I can provide a case authority to prove that dishonesty is a jury question	
I can split the *Ghosh* judgment up into a clear two-part test	
I can identify the objective and subjective elements of the *Ghosh* test for dishonesty	
I can list three problems with the *Ghosh* test	
I can explain why borrowing is not theft	
I can describe the instances in which borrowing may be an intention to permanently deprive under s.6(1) and *Lloyd* (1985)	

Section:	Relevance:	Cases:
Section 1(1)	Definition of theft	*Treacy v DPP* (1971)
Section 2(1)	Definition of 'dishonesty'	*Turner* (1971) *Small* (1987) *Brutus v Cozens* (1972) *Feely* (1973) *R v Ghosh* (1982) *DPP v Gohill and another* (2007)
Section 3(1)	Definition of 'appropriation'	*Pitham v Hehl* (1977) *Corcoran v Anderton* (1980) *R v Morris* (1983) *Atakpu v Abrahams* (1994) *Lawrence* (1972) *Hinks* (2000) *Dobson v General Accident* (1990) *Osman* (1989) *Ngan* (1998)

Section:	Relevance:	Cases:
		Governor of Brixton ex p Levin (1997) *Gomez* (1993) *Wheeler* (1990)
Section 4(1)	Definition of 'property'	*Kelly and Lindsay* (1998) *Cresswell v DPP* (2006) *Kohn* (1979) *A-G of Hong Kong v Chan Nai-Keung* (1987) *Oxford v Moss* (1979)
Section 5(1)	Definition of 'belonging to another'	*Turner* (1971) *Meredith* (1973) *Woodman* (1974) *Bonner* (1970) *Hall* (1972) *Klineberg and Marsden* (1999) *Gilks* (1972) *Davidge v Bunnett* (1984) *Wain* (1995) *A-G's Reference (No. 1 of 1983)* (1985)
Section 6(1)	Definition of 'intention to permanently deprive'	*Turner* (1971) *Small* (1987) *Brutus v Cozens* (1972) *Feely* (1973) *R v Ghosh* (1982) *DPP v Gohill and another* (2007)

Potential exam question:

Apply the definition of theft under s.1(1) of the Theft Act 1968 to the following scenario:

Alex took his brother's (Ali's) new Lexus out for a drive when Ali was at work. Ali's new laptop was also in the back of the car. Alex drove the Lexus across the countryside on rough terrain. He eventually crashed the Lexus into a tree, and ran off with the laptop.

Alex played with the laptop for a while before realising that it was running on a new and expensive program that his friends wanted to buy. Alex removed the hard drive, knowing that his father could find a cheap replacement, and returned the laptop to Ali that evening along with the bad news that his new Lexus was wrapped round a tree 25 miles away. Ali called the police immediately.

Has Alex committed theft?

Chapter 12

Robbery, burglary and other offences under the Theft Acts

This chapter will look in detail at the other offences contained under the Theft Acts (from 1968 and 1978). These other offences include robbery, burglary, aggravated vehicle-taking and handling stolen goods. All of these offences revolve around the taking of property.

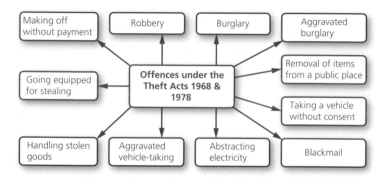

12.1 Robbery

• Robbery is the equivalent to theft aggravated by the use or threat of force.

Workpoint

The offence of robbery is provided below. What are the relevant physical components to be completed by the defendant?

Section 8: A person is guilty of robbery if he steals, and immediately before or at the time of doing so, and in order to do so, he uses force on any person or puts or seeks to put any person in fear of being then and there subjected to force.

• The word 'steal' means 'theft'.
• There must be a complete theft in order for a robbery to be charged.
• If the defendant believes he has a lawful right to the property, the

mens rea for theft is not made out and so the robbery is not made out – *Robinson* (1977).

- If force is used during the theft, the robbery is complete at the moment of the theft – *Corcoran v Anderton* (1980).
- The use of force is left to the jury to decide – *Dawson and James* (1976).

Research Point

Look up the case *Clouden* [1987] Crim LR 56, which discusses the use of force upon a victim during a theft. What happened to the victim in this case? Was it held to be 'force' for the purposes of robbery? Who decided the question of force?

- Putting someone 'in fear' of force is sufficient for robbery.
- This includes threatening words such as 'I have a knife and I'll use it if...'.
- In *Bentham* (2005) the defendant pretended to have a gun in his pocket and he was convicted of robbery.
- The victim does not need to be frightened by the threat of force – *B and R v DPP* (2007).

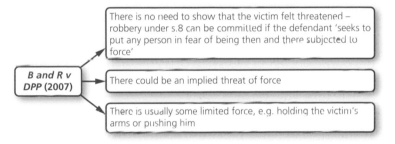

B and R v DPP (2007)

There is no need to show that the victim felt threatened – robbery under s.8 can be committed if the defendant 'seeks to put any person in fear of being then and there subjected to force'

There could be an implied threat of force

There is usually some limited force, e.g. holding the victim's arms or pushing him

Workpoint

The physical components of robbery are below. Components (1) and (5) both have to be met, and either (2), (3) or (4) have to be met. Apply them to the scenario. Has a robbery taken place? Give reasons for your answer.

Scenario: Alan breaks into Jenny's house to steal a bank safe combination code and bank keys. Jenny tries to push Alan out of the house but he barges past her and knocks her out. Alan breaks into the bank with the keys the next night and steals £10,000. Has there been a robbery in relation to the code, the keys and the £10,000?

Workpoint continued

Components:

(1) A defendant steals and...
(2) immediately before or during the theft he *uses* force; OR
(3) immediately before or during the theft he *puts* the victim in fear of force then and there; OR
(4) immediately before or during the theft he *seeks* to put the victim in fear of force then and there;
(5) ...and the force element is applied *in order* to steal.

12.1.1 Force

• The immediacy of the force has not been decided by the courts.

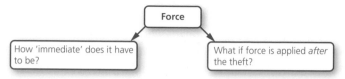

Case:	
Hale (1979)	Facts: the defendants stole the victim's jewellery box and then tied her up and gagged her before leaving. On appeal against conviction for robbery the defendants argued that the theft was complete at the time of taking the jewellery box and so the force was applied too late to turn it into robbery.
	Held: 'To say that the conduct is over and done with as soon as he laid hands on the property is contrary to common sense...appropriation does not suddenly cease. It is a continuous act.'

• In *Hale* (1979), appropriation was deemed a continuing act in order to make the force applicable.
• The force used must be used in order to steal.

Workpoint

In the two scenarios below, has the force been used to steal? Give reasons for your answer.

(a) Craig punches Mike during a heated argument and knocks him out. While Mike is lying on the floor unconscious, Craig notices that there is a wallet falling out of his jeans and takes £50.
(b) Lucy steals sweets from her corner shop and uses force when she tries to escape.

12.1.2 The *mens rea* of robbery

- The *mens rea* of robbery is that of theft: an intention to permanently deprive the victim of their property.
- The appropriation must also be dishonest – *Ghosh* (1982).
- Robbery under s.8 merely adds the physical element of force.

Research Point

Possible reforms were suggested by Andrew Ashworth in his article: 'Robbery Reassessed' [2002] Crim LR 851. What did he suggest?

Checkpoint - robbery

Item on checklist:	Done!
I can define robbery under s.8 of the Theft Act 1968	
I can explain the difference between theft and robbery	
I understand that the theft has to be complete for the robbery to take place	
I can describe the judgment in *B and R v DPP* (2007) in relation to force	
I can explain the influence of *Hale* (1979) on the immediacy of force	
I can define the *mens rea* of robbery	

12.2 Burglary

- Burglary is an offence under s.9 of the Theft Act 1968.

'Section 9(1) A person is guilty of burglary if -

(a) he enters any building or part of a building as a trespasser and with intent to commit theft, grievous bodily harm, or unlawful damage;
(b) having entered a building or part of a building as a trespasser he steals or attempts to steal anything in the building or that part of it or inflicts or attempts to inflict on any person therein any grievous bodily harm.'

• The offence of burglary is split into two parts: (a) and (b).

Burglary under s.9 of the Theft Act 1968	
Section 9(1)(a)	Section 9(1)(b)
Enters a building or part of a building as a trespasser with intent to...	Having entered a building or part of a building as a trespasser...
• Steal • Cause grievous bodily harm • Do unlawful damage	• Steals or attempts to steal • Inflicts or attempts to inflict grievous bodily harm

Workpoint

What is the main difference between the offences under 9(1)(a) and 9(1)(b)?

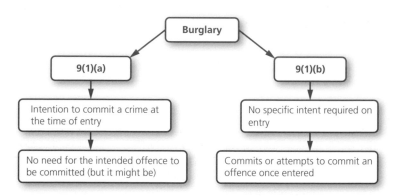

Workpoint

Evan climbs into Zara's bedroom window. On entering her bedroom he finds her laptop and picks it up. Zara's father bursts into the room and Evan drops the laptop and runs away. Has he committed an offence under s.9(1)(a) or s.9(1)(b)? Give reasons for your answer.

12.2.1 Entry

• 'Entry' is not defined in the 1968 Act.
• An 'effective and substantial entry' was required in *Collins* (1972).
• Leaning in through a window was held to be an 'effective' entry in *Brown* (1985).

Case:	
Ryan (1996)	Facts: the defendant was trapped when climbing into a house at 2:30am. His head and right arm were inside the house but the rest of his body was outside. The fire brigade had to release him.
	Held: the Court of Appeal upheld his conviction for burglary because there was evidence upon which a jury could find that he had entered.

- A 'building' or 'part of a building' includes inhabited vehicles (e.g. caravans) – s.9(4).
- The building in question must be intended to be permanent – *Stevens v Gourley* (1859).
- A 25ft-long freezer with its own door and electricity supply was held to be a building in *B and S v Leathley* (1979).
- A lorry trailer is not a building even if it has its own electricity supply – *Norfolk v Seekings* (1986).
- A shopper has permission to be in one part of the shop, but not another part (e.g. behind the till) – *Walkington* (1979).

12.2.2 As a trespasser

- A person who has permission to enter is not a trespasser.

Case:	
Collins (1972)	Facts: the defendant, who was drunk, entered a bedroom window with intent to rape. The victim thought he was her boyfriend and helped him in. They also had intercourse. He was convicted of burglary under s.9(1)(a). He argued he had permission to enter.
	Held: there cannot be a conviction for burglary under s.9 unless the defendant enters knowing that he is a trespasser or at the very least is reckless as to whether he is trespassing.
	Conviction quashed.

- Even if a person is given permission to enter, if he goes **beyond** that permission he is trespassing – *Smith and Jones* (1976).

Workpoint

Jeremy entered the local bakery to take some bread. He was banned by the Magistrate's Court a month ago because of a previous conviction of theft. He took three bread rolls and ran away. Which section would you charge him under for burglary, if any? Give reasons for your answer.

12.2.3 The *mens rea* of burglary

- It depends on the section charged as to what the *mens rea* is.

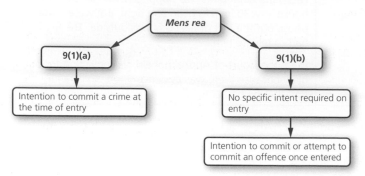

- The burglary of a dwelling (i.e. private home) attracts a steeper penalty than a burglary of any other building – s.9(3).

Workpoint

Kevin and Laura have had an argument in their shared student accommodation about his cannabis use and he has been kicked out by the university. He needs to return for his belongings and so uses his secret spare key. When he is in the flat, Laura returns home. They have a huge argument and Kevin beats up her new boyfriend who is now inhabiting his old room. Has a burglary been committed? Provide a section under the 1968 Act and give reasons for your answer.

12.2.4 Aggravated burglary

- This is a more serious form of burglary under s.10 of the 1968 Act where the defendant carries an article (e.g. knife or gun) to inflict injury.

> *'Section 10: A person is guilty of aggravated burglary if he commits any burglary and at the time has with him any firearm or imitation firearm, any weapon of offence, or any explosive.'*

A 'firearm' does not have to be capable of being discharged – s.10(1)(a)

A 'weapon of offence' means any article made or adapted for causing injury or incapacitating a person – s.10(1)(b)

This might include rope or masking tape

- The defendants must have the weapons on them at the time of the burglary.

Case:	
Francis (1982)	Facts: the defendants were armed with sticks when they gained entry. They put the sticks down and stole items from the house. They were convicted of aggravated burglary under s.10. The burglary itself was under s.9(1)(b).
	Held: although the defendants had the weapons with them on entry, there was no evidence that they intended to steal at that point. When they did steal under s.9(1)(b), they did not have the weapons with them. Convictions quashed.

- If a defendant picks up a weapon from inside the house and uses it he can be convicted of aggravated burglary – *O'Leary* (1986).
- In a joint enterprise of burglary, if one defendant has a weapon, all the defendants will be guilty under s.10 if they are aware of it and they are all in the building together – *Klass* (1998).

Workpoint

Nadia breaks into her school late at night. She goes into the chemistry lab. She smashes all of the equipment causing £20,000 worth of damage. The caretaker bursts into the lab and she throws a tripod at him, which pierces through his eye and causes brain damage. Nadia runs away empty-handed. Which offence would you charge Nadia with? Section 9(1)(a), 9(1)(b) or section 10? Give reasons for your answer.

Checkpoint - burglary

Item on checklist:	Done!
I can define burglary under s.9 of the 1968 Act and split it up into two parts	
I can distinguish burglary under s.9(1)(a) from burglary under s.9(1)(b)	
I can explain 'entry' in light of *Ryan* (1996)	
I can clarify the test for 'trespassing' after *Collins* (1972)	
I can define the *mens rea* for burglary under s.9(1)(a) and s.9(1)(b)	
I can describe aggravated burglary under s.10 of the 1968 Act	
I can explain the rule in *Francis* (1982) in reference to aggravated burglary	

12.3 Blackmail

- Blackmail is an offence under section 21 of the Theft Act 1968.
- It involves the threat of loss to another.

> 'Section 21(1): A person is guilty of blackmail if, with a view to gain for himself or another or with intent to cause loss to another, he makes any unwarranted demand with menaces, and for this purpose a demand with menaces is unwarranted unless...

...the person making it does so in the belief:

(a) that he has reasonable grounds for making the demand, AND...

(b) ...that the use of the menaces is a proper means of reinforcing the demand.

Definition

Menaces: threats.

- There are four elements to be proved under s.21:

1) A demand → 2) which is unwarranted → 3) made with menaces → 4) with a view to gain or loss

12.3.1 Demand

- There must be a demand made to the victim, but this can take any form: words, conduct, writing or email (or maybe even social networking sites).
- The demand does not have to be made directly to the victim's face – *Collister and Warhurst* (1955).
- A written demand constitutes the *actus reus* of blackmail as soon as it is posted and the demand continues until it reaches the victim – *Treacy* (1971).

12.3.2 Unwarranted demand

- If grounds 21(1)(a) and 21(1)(b) (above) are made out, the demand is warranted.
- If they are not made out, the demand is unwarranted.

- Sections 21(1)(a) and 21(1)(b) are *subjective* tests (i.e. through the eyes of the defendant).
- Both tests have to be met for the demand to be warranted.

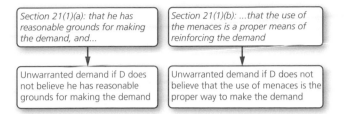

Section 21(1)(a): that he has reasonable grounds for making the demand, and...	Section 21(1)(b): ...that the use of the menaces is a proper means of reinforcing the demand
Unwarranted demand if D does not believe he has reasonable grounds for making the demand	Unwarranted demand if D does not believe that the use of menaces is the proper way to make the demand

Case:	
***Harvey* (1981)**	Facts: the defendants gave the victim £20,000 for cannabis but did not receive what they paid for. They felt they had a right to recover the money but reinforced their demands for a refund by kidnapping the victim, his wife and child, and threatening serious injury upon them all. Held: their menaces (i.e. threats) were not the proper way to reinforce the demand. They were all found guilty of blackmail.

Research Point

Look up the Eighth Report of the Criminal Law Revision Committee, *Theft and Related Offences*, Cmnd 2977 (1966). What did they intend to happen in the subjective test for unwarranted demands?

12.3.3 View to gain or loss

- The *mens rea* of blackmail requires the defendant to act with a view to:

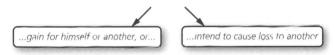

...gain for himself or another, or...	...intend to cause loss to another

- Gain and loss is defined under s.32(2)(a) of the 1968 Act.
- Gain and loss must involve money or property but can be temporary.
- Both a gain and a loss may be present – *Bevans* (1988).

12.3.4 Menaces

- Menaces are threats.
- The blackmail/demand must be made with menaces.

Case:	
Thorne v Motor Trade Association (1937)	Lord Wright: 'I think the word "menace" is to be liberally construed and not as limited to threats of violence but as including threats of any action detrimental to or unpleasant to the person addressed. It may also include a warning that in certain events such action is intended.'
Clear (1968)	The menace must either be 'of such a nature and extent that the mind of an ordinary person of normal stability and courage might be influenced or made apprehensive by it so as to unwillingly accede (i.e. surrender) to it.'

Workpoint

Arun and Daveed were known criminals in their local area. They had received over 1kg of pure cocaine from the harbour in their town and were intending to sell it on the streets for a value of £250,000. Arun gave the shipment to Daveed to look after until the weekend but, when the weekend came around, Daveed had sold most of it on his own and put all of the profits into his back account. Arun was furious and asked for half of the profits to reflect the joint arrangement, but Daveed refused. Arun threatened Daveed that if he didn't hand over half of the profits, he would 'out' Daveed as a homosexual, knowing that his strictly religious family would disown him and that he would lose his job.

Has there been an unwarranted demand which is made with menaces with a view to gain or loss under s.21(1) of the Theft Act 1968? Give reasons for your answer.

Checkpoint - blackmail

Item on checklist:	Done!
I can define blackmail under s.21(1) of the Theft Act 1968	
I can define 'menaces'	
I can list the four main elements to be proved under s.21(1) of the 1968 Act	

Item on checklist:	Done!
I can define 'demand' and list a case authority to support my answer	
I can explain the two grounds under s.21(1)(a) and s.21(1)(b) which allow a demand to be warranted	
I can explain what must be gained or lost by the defendant or the victim under s.32(2)(a) of the 1968 Act	
I can define 'menaces' in light of *Thorne v Motor Trade Association* (1937) and *Clear* (1968)	

12.4 Handling stolen goods

- Handling stolen goods is not the offence of theft, but it is a knowledge of a theft.
- This knowledge makes the defendant blameworthy.

> 'Section 22(1) of the Theft Act 1968: A person handles stolen goods if, knowing or believing them to be stolen goods, he dishonestly receives the goods, or dishonestly undertakes or assists in their retention, removal, disposal or realisation by or for the benefit of another person or he arranges to do so.'

Definition

Realisation: selling.

Actus reus of handling stolen goods:
- ❑ They must be 'goods' as defined under s.34(2)(b)
- ❑ Goods were stolen at the time of handling
- ❑ Defendant received, undertook or assisted...
- ❑ ...in their retention, removal, disposal or realisation
- ❑ Where the defendant assisted, he must be assisting another to retain, remove, dispose or realise

Mens rea of handling stolen goods:
- ❑ The defendant knew or believed the goods were stolen
- ❑ The defendant was dishonest

- 'Goods' are defined as 'money and every other description of property except land and includes things severed from land' – s.34(2)(b).
- The definition of 'goods' under s.34(2)(b) may include a thing in action – *A-G's Ref (No. 4 of 1979)* (1981).

12.4.1 'Stolen'

- The goods must be stolen under the s.22(1) definition.
- A defendant may believe that the goods are stolen (even though they are not) and then attempt to handle them – *Shivpuri* (1986).
- The stolen goods can be obtained by theft, deception and blackmail – s.24(4).
- Under s.24(2)(a), if stolen goods are sold for cash, the cash is also deemed to be stolen goods – *A-G's Ref (No. 4 of 1979)* (1981).

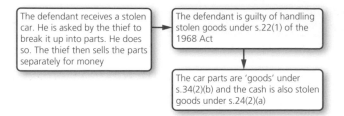

- Under s.24(3), if stolen goods are restored to the owner or other lawful possession or custody, they are no longer stolen goods – *Greater London Police v Streeter* (1980).

12.4.2 Handling

- Various methods of handling are provided under the definition in s.22(1):

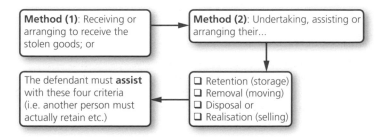

- 'Retention' means 'keep possession of, not lose, continue to have' – *Pitchley* (1972).
- The retention, removal, disposal and realisation must be for the benefit of another.

Case:	
Bloxham (1982)	Facts: D purchased a car which he later believed was stolen. He cheaply sold it on to another and was charged under s.22(1) on the basis that he had disposed of or realised the car for another's benefit.
	The House of Lords: he had been wrongly convicted – the disposal was for the defendant's own benefit, not another's.

Workpoint

Laura received money from her father, who was in prison. Laura put the money into her bank account. Three months later, she learnt that the money from her father was actually stolen from a bank robbery. She did nothing about it and left the lump sum in her bank account. Has Laura 'handled stolen goods'? Give reasons for your answer.

Laura later received a phone call from her father from prison. He learnt that Laura was in trouble for handling stolen goods so he pleaded with her to withdraw the money and burn it for him. She did so, thinking that she is no longer guilty of handling stolen goods. Has Laura's actions of withdrawing and burning still constituted a handling of stolen goods? Give reasons for your answer.

12.4.3 Assisting

- Knowing that stolen items are being kept in your neighbour's garage is not enough to undertake or assist – *Sander* (1982).

Case:	
Kanwar (1982)	Facts: D's husband used stolen goods to furnish their home. She was aware that the items were stolen. She lied to the police about it. She was convicted for handling stolen goods on the basis that her lies were assisting the retention of the goods.
	The Court of Appeal: 'to constitute the offence, something must be done by the offender, and done intentionally and dishonestly, for the purpose of enabling the goods to be retained. Such conduct must be done knowing or believing the goods to be stolen and done dishonestly and for the benefit of another. The requisite assistance need not be successful in its object.'

- *Kanwar* (1982) tells us two things – the assistance must be intentional and dishonest, and the assistance does not have to be successful.

12.4.4 *Mens rea* of handling stolen goods

- According to s.22(1) of the 1968 Act, the defendant must know or believe the goods to be stolen at the time of handling.
- This is a subjective test (i.e. from the defendant's point of view).
- In *Pitchley* (1972) the defendant only became guilty when he became aware that the goods he had received were stolen.

Case:	
Hall (1985)	'"Believe" means that the defendant may state to himself: "I cannot say I know for certain that these goods are stolen, but there can be no other reasonable conclusion in the light of all the circumstances."'

- Suspicion is not enough – *Forsyth* (1997).

Case or statute:	Rule:
Section 22(1) of the 1968 Act	Definition of handling stolen goods
s.34(2)(b)	Definition of 'goods'
A-G's Ref (No. 4 of 1979) (1981)	'Goods' can include a thing in action
Shivpuri (1986)	Defendant can believe goods to be 'stolen'
Section 24(4) of the 1968 Act	Stolen goods can derive from theft, deception or blackmail
Section 24(2)(a) of the 1968 Act and *A-G's Ref (No. 4 of 1979)* (1981)	If stolen goods are sold for cash, the cash is stolen goods
Section 24(3) of the 1968 *Act* and *Greater London Police v Streeter* (1980)	Goods no longer 'stolen' if returned to owner, in lawful possession or custody
Pitchley (1972)	Definition of 'retention'
Bloxham (1982)	'Handling' must benefit another
Sander (1982)	'Knowing' is not enough for assisting
Kanwar (1982)	Guidance on 'assisting'
Hall (1985)	Definition of 'believe' – *mens rea* of offence
Forsyth (1997)	Suspicion is not enough for the *mens rea*

Checkpoint - handling stolen goods

Item on checklist:	Done!
I can define handling stolen goods under s.22(1) of the Theft Act 1968	
I can define 'goods' under s.34(2)(b)	
I can explain the relevance of *A-G's Ref (No. 4 of 1979) (1981)* to 'goods'	
I understand that the goods don't have to be stolen but the defendant may believe that this is the case under *Shivpuri* (1986)	
I can list the crimes which the stolen goods must derive from and provide a statutory reference for this rule	
I can provide a statutory reference and a case to confirm that any products (e.g. money) that represent or derive from the stolen goods are themselves stolen goods	
I can provide a statutory reference and a case to confirm that goods are no longer stolen if they return to the owner, lawful possession or custody	
I can elaborate on the definition of 'retention' with the help of *Pitchley* (1972)	
I can explain the influence of *Bloxham* (1982) on the definition of 'handling'	
I can confirm with two case authorities that 'knowing' is not enough for 'assisting'	
I can define the *mens rea* of handling stolen goods with the help of two case authorities	

12.5 Going equipped for stealing

• This is an offence under s.25(1) of the Theft Act 1968.

> 'Section 25(1): A person shall be guilty of an offence if, when not at his place of abode, he has with him any article for use in the course of or in connection with any burglary, theft or cheat.'

• The defendant must have the article on his person or he may have possession or control of an article.

- The defendant may simply pick something up at the scene – *Minor v DPP* (1988).

Workpoint

List any 'articles' that you believe a person may have with them to use in a burglary or a theft (big or small).

Research Point

The Criminal Law Revision Committee in their Eighth Report, *Theft and Related Offences*, Cmnd 2977 (1966) listed some potential articles at paragraph 148 and said that they would be relevant to s.25(1) if they were intended for use in a burglary or theft. List them.

- The term 'article' has been interpreted very widely by the courts to include a bottle of wine in a restaurant – *Doukas* (1978).
- The articles must be 'for use' in an upcoming criminal offence, not an offence which has already been committed – *Ellames* (1974).
- If the article was made or adapted for use in a crime, this is good evidence that the defendant had it with him for such a purpose – s.25(3).
- The *mens rea* of s.25(1) is that the defendant knows he has the article and intends to use it in the course of one of the listed crimes.

Workpoint

Laura, Wendy and James are planning to break into their high school biology lab and cause significant damage (i.e. a burglary). What items must they have with them and under what circumstances in order to satisfy the criteria under s.25(1)?

12.6 Making off without payment

- There was a gap in the Theft Act 1968 where the defendant did not steal anything but his behaviour was still blameworthy.
- For example, individuals who filled their tank with petrol and then drove away without paying were not charged with theft because ownership of petrol had already transferred – *Greenberg* (1972).
- The Criminal Law Revision Committee in its Thirteenth Report, *Section 16 of the Theft Act 1968*, Cmnd 6733 (1977) recommended a new law to fill the gap.
- The Theft Act 1978 was passed (it did **not** repeal the 1968 Act; they work together).

> 'Section 3(1) of the 1978 Act: A person who, knowing that payment on the spot for any goods supplied or service done is required or expected from him, dishonestly makes off without having paid as required or expected and with intent to avoid payment of the amount due shall be guilty of an offence.'

- The goods or service that is supplied must be lawful – s.3(3) of the 1978 Act.

Workpoint

Copy and complete the diagram, listing instances you can think of where a customer receives a service and then might leave before paying.

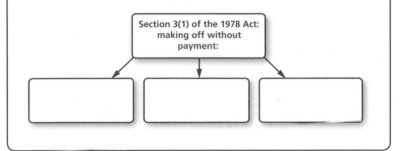

Section 3(1) of the 1978 Act: making off without payment:

- It is vital that payment on the spot is required or expected: a customer may sometimes arrange to pay later – *Vincent* (2001).
- The defendant must 'make off' which means leave the scene or the building – *McDavitt* (1981).
- In terms of *mens rea* under s.3(1), the defendant must know that payment on the spot is required and he must intend to avoid payment.

Case:	
Allen (1985)	Facts: the defendant owed £1,286 for a stay in a hotel. He left without paying but his defence was that he genuinely intended to pay in the near future as he was waiting for sufficient funds to cover the bill.
	Court of Appeal: 'The phrase "*and with intent to avoid payment of the amount due*" adds a further ingredient: an intention to do more than delay or defer, an intention to evade payment altogether.'

Workpoint

Mr Kelly had a business partner, Mr Manor. They frequently attended conferences together and went golfing on weekends. Mr Manor offered Mr Kelly a room in his Manor Hotel for a whole week in the summer. Mr Kelly accepted his offer and they agreed that Mr Kelly would pay the invoice 'whenever their next business venture comes through'. Mr Kelly books into the Manor Hotel in London, run by Mr Mike Smith. Mr Manor had not communicated to Mike Smith that Mr Kelly was staying for a week on a friendly promise and would pay at a later date.

Mr Kelly was arrested a week later when he tried to leave the Manor Hotel without paying. Has Mr Kelly committed an offence? Give reasons for your answer.

Case or statute:	Rule:
Section 25(1) of the 1968 Act	Definition of going equipped for stealing
Minor v DPP (1988)	The defendant may pick something up at the scene
Doukas (1978)	'Article' has been interpreted widely
Ellames (1974)	Article must be for use in upcoming offence
Section 25(3) of the 1968 Act	An article might be made or adapted for purpose
Greenberg (1972)	An example of making off without payment
Section 3(1) of the 1978 Act	Definition of making off without payment
Section 3(3) of the 1978 Act	Goods or services provided must be lawful
Vincent (2001)	Payment on the spot must be expected or required
McDavitt (1981)	The defendant must 'make off' from the scene
Allen (1985)	Defendant must intend to evade payment permanently

Checkpoint - going equipped for stealing and making off without payment

Item on checklist:	Done!
I can define going equipped for stealing under s.25(1) of the Theft Act 1968	
I can explain the rule in *Minor v DPP* (1988)	
I can define 'article' with reference to *Doukas* (1978) and *Ellames* (1974)	
I can explain why 'adapted for use' is important under s.25(3) of the 1968 Act	
I can define making off without payment under s.3(1) of the Theft Act 1978	
I can use *Greenberg* (1972) to illustrate the need for this new offence	
I understand that a customer can arrange to pay later under *Vincent* (2001)	
I understand that the customer/defendant must leave the scene or building under *McDavitt* (1981)	
I can explain the *mens rea* of making off without payment using *Allen* (1985) as an illustration	

Potential exam question:

Jennifer walked over to Betty's house late at night. Betty had been seen with Jennifer's ex-boyfriend and Jennifer was raging with jealousy because she was pregnant and had been left to raise the baby alone. Jennifer picked up a large twig and snapped it so that it had a sharp and ragged edge. She climbed into Betty's bedroom window using a ladder from next door, knowing that Betty was asleep in bed. Jennifer tripped up on Betty's shoes and Betty woke up. She shouted out in alarm on seeing a black shadow in her bedroom with a weapon. Jennifer recognised her ex-boyfriend's voice and lunged at the pair of them, stabbing them with the sharp stick. She stabbed Betty in the eye.

Has Jennifer committed a burglary?

Chapter 13

Fraud

This chapter explores the new deception offences brought in by the Fraud Act 2006. Many of the offences below are based on similar offences under the Theft Act 1968, such as section 6: possession of articles for use in fraud, section 7: making or supplying articles for use in frauds, or section 11: obtaining services dishonestly.

13.1 The history of fraud

- The new 2006 Act was passed as a result of loopholes in the Theft Act 1968.

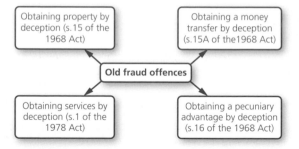

Obtaining property by deception (s.15 of the 1968 Act)

Obtaining a money transfer by deception (s.15A of the1968 Act)

Old fraud offences

Obtaining services by deception (s.1 of the 1978 Act)

Obtaining a pecuniary advantage by deception (s.16 of the 1968 Act)

Research Point

Look up the Law Commission's report, *Fraud* (2002) (Law Com. No. 276) at paragraph 3.11. What did the Law Commission think about the old state of fraud?

- Gaps in the Theft Act 1968 were found by *Laverty* (1970), *DPP v Ray* (1973), *Lambie* (1981) and *Preddy* (1996).
- The Law Commission published a Consultation Paper No. 155, *Legislating the Criminal Code: Fraud and Deception*.
- This was followed with its *Fraud* Report (2002) with a draft Bill attached.
- The draft Bill eventually became the Fraud Act 2006.

13.2 The new Fraud Act 2006

- The Fraud Act 2006 repealed sections 15, 15A, 16 and 20(2) of the Theft Act 1968.
- It also repealed sections 1 and 2 of the Theft Act 1978.
- The Fraud Act 2006 replaced these old offences with six new ones.

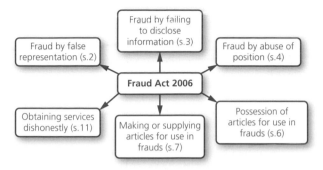

13.3 Fraud by false representation

Definition

Representation: pretending to be somebody else, representing another person.

- Fraud by false representation is contained under s.2 of the 2006 Act.

> 'Section 2(1): D commits fraud by false representation if he -
>
> (a) dishonestly makes a false representation, and
> (b) intends, by making the false representation -
>   (i) to make a gain for himself or another, or
>   (ii) to cause loss to another or to expose another to the risk of loss.'

- The *actus reus* is simple under s.2 but there are several components to the *mens rea*.

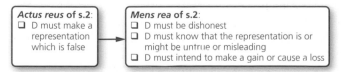

13.3.1 What is a 'representation'?

• A representation is an impersonation of somebody else.

An example of a false representation:	
Defendant: 'Hello. I am the owner of this house. I would like to sell it to you for a knock-down price.'	Truth: he is not the owner of the house and simply wants to pocket profits that are not rightfully his.

Workpoint

Now give your own example of a false representation.

• A false representation is defined under the 2006 Act as an 'untrue or misleading' statement about 'fact or law or state of mind' – s.2(2).
• The representation may also be express or implied – s.2(4).

Workpoint

There are five representations below (they are all false). Pick out which one is based on fact, law, state of mind, express or implied.

(1) Stacey wears a police uniform to gain entry into the station. She does not say anything.
(2) Henry promises that he will pay his gas bill but he and his flatmates have no intention of doing so.
(3) A car dealer states that the car has done 50,000 miles when really it has done 108,000.
(4) Melanie tells Michael, aged 10, that it is against the law not to give to charity on a Sunday while in church, so Michael hands over his pocket money.
(5) Mr Burns states in the local newspaper and on the internet that he is a member of the local library and that he will happily receive donations for its roof repairs, but this is all untrue.

• There is no limit as to how a representation may be expressed – it can be written, spoken or on the internet.
• There are many ways in which a false representation can be implied.

Definition

Implied: unspoken, understanding, inferred, assumed, believed.

Case:	
Barnard (1837)	Facts: D went into an Oxford shop wearing an Oxford University outfit. He also said he was a fellow of the university. The shop owner sold him goods on credit.
	Held: the cap and gown was an implied false representation and he also expressly falsely represented himself.

A more modern example:
A man, Mr Smith, walks into a shop with someone else's credit card. He hands it over to the cashier. The cashier reads the name on the card, Mr Khan, and asks Mr Smith what his name is. Mr Smith replies 'Mr Khan'.

Workpoint

Now give your own example of a false representation.

Case:	
DPP v Ray (1973)	Facts: D went to a restaurant with three friends. They did not have enough money and, in the end, decided not to pay for their meal. They all ran away without paying. They were charged under the old offence (now repealed) of obtaining a pecuniary (i.e. financial) advantage under s.16(2)(a) of the Theft Act 1968. The Court of Appeal quashed the conviction because the defendant's original representation – that he would pay – was genuine.
	The House of Lords: when the defendant changed his mind, this produced a deception, and his earlier genuine representation had now become a false representation.

- As a result of *DPP v Ray* (1973), a defendant will still be guilty of fraud by false representation under s.2 if he started out with a genuine representation but later turned it into a false one

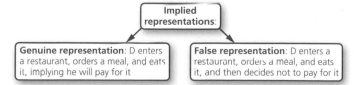

Implied representations:

Genuine representation: D enters a restaurant, orders a meal, and eats it, implying he will pay for it

False representation: D enters a restaurant, orders a meal, and eats it, and then decides not to pay for it

- Writing cheques while knowing that there are insufficient funds in the account is a false representation that you will pay for the goods – *Gilmartin* (1983).
- Presenting a cheque guarantee card is also a false representation if it is used in a way that the bank forbids – *Metropolitan Police Commissioner v Charles* (1976).

Research Point

A false representation can be made to a machine under s.2(5) of the Fraud Act 2006. Find the Explanatory Notes in your law library or on Lexis or Westlaw (they are attached to the back of the 2006 Act) and make notes as to what 'machines' are listed under the 2006 Act and why Parliament included machines under s.2(5).

13.3.2 'False'

Definition

False: untrue, lies, misleading, deception.

- The defendant's representation must be 'false' under s.2 of the 2006 Act.
- A representation is 'false' if it is 'untrue or misleading'– s.2(2).

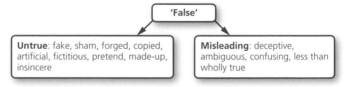

'False'

Untrue: fake, sham, forged, copied, artificial, fictitious, pretend, made-up, insincere

Misleading: deceptive, ambiguous, confusing, less than wholly true

- The victim or recipient does not have to believe the defendant.
- If a workman provides a grossly overinflated quote for repairs, this is a misleading representation – *Silverman* (1987).

Workpoint

Are the following representations false? Give reasons for your answer.

(1) Mr Rogers, who worked for Cars-R-Us, sold Mr and Mrs Jennings an Audi A4. He handed over the MOT pass certificate, which he received from the previous owner. Mr Rogers did not make any

checks to confirm that the car had been in any accidents because it looked fine. The Audi A4 was actually not roadworthy after a crash a few months ago. Mr and Mrs Jennings bought the car once they saw the MOT pass certificate.

(2) Mr Fix-it visits a pensioner's house. She needs some roof tiles replaced. Mr Fix-it writes up a quote for £21,000 to replace the whole side of the roof and fix the rot and damp. She argues she doesn't have the money so he suggests an instalments programme at £30 a month. She agrees, but her daughter informs her that she has been the victim of fraud.

13.3.3 'Gain or loss'

- The defendant must intend to make a gain or loss when he makes his false representation.
- This gain or loss can be for himself or another (e.g. a colleague, friend or family member).

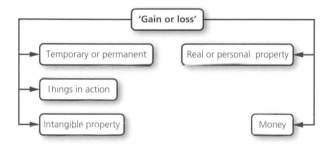

- Gain or loss – whether temporary or permanent – includes money and all other property under s.5(2).
- The defendant must simply intend the gain or loss – it does **not** have to materialise.

Workpoint

David asks Chen if he can borrow Chen's car because his own Mini has a flat battery. Chen hands over the keys to his new Porsche for David to drive for three hours. David drives around in the Porsche for three hours and then returns it. Chen is angry, having discovered that David's Mini is actually completely fine and parked in his garage after his wife went out shopping in it.

(a) Is there a false representation here?

Workpoint continued

(b) Did David intend a gain and/or loss to himself and/or another?
(c) Is there an actual gain and/or loss here? Where?
(d) Is the gain and/or loss temporary or permanent?

13.3.4 The *mens rea* of fraud by false representation

- The *mens rea* of fraud by false representation under s.2 is explained below.
- To be convicted, the defendant must make his false representation dishonestly.
- There is no definition of dishonesty, but the theft case of *Ghosh* (1982) will suffice.

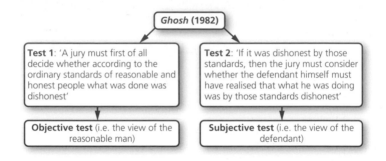

- The two-part test in *Ghosh* (1982) is the acceptable definition of dishonesty and the jury must apply the objective/subjective test.

Workpoint

Returning to David and Chen (above), apply the two-part dishonesty test to David's actions to ascertain whether his false representation was dishonest. Give reasons for your answer.

- As part of the *mens rea*, the defendant must **know** that the representation is untrue or misleading, or that it **might be**.
- 'Know' has been strictly defined as 'true belief' and should not be watered down – *Saik* (2006).
- The defendant must also **intend** to make a gain or cause a loss.

- The definition of intention is the same throughout criminal law: foresight of a virtual certainty is evidence of intention – *Moloney* (1985) and *Woollin* (1998).

Workpoint

Fred is a pensioner who has smoked 40 cigarettes a day for most of his life. He is required to fill out a health insurance form. He comes across a box which asks 'Do you or have you ever smoked?'. He ticks the box for 'No' because this will be much cheaper for him. He then sends off his health insurance form.

Has Fred *intended* to make a gain or cause a loss? Give reasons for your answer and apply *Woollin* (1998).

Checkpoint - fraud by false representation

Item on checklist:	Done!
I can list four of the new offences under the Fraud Act 2006	
I can explain what a 'representation' is in basic terms	
I can define the offence of fraud by false representation under s.2 of the 2006 Act	
I can explain what a 'false representation' must be under s.2(2) and s.2(4) of the 2006 Act	
I can explain the relevance of *Barnard* (1837) to false representations	
I can describe the decision in *DPP v Ray* (1973) and explain why it is relevant to representations	
I can define the word 'false' in my own words and under s.2(2) of the 2006 Act	
I can list the items that can be 'gained or lost' under s.5(2) of the 2006 Act	
I can write down all three *mens rea* elements of the s.2 offence	
I can define the *Ghosh* (1982) test for dishonesty	
I can define 'intention' under the criminal law with a case authority	

13.4 Fraud by failing to disclose information

- There is a new offence under s.3 of the 2006 Act of failing to disclose information.

> 'Section 3(1): D commits fraud by failing to disclose information if he -
>
> (a) dishonestly fails to disclose information to another person which he is under a legal duty to disclose; and
>
> (b) intends by failing to disclose the information:
>
>   (i) to make a gain for himself or another; or
>   (ii) to cause loss to another or to expose another to the risk of loss.'

- There are four components to be proved under s.3 – two *actus reus* and two *mens rea*:

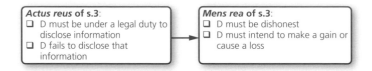

Actus reus of s.3:
- ❑ D must be under a legal duty to disclose information
- ❑ D fails to disclose that information

Mens rea of s.3:
- ❑ D must be dishonest
- ❑ D must intend to make a gain or cause a loss

- Under the Fraud Act 2006, a legal duty is required to disclose information.

Case:	
Rai (2000)	Facts: the defendant applied for a grant from the council to install a downstairs bathroom for his mother. Two days after the money was approved, his mother died. He kept the money and continued with the improvement.
	The Court of Appeal: this was obtaining property by deception under the old (repealed) s.15 of the Theft Act 1968.

- Could the facts of *Rai* (2000) lead to a conviction under the new 2006 Act?

Rai (2000): would he meet all of the criteria under the Fraud Act 2006?	
(1) Was D under a legal duty to disclose his mother's death? **Not clear – she was alive on approval**	Is D dishonest? **Yes**
(2) Has D failed to disclose that information? **Not sure – duty not clear**	Did D intend to make a gain or cause a loss? **Yes**

- The 'legal duty' is clearly an important criteria.
- The Fraud Act 2006 does not define a legal duty.
- However, the Law Commission's report on *Fraud* (2002) (Law Com. No. 276 Cm 5560) did define a legal duty – paragraph 7.28.
- The Explanatory Notes attached to the Fraud Act 2006 support the following definition from the Law Commission:

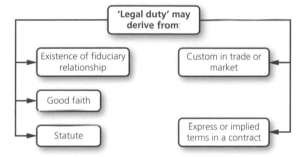

Research Point

The Law Commission gives further advice under paragraph 7.29 regarding when a legal duty exists. Look up the Law Commission's report on *Fraud* (2002) (Law Com. No. 276 Cm 5560) and list the comments.

- The *mens rea* of fraud by failing to disclose information is dishonesty and an intention to make a gain or cause a loss.
- As for fraud by false representation under s.2 (above), the *Ghosh* (1982) test will suffice for dishonesty.
- Similarly, the definition of 'gain and loss' under s.5(2) of the 2006 Act will also suffice.

Miller Bread Corporation was in negotiations with Mr Smith.
Mr Smith owned a bakery and wanted to stock Miller Bread products.
Miller Bread Corporation showed Mr Smith its accounts. They boasted
an annual turnover of £250,000 and 16 international clients. In fact,
Miller Bread Corporation was running out of money and its turnover
had dropped to £1,000 because of its debts. It had lost 12 of its inter-
national clients in the last 2 months and needed the contract with
Mr Smith to keep it afloat.

Do you believe Miller Bread Corporation has a legal duty to disclose
this financial information, based on the recommendations by the Law
Commission? Give reasons for your answer.

In addition, does Miller Bread Corporation have the *mens rea* for the
offence under s.3? Give reasons for your answer.

Checkpoint - fraud by failing to disclose information

Item on checklist:	Done!
I can define the offence under s.3 of the Fraud Act 2006	
I can split the offence into four elements – two *actus reus* and two *mens rea*	
I can apply the facts of *Rai* (2000) to the offence under s.3 of the 2006 Act	
I can list the places from which a 'legal duty' may arise	
I can define the *mens rea* requirement under s.3	

13.5 Fraud by abuse of position

• There is a new offence under s.4 of the 2006 Act of abusing a position
for the purposes of fraud.

> '*Section 4(1): D commits fraud by abuse of position if he -*
>
> *(a) occupies a position in which he is expected to safeguard, or not to act against, the financial interests of another person;*

> *(b) dishonestly abuses that position;*
> *(c) intends by means of abuse of that position:*
>   *(i) to make a gain for himself or another; or*
>   *(ii) to cause loss to another or to expose another*
>   *to the risk of loss.'*

- This offence can be committed by an **omission** as well as an act – s.4(2).
- There are four components to be proved under s.4 – two *actus reus* and two *mens rea*:

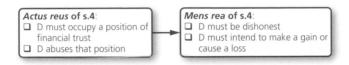

Actus reus of s.4:
- ❑ D must occupy a position of financial trust
- ❑ D abuses that position

Mens rea of s.4:
- ❑ D must be dishonest
- ❑ D must intend to make a gain or cause a loss

- Section 4(1) does not contain the word 'secretly' as was suggested by the Law Commission draft (*Fraud* – 2002) so the victim may be aware of the circumstances.

Workpoint

Can you think of an instance in which a person, who holds a particular position of trust, may abuse that position in order to gain for himself?

13.5.1 Occupies a position

- One of the requirements of the *actus reus* for s.4 is the occupation of a position of financial trust.
- The Explanatory Notes to the 2006 Act quote the following positions:

trustee and beneficiary → director and company → professional person and client → agent and principal

employee and employer → between partners → voluntary work → any partners not at arm's length

- Fiduciary duties (e.g. trustees etc.) are not essential – the judge will decide whether there is a relevant relationship and then direct the jury accordingly.

13.5.2 Abuse of position

- The word 'abuse' is left open.
- The Explanatory Notes provide some examples:
  1. An employee conducting business in a way that costs his employer a lot of expense;
  2. An employee of a software company who clones software products to sell on;
  3. A person who cares for an elderly person has access to their bank account and uses the money for his own business ventures.
- In *Doukas* (1978), an employee was a wine waiter and sold his own wine while at work to pocket the profit.

13.5.3 The *mens rea* of fraud by abuse of position

- The *mens rea* of fraud under s.4 is dishonesty and an intention to make a gain or cause a loss.
- As for the frauds under sections 2 and 3 (above), the *Ghosh* (1982) test will suffice for dishonesty.
- Similarly, the definition of 'gain and loss' under s.5(2) of the 2006 Act will also suffice.

Workpoint

Apply the four elements of the s.4 offence (*actus reus* and *mens rea*) to the scenario below.

John and Wendy were going through a divorce. They consulted their solicitor, Mr Wiggs, to help them. Mr Wiggs noticed that John and Wendy had won £1.3 million in the lottery three months ago, and that was the main source of their arguments. Mr Wiggs added a 30% supercharge onto John and Wendy's legal bill, claiming that 'big money' divorces required more admin work. When John and Wendy questioned this, Mr Wiggs said that he was the only 'big money' divorce specialist in their county, but there is no such thing as a 'big money' divorce specialist.

Checkpoint - fraud by abuse of position

Item on checklist:	Done!
I can define the offence under s.4 of the Fraud Act 2006	

Checkpoint - continued

Item on checklist:	Done!
I can split the offence into four elements – two *actus reus* and two *mens rea*	
I can define 'position' for the purposes of s.4	
I can define 'abuse' for the purposes of s.4	
I can provide my own example of an abuse of position under s.4	
I can define the *mens rea* requirement under s.4	

Workpoint

Apply one of the sections above to each of the scenarios below.

(1) Fiona used Christmas chocolate money to get her snacks out of the vending machine.
(2) Tony had recently received a heart transplant but did not mention this when filling out his life insurance form.
(3) Jenny stood on the street corner with a charity money box. She was intending to keep all of the money for herself.
(4) Larry worked for Blockbuster Video. He frequently took DVDs home and copied them to sell on to his friends.

13.6 Possession of articles for use in fraud

- It is an offence to possess or control any article for the purposes of fraud.

> *'Section 6(1): A person is guilty if he has in his possession or under his control any article for use in the course of or in connection with any fraud.'*

- The term 'article' includes any item, electronic program or electronic data.
- Fraud can take place anywhere as a result of the internet.

Theft Act 1968	Fraud Act 2006
Section 25: Going equipped for stealing	*Section 6: Possession of articles for use in fraud*
This offence must be committed when D is not at his place of abode (e.g. carrying a hammer on the way to a house)	This offence can be committed anywhere, including D's place of abode (e.g. a computer program at home)

- The *mens rea* of s.6 is a general intention to commit fraud.
- The courts may refer to cases under s.25 of the 1968 Act to help with *mens rea*.

Case:	
***R v Ellames* (1974)**	The Court of Appeal: 'The prosecution must prove that the defendant was in possession of the article, and intended the article to be used in the course of or in connection with some future burglary, theft or cheat. It is enough to prove a general intention to use it for some burglary, theft or cheat. It will be enough to prove that he had it with him with the intention that it should be used by someone else.'

13.7 Making or supplying articles for use in frauds

- It is an offence to make, adapt, supply or offer an article for the purposes of fraud.

> *'Section 7(1): A person is guilty of an offence if he makes, adapts, supplies or offers to supply any article -*
>
> *(a) knowing that it is designed or adapted for use in the course of or in connection with any fraud, or*
> *(b) intending it to be used to commit, or assist in the commission of, fraud.'*

- The *actus reus* of s.7 can be committed in a number of ways:

- Making an article for fraud
  e.g. a fake credit card
	- Adapting an article for fraud
	  e.g. a computer database

Supplying an article for fraud e.g. *machines, computers, cables etc.*	Offering to supply an article for fraud e.g. *offering to provide blank credit cards*

- The *mens rea* of s.7 can be split into two parts:

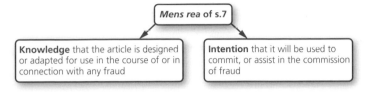

Mens rea of s.7

Knowledge that the article is designed or adapted for use in the course of or in connection with any fraud

Intention that it will be used to commit, or assist in the commission of fraud

Workpoint

Jack and Peter were both inmates at Redwood Prison. They were convicted of a bank robbery three years ago, and the third perpetrator escaped with £20,000. Jack was allowed access to the internet once a week and Peter also had connections with the 'outside'. Jack and Peter managed to retrieve the £20,000 by fraud from inside the prison. Jack is charged under s.6 and Peter is charged under s.7. What must each defendant do in terms of *actus reus* and *mens rea*?

13.8 Obtaining services dishonestly

- The new offence of obtaining services dishonestly is found under s.11 of the Fraud Act 2006.
- It replaces s.1 of the Theft Act 1968.

Workpoint

The offence of obtaining services dishonestly under s.11 of the 2006 Act is provided below. There are three elements to the *actus reus* and three elements to the *mens rea*. Copy and complete the table.

Section 11(1): A person is guilty of an offence under this section if he obtains services for himself or another -

(a) by a dishonest act, and
(b) in breach of subsection (2).

Section 11(2): A person obtains services in breach of this subsection if -

(a) they are made available on the basis that payment has been or will be made for or in respect of them;
(b) he obtains them without any payment having been made for or in respect of them or without payment having been made in full, and -

(c) when he obtains them he knows -
(i) that they are being made available on the basis described in paragraph (a), or;
(ii) that they might be,

but intends that payment will not be made, or will not be made in full.

Actus reus:	Mens rea:
(1)	(1)
(2)	(2)
(3)	(3)

13.8.1 *Actus reus* of obtaining services dishonestly

- To be charged under s.11, the services must actually be obtained by the defendant.
- The term 'services' has not been defined by the 2006 Act.
- Potential examples of 'services' are provided below.

Using a false credit card on the internet to buy a service

Climbing over a fence to watch a sporting event without paying the entrance fee

Using a false or amended bus pass to receive a travel discount

Falsely claiming to be over a certain age in order to get into the cinema

Using a stolen satellite dish to receive channels you have not paid for

Workpoint

Now give your own example of obtaining services dishonestly.

- The *actus reus* of s.11 will only be complete if the defendant does not pay for the service, or does not pay in full.
- If the full price is paid – regardless of any other circumstances – the *actus reus* is not made out.

13.8.2 *Mens rea* of obtaining services dishonestly

- The *mens rea* of s.11 is not currently supported by any case law, but words such as 'dishonest', 'knows' and 'intends' are important.
- The *Ghosh* (1982) test will probably be used for the dishonesty component.
- The prosecution must prove that the defendant intended not to pay for the services.

Workpoint

If Garry and Jill go to a restaurant, and Garry flashes his credit card at the beginning of the meal and brags that it can cover a 'feast' but then puts it away, is Jill guilty of obtaining services dishonestly if they both later leave without paying? Give reasons for your answer.

Checkpoint - possession of articles for use in fraud, making or supplying articles for use in frauds, and obtaining services dishonestly

Item on checklist:	Done!
I can define the offence of possession of articles for use in fraud under s.6 of the Fraud Act 2006	
I can distinguish the offence under s.6 of the 2006 Act from the offence under s.25 of the Theft Act 1968	
I can describe the *mens rea* of s.6 with the help of *R v Ellames* (1974)	
I can define the offence of making or supplying articles for use in frauds under s.7 of the Fraud Act 2006	
I can give at least three of my own examples of how the *actus reus* under s.7 can be completed	
I can describe the *mens rea* of s.7	

Checkpoint - continued

Item on checklist:	Done!
I can define the offence of obtaining services dishonestly under s.11 of the Fraud Act 2006	
I can give at least three of my own examples of 'services' under the *actus reus* of s.11	
I can describe the *mens rea* of s.11	

Potential exam questions:

Jerry Steiner is dating a young model named Cheryl. He wants to impress her so he takes her to *Le French* which is a very exclusive restaurant in town. Jerry orders a five course meal and expensive champagne. He visits the bar at the end of the evening to settle the bill. Jerry takes out a credit card with the name "Mr Hassan" on it. This is in fact the name of his boss, who works with Jerry on the building site down the road. Jerry saw the credit card on his boss's desk with the pin number attached and decided to take it for one night only. Jerry hands the card over and the cashier asks him what his name is. Jerry replies: "Mr Abdul Hassan" before the sale is put through the system.

Has Jerry committed fraud by false representation?

Chapter 14
Criminal damage

This chapter will explore the basic offence of criminal damage, created by the Criminal Damage Act 1971. Three other related offences include: aggravated criminal damage, arson and aggravated arson.

- The Criminal Damage Act 1971 was the result of a report by the Law Commission: *Offences of Damage to Property* (Law Com No. 29) (1970).

Section 1(1): Criminal damage (i.e. basic offence)

Section 1(2):Aggravated criminal damage (i.e. endangers life)

Section 30(1) of the Crime and Disorder Act 1998: racially aggravated criminal damage

Criminal damage

Section 1(3): Arson (i.e. damage with fire)

Section 3: Possessing anything with intent to destroy or damage property

Section 2: Threats to destroy or damage property

Section 1(3): Aggravated arson (i.e. arson endangers life)

14.1 Criminal damage

Definition

Damage: harm, spoil, smash, break, scratch, dent, impair, ruin, destroy.

- The 'basic offence' of criminal damage is enshrined into s.1(1) of the Criminal Damage Act 1971:

> *'Section 1(1):* A person who without lawful excuse destroys or damages any property belonging to another intending to destroy or damage any such property or being reckless as to whether any such property would be destroyed or damaged shall be guilty of an offence.'

- Two 'lawful excuses' are provided in section 5 of the 1971 Act (examined below).

Workpoint

Make a list of the three *actus reus* elements and list the three *mens rea* elements of the basic offence under s.1(1).

14.1.1 'Destroy or damage'

- The words 'destroy' and 'damage' are not defined by the 1971 Act.
- The same phrase was used by the old law under the Malicious Damage Act 1861.
- Trampling down grass was held to be damage in *Gayford v Chouler* (1898).

Case:	
Roe v Kingerlee (1986)	Facts: the defendant smeared mud on the walls of a police cell, which cost £7 to clean up.
	Held: whether property has been damaged 'is a matter of fact and degree for the justices to decide' and they will direct the jury accordingly. The damage need not be permanent.

- The Australian case of *Samuels v Stubbs* (1972) held that the property does not need to be 'useless' after the damage has been done.
- Paintings on concrete are damage because they need to be cleaned up afterwards – *Hardman v Chief Constable of Somerset Constabulary* (1986).
- Writing a biblical quote on a concrete pillar is criminal damage – *Blake v DPP* (1993).

Case:	
Fiak **(2005)**	Facts: the defendant put a blanket down his cell toilet and flushed it several times, leading to flooding. The blanket had to be cleaned before it was used again. Held: the cell and the blanket had to be cleaned, so this was held to be criminal damage.

- If damage or soiling can be wiped off with little effort, it is unlikely to be criminal damage – A *(a juvenile)* v R (1978).
- A scratch to a scaffolding pole was not criminal damage because this kind of damage is likely in everyday use – *Morphitis v Salmon* (1990).
- Altering or deleting computer programs was held to be criminal damage in *Whiteley* (1991).
- The Computer Misuse Act 1990 now makes it clear that a computer must be *physically* damaged in order to be charged under criminal damage – s.3(6).

Case/statute:	Issue:	Criminal damage?
Gayford v Chouler (1898)	Trampling down grass	Yes
Roe v Kingerlee (1986)	Mud on cell wall	Yes
Samuels v Stubbs (1972)	Police hat stood on and dented	Yes
Hardman v CC of Somerset (1986)	Paintings on concrete	Yes
Blake v DPP (1993)	Biblical quote on concrete pillar	Yes
A (a juvenile) v R (1978)	Policeman was spat on by juvenile	No
Morphitis v Salmon (1990)	Scratch on a scaffolding pole	No
Whiteley (1991)	Altering or deleting computer programs	Yes
Computer Misuse Act 1990	Physical damage to the computer	Yes

Workpoint

Are the following scenarios 'damage' within the meaning of criminal damage under the 1971 Act? Give reasons for your answer.

(a) Shannon finishes washing her dad's car and pours the dirty water over her neighbour Edna, ruining Edna's new cashmere jacket.

(b) Jack throws David's school bag out of the window and the shoulder strap rips off.

(c) Louise writes a malicious message about one of her friends in white chalk all over the school wall.

14.1.2 Property

- The definition of property under s.10(1) of the 1971 Act includes the following things:

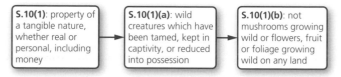

| **S.10(1)**: property of a tangible nature, whether real or personal, including money | **S.10(1)(a)**: wild creatures which have been tamed, kept in captivity, or reduced into possession | **S.10(1)(b)**: not mushrooms growing wild or flowers, fruit or foliage growing wild on any land |

- 'Real property' is included under the Criminal Damage Act 1971 definition of property.

14.1.3 Belonging to another

- The definition of belonging to another under s.10(2) of the 1971 Act includes:

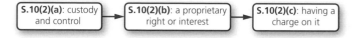

| **S.10(2)(a)**: custody and control | **S.10(2)(b)**: a proprietary right or interest | **S.10(2)(c)**: having a charge on it |

- The property must belong to another for basic criminal damage under s.1(1).
- A co-owner can also be guilty of criminal damage because the property still belongs to another – *Smith* (1974).

14.1.4 The *mens rea* of criminal damage

- Criminal damage under s.1(1) must be done intentionally or recklessly.
- It used to be 'unlawfully or maliciously' under the Malicious Damage Act 1861.
- The defendant must intend to destroy or damage property.

Case:	
Pembliton (1874)	Facts: the defendant threw a stone at some men who he'd been fighting with outside a pub. The stone missed and broke a window.
	Held: the defendant was not guilty of causing malicious damage because he did not intend to break the window.

- Under the Criminal Damage Act 1971, recklessness would probably cover the scenario in *Pembliton* (1874).
- The *mens rea* will **not** be met if the defendant mistakenly believes that the property belongs to himself – *Smith* (1974).
- Criminal damage requires subjective recklessness – *Cunningham* (1957).

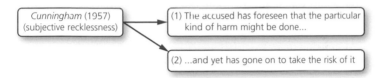

Cunningham (1957)
(subjective recklessness)

(1) The accused has foreseen that the particular kind of harm might be done...

(2) ...and yet has gone on to take the risk of it

- A jury must ask themselves if the **defendant** saw the risk – *Stephenson* (1979).
- The test briefly switched to objective recklessness and whether the **reasonable man** would have foreseen the risk – *Caldwell* (1981).

Case:	
R v G (and another) (2003)	Facts: two young boys aged 11 and 12 set fire to a wheelie bin and left the scene. The resulting fire caused £1 million damage. They were convicted using *Caldwell* recklessness (objective) because the reasonable man would have known the risk.
	Held: the objective test is inappropriate for young defendants. Subjective recklessness as in *Cunningham* is more appropriate as it asks the jury to consider if the defendants foresaw the risk of damage.

Research Point

According to the facts in *Stephenson* [1979] 2 All ER 1198, the defendant was a tramp who lit a fire in a haystack to keep warm. He was also schizophrenic. The fire he lit caused criminal damage.

(a) Which approach do you think is best for this defendant when it comes to a recklessness test? Objective, or subjective? Give reasons for your answer.
(b) Look up the held of the case. Why did the Court of Appeal decide that the recklessness test was the right one for the defendant?

14.1.5 'Without lawful excuse'

- Under s.1(1) of the 1971 Act, a defendant has access to two lawful excuses – s.5(2).
- These are available for the basic offence of criminal damage – s.1(1).

'Section 5(2) A person charged with an offence to which this section applies shall be treated as having a lawful excuse -

(a) if at the time of the act the person who he believed to be entitled to consent to the destruction or damage had so consented, or would have so consented had he known; or
(b) if he destroyed or damaged property in order to protect property belonging to himself or another, and at the time of the act he believed -

(i) that the property was in need of immediate protection; and
(ii) the means of protection adopted would be reasonable in all the circumstances.

Section 5(3): It is immaterial whether a belief is justified or not if it is honestly held.'

- The two lawful excuses above can be split into two provisions: section 5(2)(a), and s.5(2)(b).

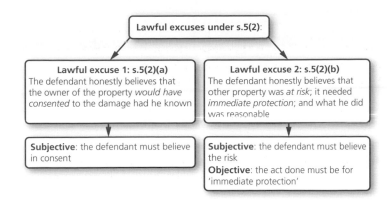

Workpoint

You hear gossip in your university canteen that there is a bomb hidden within your favourite lecture hall. The entire lecture hall could explode, causing millions of pounds worth of damage. You enter the empty lecture hall and smash up the computer, hoping to destroy the bomb. It turns out that there was no bomb.

Which lawful excuse would you like to use under s.5(2)? Can you satisfy the subjective/objective elements within the lawful excuse?

- If the defendant believes that his employer encouraged him to destroy property, this is a defence under s.5(2)(a) – *Denton* (1982).
- Section 5(3) allows an unjustified mistake as long as it is honestly held, allowing for intoxication, stupidity, forgetfulness and inattention – *Jaggard v Dickinson* (1980).

Case:	
Jaggard v Dickinson (1980)	Facts: D, who was drunk, went to what she thought was a friend's house. She broke a window to get in and believed (accurately) that her friend would have consented to this.
	Held: her conviction for criminal damage was quashed – she had an intoxicated belief in consent according to the defence under s.5(2)(a).

- Under s.5(2)(b), a defendant may believe that the damage of property is needed for the immediate protection of other property.

| Example 1: a computer is destroyed to prevent the spread of a virus | Example 2: a crop is destroyed to prevent a swarm from spreading |

Workpoint

Now write your own example of lawful criminal damage.

- There is an objective element to s.5(2)(b) – the other property must require 'immediate protection'.

Case:	
Hunt (1977)	Facts: D set fire to some bedding in a block of flats in order to illustrate that the fire alarm wasn't working. He was charged with criminal damage and the trial judge refused to allow a defence under s.5(2)(b).
	The Court of Appeal: the 'immediate protection' criteria is an objective test, and the reasonable man would not consider the criminal damage to be protecting other property but simply drawing attention to a defective fire alarm.

- From an objective perspective, cutting the perimeter fence to a naval base would not protect the surrounding homes from a nuclear attack – *R v Hill* (1988).
- A defendant may raise both defences – *Blake v DPP* (1993).

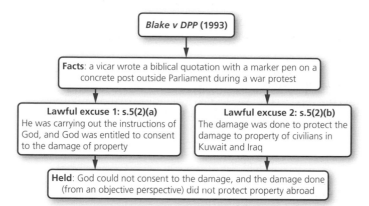

Blake v DPP (1993)

Facts: a vicar wrote a biblical quotation with a marker pen on a concrete post outside Parliament during a war protest

Lawful excuse 1: s.5(2)(a)
He was carrying out the instructions of God, and God was entitled to consent to the damage of property

Lawful excuse 2: s.5(2)(b)
The damage was done to protect the damage to property of civilians in Kuwait and Iraq

Held: God could not consent to the damage, and the damage done (from an objective perspective) did not protect property abroad

- Wild badgers are not 'property' to protect under s.5(2)(b) – *Cresswell v DPP* (2006).
- The protection of persons is **not** included under s.5(2)(a) or 5(2)(b) – *Baker and Wilkins* (1997).

Research Point

Look up the Law Commission's report, *Legislating the Criminal Code: Offences against the Person and General Principles*, (1993), Law Comm No. 218, paragraph 37.6. What are its views about including 'protection of others' within the defences under s.5(2) of the 1971 Act?

Checkpoint - basic criminal damage

Item on checklist:	Done!
I can list five offences from the Criminal Damage Act 1971	
I can define the basic offence under s.1(1) of the 1971 Act	
I can illustrate what is meant by 'destroy' or 'damage' under s.1(1) using six legal authorities	
I can define the term 'property' under s.10(1) of the 1971 Act	
I can define the phrase 'belonging to another' under s.10(2) of the 1971 Act	
I can explain the relevance of *Cunningham* (1957) to the *mens rea* of criminal damage under s.1(1) of the 1971 Act	
I can distinguish the tests of objective and subjective recklessness on defendants who commit criminal damage	
I can define the two lawful excuses under s.5(2) of the 1971 Act	
I can give my own example of a lawful excuse under s.5(2)(a)	
I can explain the applicability of *Hunt* (1977) to the lawful excuse under s.5(2)(b)	
I understand that *Blake v DPP* (1993) illustrates that both defences under s.5(2) may be raised simultaneously	

14.2 Aggravated criminal damage

Definition

Aggravated: endangering life, dangerous to life, causing injury.

- Aggravated criminal damage is a much more serious offence under s.1(2) of the 1971 Act.
- The maximum penalty is life imprisonment.

> 'Section 1(2): A person who without lawful excuse destroys or damages any property, whether belonging to himself or another -
>
> (a) intending to destroy or damage any property or being reckless as to whether any property would be destroyed or damaged; and
> (b) intending by the destruction or damage to endanger the life of another or being reckless as to whether the life of another would be thereby endangered; shall be guilty of an offence.'

Workpoint

List what you think are the *actus reus* and *mens rea* elements of aggravated criminal damage under s.1(2).

14.2.1 Endangering life

- The danger must come from the destroyed or damaged property, not from the aggressive act itself – *Steer* (1987).

Workpoint

Why is it important under s.1(2) of the Criminal Damage Act 1971 that the *criminal damage* causes the danger to life, rather than the act of the defendant?

- If the defendant directly intends to injure the victims, s.1(2) will **not** be activated.

- However, if the defendant intends to injure his victims *through his criminal damage*, s.1(2) **would** be engaged.
- This loophole in the statute has caused controversy in the courts – *Warwick* (1995).

Case:	
Warwick (1995)	Facts: the defendant rammed a police car and threw bricks, causing the rear window to smash and broken glass to shower the officers.
	Lord Taylor CJ: (describing the facts of *Warwick* 1995) 'If the defendant's intention is that the stone itself should crash through the roof of a train and thereby directly injure a passenger the section would not bite...if however, the defendant intended or was reckless that the stone would smash the roof of the train so that metal struts from the roof would descend upon a passenger, endangering life, he would be guilty. This may seem a dismal distinction.'

Workpoint

Distinguish the scenarios below and decide whether aggravated criminal damage under s.1(2) would be applicable or not.

(a) Callum had a huge argument with his ex-girlfriend Shelly over her new partner Ben, who had moved in with Shelly and was looking after Callum's baby son. Callum went to the house one night in a rage after a threatening text message from Ben and threw bricks through all of the windows to injure Ben and Shelly.

(b) Down the road, Craig was also throwing bricks through the windows of his ex-girlfriend Sally's house. He made sure he smashed the living room window because he knew that Sally liked to sit there to watch the TV so that she would be injured by the glass.

- The property can be the defendant's own under s.1(2), because the aim of the section is to make him guilty if he intends or is reckless as to endangering the lives of others.

Case:	
Merrick (1995)	Facts: the defendant was employed by a house-owner to remove electrical wires. While removing the cable he was 'damaging' it and he left the live wires exposed for six minutes, thus endangering life also.
	Held: his conviction was upheld under s.1(2). If the householder had done the same thing, he would have been guilty under s.1(2) too.

14.2.2 The *mens rea* of aggravated criminal damage

- The *mens rea* of aggravated criminal damage under s.1(2) is intention or recklessness as to the damage **and** the endangering of life.

Section 1(2) *mens rea*: intention or recklessness as to...

Destroying or damaging property **and**...

...whether life is endangered by the destruction or damage

- Life does not *have* to be endangered, the defendant must simply intend for it to be or realise that it might be – *Sangha* (1988).
- The recklessness is subjective – *Cunningham* (1957), *R v G* (2003), *Cooper* (2004) and *Castle* (2004).

Workpoint

If a defendant, D, throws a petrol bomb at a house where he knows five occupants are inside watching TV, what, as a bare minimum, must he be thinking at the time in order to be convicted under s.1(2) of the 1971 Act? Write down his required *mens rea*.

Checkpoint - aggravated criminal damage

Item on checklist:	Done!
I can distinguish the *actus reus* of aggravated criminal damage under s.1(2) of the 1971 Act from the *actus reus* of basic criminal damage under s.1(1)	
I can explain the concept of 'endangering life' with the help of *Steer* (1987)	
I can critically examine the 'endangering life' loophole in s.1(2) as highlighted in *Warwick* (1995)	
I can define the *mens rea* of aggravated criminal damage under s.1(2) of the 1971 Act	
I can describe the recklessness test for aggravated criminal damage and can cite three legal authorities as support	

14.3 Arson

- Under s.1(3) of the 1971 Act, if **basic** criminal damage under s.1(1) is committed with fire, the offence becomes **arson**.
- The *actus reus* and *mens rea* elements are all the same.
- This is a serious offence and the maximum penalty is life imprisonment.

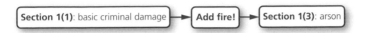

Section 1(1): basic criminal damage → Add fire! → **Section 1(3)**: arson

- Under s.1(3) of the 1971 Act, if **aggravated** criminal damage under s.1(2) is committed by fire, the offence becomes **aggravated arson**.
- This is a very serious offence and the maximum penalty is life imprisonment.

Section 1(2): aggravated criminal damage → Add fire! → **Section 1(3)**: aggravated arson

Research Point

Look up the case of *Miller* [1983] 1 All ER 978. What did the defendant do (in terms of destroying or damaging property)? What was he charged with? What were the unique circumstances of this case?

14.4 Threats to destroy or damage property

- Under s.2 of the 1971 Act, a defendant commits an offence if he threatens to commit basic criminal damage or aggravated criminal damage.

> *'Section 2: A person who without lawful excuse makes to another a threat, intending that that other would fear it would be carried out -*
>
> *(a) to destroy or damage any property belonging to that other or a third person; or*
> *(b) to destroy or damage his own property in a way which he knows is likely to endanger the life of that other or a third person, shall be guilty of an offence.'*

- The defendant must **intend** for the victim to fear that the threat will
be carried out.
- There is no alternative *mens rea* of recklessness – *Cakman and others*,
The Times, 28 March 2002.

14.5 Possessing anything with intent to destroy or damage property

- Under s.3 of the 1971 Act, it is an offence to possess anything with an
intent to destroy or damage property.

> 'Section 3: A person who has anything in his custody
> or under his control intending without lawful excuse to
> use it or cause or permit another to use it -
>
> (a) to destroy or damage any property belonging to some
> other person; or
> (b) to destroy or damage his own property in a way which
> he knows is likely to endanger the life of some other person;
>
> shall be guilty of an offence.'

- There is no time limit under this provision – the offence may take
place at any time.

- Similar to s.2 (above), the *mens rea* requires intention and omits recklessness.

Workpoint

What kind of scenario do you think could fall under s.3(b)?

Workpoint

Jack and his band, 'Depths of Doom', are now planning to break into a solicitor's office as part of their human rights protest. Jack and James plan the break-in and use their contacts to attain crowbars, petrol, knives and hammers. Jack and James share the items out among the band. The two other members, Xin and Zack, break into the office using the items and destroy documents and furnishings as Jack and James look out for police. The secretary was in the building at the time and she was frightened by the smell of petrol.

Who can be charged under s.3 of the 1971 Act? Check the provisions carefully, and give reasons for your answer.

14.6 Racially aggravated criminal damage

- It is an offence under s.30(1) of the Crime and Disorder Act 1998 to commit racially aggravated criminal damage.
- Basic criminal damage under s.1(1) is required, along with special circumstances set out under s.28(1) of the Crime and Disorder Act 1998.

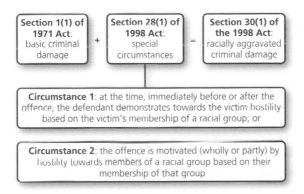

- This offence is aimed at property, not a person.
- However, under s.30(3) of the 1998 Act, the owner of the damaged property is deemed to be the 'victim' for the purposes of the offence under s.30(1).

Give an example of when basic criminal damage, plus one of the special circumstances under s.28(1) of the 1998 Act, might come together to form an offence of racially aggravated criminal damage under s.30(1) of the 1998 Act.

- Only basic criminal damage under s.1(1) of the 1971 Act is required under the s.30(1) offence.
- The maximum penalty under s.30(1) of the 1998 Act is 14 years' imprisonment, compared to 10 years for basic criminal damage under s.1(1) of the 1971 Act.

Checkpoint - arson, threats to destroy or damage property, possessing anything with intent to destroy or damage property, racially aggravated criminal damage

Item on checklist:	Done!
I can define the offence of arson under s.1(3) of the 1971 Act	
I can distinguish between arson and aggravated arson	
I can define the offence of threats to destroy or damage property under s.2 of the 1971 Act	
I can describe the *actus reus* and *mens rea* elements of the s.2 offence	
I can define the offence of possessing anything with intent to destroy or damage property under s.3 of the 1971 Act	
I can describe the *actus reus* and *mens rea* elements of the s.3 offence	
I can cite the correct statutory provision for the offence of racially aggravated criminal damage	
I can describe the two circumstances under s.28(1) of the 1998 Act that convert basic criminal damage (under s.1(1) of the 1971 Act) into racially aggravated criminal damage	

Potential exam question:

Max and his friend Nabeela, both aged 16, were standing on a bridge above a busy motorway. Max had collected 20 bricks from a local construction site and brought them along in a wheelie basket. Max and Nabeela took some time to scrawl a message onto the bricks – 'army out of Afghanistan' – and pile them up on the bridge. They then began dropping the bricks down onto the busy motorway below every time a white man drove by, shouting 'You destroyed our property, we will destroy yours!'. Fifteen cars were damaged during the attack, and three drivers were also hurt.

Advise Max and Nabeela on whether they have committed criminal damage under s.1(1) of the 1971 Act and aggravated criminal damage under s.1(2) of the 1971 Act.

Glossary

A thing in action: a right to do something i.e. withdraw money from your own account.

Actus reus: physical act of the crime.

Affray: scuffle, fight, brawl, disturbance, commotion, threats.

Aggravated: endangering life, dangerous to life, causing injury.

Appropriate: take, acquire, obtain, grab, seize, get, steal, rob, pinch.

Attempt: try, effort, plan, endeavour.

Basic intent crimes: criminal offences in which recklessness will suffice as a *mens rea*.

Capacity: understanding, awareness, capability, clear mind, reasoning, ability.

Causation: the defendant must *cause* the outcome.

Coercion: force, intimidation, bullying, oppression, cruelty.

Coincidence in crime: the physical act and mental element must happen at the same time, or at least meet at some point.

Conspiracy: plot, scheme, plan, agreement.

Constructive manslaughter: unlawful act manslaughter, doing a dangerous act that causes death.

Conveyance: any vehicle constructed or adapted for the carriage of a person or persons whether by land, water or air - s.12(7)(a).

Corporation: A non-human body or entity with a separate legal personality from its human members (according to *Salomon v Salomon* 1897).

Counsel: advise, solicit, direct, guide, help, support.

Damage: harm, spoil, smash, break, scratch, dent, impair, ruin, destroy.

De minimis: ignore trivialities

Diligence: take reasonable care to avoid an outcome, be careful, take steps to avoid harm.

Diminished responsibility: an abnormality of mental functioning which substantially impairs a person's ability to understand, rationalise, or exercise self-control.

Direct intention: the defendant directly aims or desires the consequence (i.e. death).

Dishonest: intentionally deceptive, a desire to trick or defraud people.

Doli incapax: incapable of wrong.

Dutch courage: drinking alcohol in order to give oneself the confidence to act or commit a crime.

Factual causation: it is a physical fact that the defendant caused the outcome.

False: untrue, lies, misleading, deception.

Gross negligence manslaughter: grossly negligent behaviour that leads to a death.

Implied: unspoken, understanding, inferred, assumed, believed.

Inchoate: beginning, incomplete, undeveloped, early stages.

Incite: provoke, spur on, motivate, persuade, encourage.

Infanticide: an offence/defence where a mother kills her child under 12 months old.

Intention: desire, foresight, virtually certain consequence, purpose, goal, objective.

Joint enterprise: working together, group work, shared effort, equal participation.

Legal causation: this is concerned with the *number* of causes, *who* was the significant cause, *which* cause was operating (i.e. "active") at the time of injury/death, etc.

Loss of Control: a loss of control due to a qualifying trigger in response to which a person of the same age and sex would have reacted the same

Malice aforethought: an intention to kill.

Menaces: threat

Mens rea: mental element of the crime.

Mens rea: guilty mind

Murder: the unlawful killing of a human being with malice aforethought.

Negligence: mistake, ignorance, failing to appreciate consequences that would have been appreciated by a reasonable man.

Objective: through the eyes of the reasonable man (i.e. who is 'objective')

Oblique intention: the defendant foresees the consequence (i.e. death) as virtually certain so therefore the jury may conclude that intention was present.

Omission: failure to act.

Penetration: a continuing act from entry to withdrawal s.79(2) of the 2003 Act.

Principle of identification: a person must be identified within the company structure who is the "directing mind and will" of the company (*Lennard's Carrying Co v Asiatic Petroleum* 1915).

Procure: bring about, cause, make happen.

Property: possessions, belongings, goods, assets, materials, goods, land, items.

Rape: forced sexual intercourse.

Real property: land, property, building, site, field, house, factory.

Realisation: selling

Representation: pretending to be somebody else, representing another person.

Restoration: pay back, restore, return.

Riot: uprising, disturbance, unrest, demonstration, rebellion, group, gathering.

Special jury verdict: "not guilty by reason of insanity".

Specific intent crimes: criminal offences that specifically require intention for a *mens rea*;

Subjective: through the eyes of the defendant (i.e. the 'subject')

Suicide pact: several people agree to kill each other, but one remains alive.

Transferred malice: malicious intentions towards one victim is transferred to another victim.

Violent disorder: three or more persons, present together, using or threatening violence.

Withdrawal: removal, pulling out, departure, leaving, abandonment.

Index

INDEX